MW01065885

"Arise, Shine; for thy light is come"

–ISAIAH 60:1

ISBN Hardcopy: 978-1-7323262-0-0
ISBN Paperback: 978-1-7323262-1-7
ISBN E-Book: 978-1-7323262-2-4

Anita Joe Ministries
www.anitajoeministries.com
anitajoeministries@gmail.com

Printed in the United States of America

DEDICATION

This book is dedicated to my redeemer, Jesus Christ, who graced me to write as a testimony of the glorious work He has done in me. Had it not been for the cross of Calvary and the shedding of His precious blood, I would have remained in a state of brokenness without hope. Therefore, with all of my soul, I give to my God and King all the praises, honor and glory.

This book is also dedicated to all who have been broken. It is written not to gain sympathy, but to encourage you to feed on the words of Jesus and trust Him to bring divine healing to your soul. I hope my style of conversational writing will make it easy for you to start your journey, so that you may receive all the blessings your heavenly Father has in store for you.

"Trust in the Lord with all thine heart."
—Proverbs 3:5

ACKNOWLEDGMENTS

Thanks to Bishop H. M. Bolden for preaching the unadulterated gospel of Jesus Christ.

Thanks to my third-grade teacher, Mrs. McConoughey, for letting me read the first book I ever wrote in front of the class.

Thanks to Lorraine DarConte for photography and compilations.

Thanks to Melissa Walker for permission to use Brylee Walker's photo.

Thanks to my adopted son, Sergeant Anthony Moore, for godly encouragement.

Thanks to Diana Grabau for the grueling hours of editing in pursuit of accuracy to make this book a good read. You are a blessing.

CONTENTS

FOREWORD

Anita Joe crafts a page-turning story that will motivate Christians as well as those seeking Christ. An inspiring story of pain, suffering, courage, and strength, this book exemplifies the power of the Lord to RISE above!

As I read this book I found myself inspired by the well-written story of struggle and perseverance. It became clear that this book was a reflection of life and its many obstacles, such as abuse, poverty, lack of love, and a season of turmoil. This book touched on many areas facing our youth: gender confusion, peer pressure, relationship woes, stealing, jealously, and false prophets.

Anita's story of childhood abuse at the hands of her father caused me to view my own alcoholic father as more endearing to me, and my Pentecostal minister mother as even more loving compared to her mother. I found myself celebrating Anita's victories in the Lord while she continued to weather life's struggles.

My favorite character in the Bible is King David. Anita summarized his many stories using the analogy of overcoming pits. That was so profound and inspirational that I find I love the Lord even more.

The father of lies—Satan—has a way of allowing one's own free will to dictate in a negative way how one interprets the evils of the world. Anita's words add up to a roadmap of diligence and faith that will reinforce those struck in such a struggle.

The personal reflections after each section were an interesting way to use pointed questions to challenge the reader to reflect on the chapter and provide an opportunity for readers to write down their own perspectives.

Finally, *Dare to Rise?* is a challenge that gives the reader a reason to rise up over all the evil in their lives and to allow God to lift them through it. God takes us through our worst to get to our best!

Nathan Keith Stephens, MPA
Academic Advisor/Adjunct Instructor;
Wayland Baptist University
Author of *A Different Breed of Brother*

INTRODUCTION

I wrote this book to share my life story of how a loving God, through Jesus Christ, brought an abused little girl from brokenness to wholeness. I can truly say God wonderfully delivered me. When I look back at all of the abuse I suffered, I do so with joy. I can now laugh at many of the things that had me bound.

My healing did not come overnight, nor did it come easy. It was a progressive journey. I thank the Lord for that. I don't feel anyone is mentally or emotionally capable of handling such abuse otherwise. Along the way, I learned who I was and what, in Him, God purposed me to be. It was astonishing, to say the least, because I had no inkling that God would call me, of all people, a rejected little girl from Tucson, Arizona, to be a pastor and to preach the gospel.

With no formal Bible-school training, I found it to be a scary thing. I didn't feel I was good enough or even qualified, for that matter. As I matured in the Lord, I realized one very important thing—I was HIS choice. As Jesus' spoken words state:

> *Ye have not chosen me, but I have chosen you, and ordained you.*
> *—John 15:16*

When the Lord chooses us, He doesn't need to consult with the opinions of human beings. He is the all-wise God. Throughout the Holy

Scriptures, we see that His choice is often the rejected, the weak, and the base things of the world, so that He may display His glorious power in us.

Yes, I was a reject—a misfit, if you will. Looking back, it was the best thing that could have ever happened to me, for this reason: it drove me straight into the loving arms of my heavenly Father. His love, coupled with His grace, caused me to rise and move forward. As a result, I overcame all the hurts that left me emotionally and spiritually damaged.

The Lord Jesus taught me to finally accept and love the "me" that He had made. In His image and in His likeness, He made me. I can now love others as I love myself, which is the second greatest commandment.

If someone were to ask me what was the most difficult thing to overcome, I would have to say the pain of brokenness. This pain is like none other, leaving deep wounds that can freshly recall traumas. Healing for this kind of emotional damage has to be progressive. All who desire to be healed must be willing to go through it, no matter what it takes. For me, the process began the moment I surrendered my life to Jesus. I gave Him my life and He gave me His life. Jesus took all my broken pieces and put me back together again. I am a true witness that the mighty power of Jesus can heal you completely, no matter how traumatic your experience. He did it for me, and I know He will do it for you.

You see, it happens little by little. Just as the sun rises to the dawning of a new day—have you seen this happen? Early in the morning just before the sun comes up, you look out and see the darkness giving way to blue skies. Though it is a bit obscure, you know something is happening. Then you wait a little while, and the next thing you see is a beam of light peaking over the horizon. A little more time passes and you look again—what do you see now? The rays of light, shining brighter and brighter. It's the full grandeur of the sun telling you to get ready; the future is going to be gloriously bright!

My dear friend, that's exactly the way your healing will come. Can't you feel it? Jesus Christ, the SON of the Living God, the LIGHT of the world, is coming right where you are. He has come to heal and restore every part of you and fill you with His love.

I want you to realize that your light has come, that you may experience the Father's unconditional love, as I have. You, beloved, are precious to Him, and He wants me to tell you there is good news. Right now, your world may be filled with pain, but it doesn't have to remain. The Lord Jesus is able to turn your greatest pain into your greatest victory!

May God bless you greatly as you read this book. In Jesus' mighty name, amen.

—Pastor Anita Joe

To Everything there is a season,
A time for every purpose under heaven:
A time to be born, And a time to die;
A time to plant, And a time to pluck what is planted;
A time to kill, And a time to heal;
A time to break down, And a time to build up;
A time to weep And a time to laugh;
A time to mourn, And a time to dance;
A time to cast away stones, And a time to gather stones;
A time to embrace, And a time to
refrain from embracing;
A time to gain, And a time to lose;
A time to keep, And a time to throw away;
A time to tear, And a time to sew;
A time to keep silence, And a time to speak;
A time to love, And a time to hate;
A time of war, And a time of peace."

—Ecclesiastes 3:1–8

CHAPTER I

A TIME TO BE BORN

To Everything there is a season,
A time for every purpose under heaven:
A time to be born, And a time to die;
A time to plant, And a time to pluck what is planted;

A Time to be Born...

This is one of the most fascinating scriptures in the entire Bible. I say so because it helps us to see that God is "one who plans." The writer of Ecclesiastes starts off with three profound words: season, time, and purpose. These three words speak to the great wisdom of God; how He is the orchestrator of all that happens under the sun. It is God who created seasons as a set time in which to accomplish His purpose in the earth. This, beloved, includes your birth, which is what this chapter is about. Ah, what a wonderful thought. Yes, the God of heaven methodically planned out your birth. Pause with me for a moment and think. You started out as a thought in the mind of your Creator. What does that mean, to be on God's mind and in His thoughts? Let's look at it in the natural or practical sense.

I was talking with a young Christian gentleman by the name of Anthony Moore about his beautiful little daughter Kyndall. I mentioned how much she looked like Disarae, his wife. The child had such a striking resemblance to her mother, it was as though Disarae had spit Kyndall out of her own mouth.

Anthony, having also been moved by their resemblance, began to tell me his story. "I was so amazed because I had told God I wanted a wife and a daughter who looked like her mother, but I didn't think He would make my daughter look exactly like her," he said. As he spoke, I could see how much he cherished this wonderful gift from God; he was a proud papa.

He and his wife both served in the military and were looking forward to retirement, which was right around the corner. Despite all the grueling tasks and demands that came with military service, they had endured. It would prove to pay off in the end, because of the benefits they could pass on to their children.

Anthony, obviously excited about their plans for their children, said with a smile, "I got something to show you." He turned and ran upstairs, then reentered the room waving a piece of paper in his hand. "You see this? This document shows my children's college is already paid for in full. That's why we worked so hard all these years." The young man's child had started out as a thought in his mind, including her gender and what he wanted her to look like, after which he began to plan out her little life before she could even utter a word.

So it is with the God of heaven, who is the creator of all things. He had you and me on His mind way before the earth was formed. Ephesians 1:4 says, *"Just as He chose us in Him before the foundations of the world."* Incredibly powerful, right? It gets better; you'll see.

God spoke to Jeremiah, confirming that he was approved and accepted before he was born, declaring, *"Before I formed you in the womb I knew you; Before you were born I sanctified you; I ordained you a prophet to the nations"*—Jeremiah 1:5. This prophecy is astonishing! It's no wonder the young man felt overwhelmed as he answered back, *"I! A prophet to the nations? I cannot speak: for I am a child."* Though the common human response may be a feeling of inadequacy, nonetheless, just like Jeremiah, God knew us and approved us before we entered the womb. He then brought us into being and set us apart for a specific task.

His knowledge of us before we took on flesh and bone proves two things: 1) Our preexistence with our Creator—like God, we existed as spiritual beings; and 2) You and I are not some human's mistake—we came forth from God, and we will return to Him.

Some have suggested that our souls are stored in heaven somewhere. In my opinion, we are in the heart of the Father until He brings us forth into time. I must put emphasis on this verse: *"Before I formed you in the womb I knew you."* The Hebrew word for *before* is TEREM: *the'-rem* means to interrupt or suspended. One thing we know from this passage is that something takes place that brings about an interruption. I envision that when the preexistent self meets time, there is an atomic transference and destiny is birthed. This is called "life," as we know it. Though precisely and divinely ordained, strong opposition is certain. So, when external pressures arise, just present these questions. "Where were you, hindrance, when God approved and call me forth into existence? Where were you, when He designed a set of matchless fingerprints and a DNA unlike any other? Where you there? Do you have the power to retract the order of God? The words of David are the muse to silence such annoyance. For he said:

> *You saw me before I was born. Every day of my life was recorded in Your book. Every moment was laid out before a single day had passed. How precious are your thoughts about me O God. They cannot be numbered!*
>
> —Psalm 139:16–18

This passage of scripture is a lot to wrap our minds around. Even so, it reveals the upfront and personal role our heavenly Father displays. I want to encourage you to take a deep breath and take it all in slowly.

The question is, what did your heavenly Father see? I will tell you. He saw nothing less than greatness. You are the predestination of Jehovah's secret council to be His great instrument. Thus, He saw your future. He saw what you would look like before you came into existence. And at the moment of conception, His purpose for your life began to unfold, ergo, it is absolutely absurd to believe that life starts after birth. That's a lie from the pits of hell. God is not watching over dead things; dead things can't grow.

He watched as your eyes and ears formed. He saw your mouth and nose take shape. Even when you were the size of a pea, He saw all of your inner parts. A sonogram ain't got nothing on God; it can only record an image after the fact. God sees the end of life from the beginning. In addition, every moment of your life was laid out and written down in heaven's hall of fame for the angels to behold.

Your birth was a prodigious announcement of what God has already ordained. In other words, in His divine wisdom, God preplanned your destiny way before your arrival date. Wow! That's deep.

If we could only see what has been recorded on heaven's scrolls about us, I believe we would see that our God-given plan is to be great, extraordinary, and unique. We would no doubt live life very differently. We would better understand that what God sees and wants is vastly superior to man's desires. If we could but see, there would be no reason for us to compare ourselves one with another. If we could only see, there would be all the more reason to live life with vigor and purpose.

David, no doubt, had a revelation when he declared, *"How precious are Your thoughts about me O God."* What thoughts? Thoughts of God's wonderful love toward him, so many that one can't even begin to count them all. Talk about being mindful. There is no love like God's love on planet Earth; it is unfathomable. This love is so sweet that one can't help but embrace it, yet it is so powerful that it can make a grown man bow down on his knees in tears. It's the kind of love that makes you forget your worst mistakes in life so that you feel renewed like a newborn baby.

Herein lies the beauty of our heavenly Father—He is immutable. His thoughts of love toward you and me are not fleeting, but everlasting. He loved us when we were in the womb, when there was no relationship to be had. It was God who initiated love toward you and me. He loved us even though there was no guarantee that we would ever love Him back. The words of Jeremiah come to mind, those that he declared concerning Israel:

> *The Lord hath appeared of old unto me, saying, Yea, I have loved thee with an everlasting love: therefore with lovingkindness have I drawn thee.* —Jeremiah 31:3

Just as the Lord extended loving-kindness to Israel in their exodus and so many other times throughout history, He does so with us today. With this same affection, He's drawing us near. If we desire to experience God's kind of love, it is for us to respond by drawing near to Him. We are taught in scripture that His love is everlasting; not only so, but unequivocally unconditional. That alone is praise worthy. Hallelujah!

Now that we have been brought forth, His plans for us are to know Him and experience all His goodness. Listen again to the words of the prophet Jeremiah:

> *For I know the plans I have for you," says the Lord. "They are plans for good and not for disaster, to give you a future and a hope.*
>
> —Jeremiah 29:11

Remember my opening words? "God is one who plans." Beloved, imbibe the words of Jeremiah until you become intoxicated with them, that they may become more real than anything else.

My prayer for you today is that

> *the heavenly Father will give to you a revelation of His divine plans for your life, in the name of JESUS! Amen.*

MARVELOUS ARE YOUR WORKS!

"I will praise You, for I am fearfully and wonderfully made; Marvelous are Your works; And that my soul knows very well."
—Psalm 139:14

The Holy Scriptures declare that the works of God are marvelous, meaning they are astonishing and extraordinary. Aren't we one of His works? So then, if we can praise God for all the wonderful things His hands have made, shouldn't we also praise Him for how fearfully and wonderfully He has made us? The New Living Translation (NLT) says it on this wise: *"Thank you for making me so wonderfully complex! Your workmanship is marvelous—how well I know it."* You see, beloved, you have to know it and declare it, even as David did. God doesn't make junk! He can't; neither does He know how (see Genesis 1).

It is amazing how many people I've come across who wish they could look like someone else or had something another person possessed. Most of us, if not all, have been there. However, it's the very thing you may not appreciate about yourself that God will use (see Exodus 4:10).

Listen to the words of the prophet Isaiah: *"Woe to him who strives with his Maker! Shall the clay say to him who forms it, what are you making?"*—Isaiah 45:9

What an insult it is for the creature to question the great wisdom of his or her Maker. We understand according to the Holy Scripture that God is Lord of creation. He is not walking around displeased about how and who He created us to be. Therefore, you must get to the place of being comfortable with it. But how? By simply believing what God's word says about you and rejecting all the rest. You and I both know that the world is filled with opinions and suggestions of what is sociably acceptable, beautiful, and so on. If you feed into them, you will never measure up; and if by chance you should, it will be short-lived. Take it from me, one who has worked in the fashion and beauty industry for a number of years. One day you are praised, and the next day you are criticized. Besides, I wouldn't want to be accepted by the fiascoes of a fickle society. You can rest assured, when one rises and decides to feed on what their Creator says about them, they will not be found wanting. This is of highest importance. I challenge you to start declaring out loud, "I am Your marvelous work, and this my soul knows very well!"

A REASON TO CELEBRATE

> *"By You I have been upheld from birth; You are He who took me out of my mother's womb. Praise shall continually be of You."*
>
> —Psalm 71:6–7

This passage also speaks to the sovereignty of God. By His power, you were preserved in your mother's womb until a set time. She experienced the discomfort of excruciating labor pain, but when it was time for her to push, God brought you forth. I don't have any children of my own, but I've had several opportunities to assist with this wonderful phenomenon called labor and delivery. It's amazing to see.

First, I couldn't help but go on an emotional roller coaster ride; it's as if I too was feeling the pains of labor. Second, I found myself physically pushing along with the mother-to-be until I came to myself and said, "Hey, I'm not the one giving birth here!" Next thing you know, out comes a beautiful little creature encountering the world for the first time. In those few moments of birth, babies have a lot of firsts—their first human touch, their first breath of air, their first cry, their first bath, and so on.

When I think on the word birth, what comes to mind is newness, beginnings, and oh, of course, life! Life is a miracle created by God. So it is; your birth was His miraculous gift to the world. You have a birth date and every reason to celebrate! If there is ever a time to sing "happy birthday," your entrance into the world is the time to do so.

Our lives are so precious to God that scripture gives an account of Him singing and rejoicing over us (see Zephaniah 3:17). Wouldn't you like to hear the wonderful sound of our Lord's voice singing about you! I imagine the songs would tell of His love and great promises which He has bestowed upon each of us.

Think of the greatest love song you've ever heard and how it moved you, then multiply it by ten thousand times ten. It still cannot compare to the glorious songs God sings over His children. What depth of intimacy! We won't know the fullness of God's affection until we get to heaven; even so, without the shadow of a doubt, we have an awesome and caring Creator who is so into you and me that He pauses to sing divine lullabies over us. He is so incredibly acquainted with us that the hairs on our head are numbered (see Matthew10:30).

The doctors and midwives looked you over real good. They gently took hold of your hands and feet, counted your fingers and toes and made sure all ten were there, then recorded your first little footprint on your birth certificate. God, on the other hand, placed gifts and talents in your little hands and ordered your steps, knowing exactly the place where you would flourish in life. I believe David took all of this into consideration as he reflected on his birth and concluded praise was due.

Praising God is how we celebrate; thanking God for bringing us into the world is reason to celebrate. For in Him, we live and move and have our being (see Acts 17:28). The act of celebrating simply starts with an attitude of gratitude. It doesn't matter where you come from or what your family background is. Whether you are like David, a king over a nation, or a country bumpkin working on a farm, CELEBRATE!

THE VASTNESS OF CREATION

> *When I consider Your heavens, the work of Your fingers, The moon and the stars, which You have ordained; What is man, that You are mindful of him? and the son of man, that You visit him?*—Psalm 8:3–4

David could hardly take in the vastness of creation in comparison to man, leaving him with the question, "What is man?" If anyone would take the time to consider how miniscule mankind is, I believe all would ask the same question: Why would God be mindful of such a minute part of His creation?

The Creator doesn't measure things as humans do. It's not about size; it's about relationship. Why do I say this? Well, God could have made us to walk around with our arms continually raised toward the heavens, like the limbs on a tree. He could have put our eyes on top of our head so that we would constantly look up to Him, but He didn't.

He fashioned our eyes on the fronts of our faces and our arms to hang down at our sides. He gave us a heart and an intellect so that we may choose to love Him with our own free will, lifting our eyes and hands out of pure adoration to Him in worship. This is what real relationship is all about. It's not forced; it's by choice.

I want to expound on the word "mindful" in this text. The Hebrew meaning is "to remember, to call to mind and to visit." It was never God's plan to send us into the earth and leave us to figure things out on our own and hope for the best. Neither did God intend for us to wander aimlessly through life like nomads without a plan and purpose.

God the Father is your overseer; He loves and cares for you. First and foremost, He demonstrated it through the blood sacrifice of His only Son in order that we might have life. Knowing God through Jesus Christ is life (see John 17:3). It is life eternal and life in the here and now. With that being said, every time He looks on us, He remembers and bestows new mercies.

As a matter of fact, in Isaiah 49:15–16, God declares, *"Yet will I not forget you. Behold I have graven you upon the palms of My hands."* You and I are continually before His face. That is a depth of mindfulness we cannot comprehend, especially with the millions and trillions of people passing through the planet. Third, because He is so mindful, He is constantly at work in our lives, so much so that He has assigned angels to aid us in reaching and living out our destinies (see Psalm 91:11). David was overwhelmed at the thought of it all, which gave his question merit.

Here is the reason you and I are constantly on God's mind—simply because we are His offspring. And it doesn't stop there; He takes it upon Himself to visit us! Listen again: *"And the son of man that You visit him."*—Psalm 8:4

In the book of Job, he declares that God visits man every morning (see Job 7:18). This word—visit—has a wide description; the one I want to expound on is "to look after." In order to look after someone, you would have to be mindful of them, and God is just that.

Our Creator wants us to understand that He is concerned about every aspect of our lives, so much so that He looks in on us every morning. With a gentle kiss of His mercy, He awakens us to another day, then graces us to carry out our tasks. The sovereign Lord is responsible for you—He really is! It is important to know this right from the start.

I need you to grasp this—He made you and He will see after you. This important knowledge is what the devil doesn't want you to know; he'd rather you look to ungodly sources, sending you into a lifelong tailspin of anxiety and depression. We've all met folk who have the propensity to worry excessively about nothing; we call them worry-warts—they're enough to drive you insane. It's only because they don't understand that there is someone greater whom they can turn to and cast their cares upon.

Unfortunately, you have those who turned their backs and walked away from their God because of some unfortunate mishap in life. When ministering on the street, I come across countless people like this. I leave their presence wondering, how does a person walk away from the Lord in times of trouble when that is the time to draw closer? And where would they be going, anyway? Listen. When an individual turns away from the Lord, they turn back to sin and sin is an infringement of purpose.

My goodness, this is not wise; neither is blaming God for the evil in the world when the real culprit is Satan. Understanding that God is looking after you is a cure for such a mindset. I like the way Job puts it:

> *What is man, that thou shouldest magnify him? And that thou shouldest set thine heart upon him?* —Job 7:17

Even though Job was in the midst of severe hardship, he knew he was the center of God's heart. You're familiar with the story of Job, how his end was greater than his beginning? God was looking after him.

The next meaning for the word "visit" is "to deposit." It has an even deeper meaning. It is very important that you understand this also. You see, every time God visits us, He makes a deposit in us, which is reflected in our lives. It is His way of directly investing a part of Himself in us, which will bring Him glory.

I recall the times my grandfather Carey would come and visit us in Tucson. He lived in Los Angeles, California, and he would usually stay about two weeks. My siblings and I would be so excited.

After he arrived, all the children would run out to the car to greet him. We would assist him with his bags and help him get settled in his room.

Grandfather was what we called him. He was petite in stature but thickly built. He smoked a pipe and wore a toupee. His naturally kinky hair that showed at the edges did not match with his bone-straight hair piece. In retrospect, seeing him through the eyes of a hairstylist, he needed a makeover. Grandfather seemed to be trying to hold on to his youth, but it was long gone.

Once he got settled in, we couldn't wait to gather around to hear him tell stories; some of them made us laugh and some were scary. Then sometime during his stay, he would reach into his pocket, pull out a bunch of coins, and start handing them out to all eight children. Boy, did that put a smile on our faces.

Soon after he left for California, he was missed. He had made a deposit in his grandchildren's lives. What was it? Love—and we wanted more of it. For me, the understanding that he spent time and shared what he had, even though it wasn't much, meant a whole lot. We couldn't wait until his next visit.

So it is with God, when He visits us. He is doing phenomenal, supernatural work that is preparing us to live out the very purpose for which we have been born. The question is, do you know your purpose? Job declared, *"You have granted me life and favor, and your visitation has preserved my spirit."*—Job 10:12.

Listen. God does not grant us favor and life and then sit by idly. He has preserved us for a special purpose and is watching and working on our behalf to accomplish it. You can best believe that nothing happens concerning you and me that He is not aware of.

IT DOESN'T GET ANY PLAINER THAN THAT

You made him a little lower than the angels,
And you crowned him with glory and honor.
—Psalm 8:5

How's that for clarity? You were made a little lower than the angels. It doesn't get any plainer than that. You did not evolve from an ape. Trust me; they aint yo' cousins, honey.

People today still believe and teach evolution nonsense. That's their choice, I guess. But think about it for a moment. If that were the case, why then are the monkeys no longer evolving? Why are humans no longer evolving? According to Genesis, every living thing God created was to reproduce after its kind.

There is no logical reason why any part of creation needed to evolve. To add to that, our DNA is not compatible with that of a monkey; therefore, breeding is impossible. Perhaps scientists have tried to conjure up genetically modified creatures in some lab—I don't know—but that can't compete with the creation of God. As far as I'm concerned, the whole idea of evolution is nothing more than a pitiful, pride-filled mindset of individuals who decided to believe in the imagination of his or her own limited knowledge of nothingness.

These are people who have a so-called scientific mind that the world looks up to. It is an attempt to explain away the rationale of God. My goodness gracious, even the mind of a child understands God as creator.

In a conversation with one of my clients, she expressed her fascination with monkeys. She happened to be watching a documentary of how much they display humanlike characteristics. I, for one, like to watch monkeys parade around in their habitat. But no matter how humanlike they act, they are but monkeys.

Here's my simple explanation: All of your car manufacturers create an engineered design called the automobile, which is a process used to develop a functional product. Whether it's Chrysler, Ford, or Mercedes, each make and model has something in common, on purpose. When you see the models, though they have different names, there is something in the design from which you will be able to recognize its maker.

This is called the "signature," which says that the same designer who designed the T-Bird also designed the Lincoln Continental. So it is with creation; God's signature is all over it. No need to marvel at a monkey; the same God who created the man also created the monkey. Which brings me to the second half of this verse.

YOU ARE SIGNIFICANT

This psalm declares that we are *"crowned with glory and honor."* Crowning man with glory and honor is God's way of showing off, and He likes to show off. What was God's purpose? To adorn you with splendor, magnificence, and beauty for display, just as He is all of these. Ah, so then your birth is God's way of duplicating Himself; i.e., displaying His image in the earth. You need to pause for a shout on this one. Here's why. The Lord has endowed every human being with dignity, in that every time we see each other, we are seeing God!

I feel sorry for people who have been taught to hate on others because they are of a different race or gender and who think one skin color is better than another. These false assumptions are steeped in pride. A culprit causing one's own heart to become puffed up, lending support to feel he or she has the right to despise what God has deemed as *His* image. What foolishness. What bitter hatred to live with every day of one's life. It's an even bigger disgrace to see it displayed in our churches today. This is partly because some denominations have reduced Christ to mere skin color.

Here's my question: if God made one skin color better than another, why is it that we see all skin colors lying sick in the hospitals, nursing homes, and yes, the morgue? Sickness and disease are not partial, neither does poverty have any favorites. Trust me—we are all made of the same lump of clay. And when we die, our mortal bodies go back to the dirt.

Jesus didn't display partiality on the cross; He died for all of humanity. Let's repent and get over the foolishness of prejudice once and for all. Because when we stand before the judgment seat of Christ, we won't be judged by the color of our skin. We will be judged by the deeds we have done in our hearts.

The God I've come to know loves diversity. Look around you. Everything He created speaks to that—from the wide array of flowers and trees, to the different animals such as birds and all their kinds, to the fish in the sea. God is diverse!

Now, being that He has crowned you above all creation with glory and honor, doesn't that speak volumes to the fact that you are of special value? You are significant—yes, you! Beloved, you must comprehend this. Seeing ourselves the way God sees us is crucial, and is the foundation for success.

The Hebrew meaning for *glory* is "weightiness," meaning that which is substantial or heavy. You've heard of the idiom "worth its weight in gold," an expression first used in early Roman times. It simply means to place value on an object or a person, which is what God had done. Though mankind was created last, look at what God bestowed upon him. He gave man "dominion" over the works of His hands. When I observe little children who are spoiled with the love of their fathers, they act as if everything Daddy possesses is theirs. They roam around the family home as if they own it. When bedtime rolls around, the child skips past his own bedroom, runs and jumps right in the middle of Mommy and Daddy, snuggles up, and goes to sleep. You see, even though they are children, they are practicing dominion.

In their little hearts they know Daddy adores them, and in his eyes, they are most precious. Are you feeling me? Of how much more value are we to God, our Father? We were created to rule and reign as He does. No other creature was given this blessing. Your life was designed from the very beginning to have meaning and special purpose, regardless of your experience. The sooner you know it, the better. Because then and only then will you become unstoppable in all that you are called to do.

IT'S IN THE SCRIPT

What do I mean by *unstoppable*? God's plan for your life cannot be altered by any outside forces. It's in the script. But you are free to choose another path—your own path—forfeiting all of what God has in store. At times, it may appear that all hell has broken loose and the purpose and promises of God will never happen.

Remember, beloved, He cannot lie. The promises and the seasons belong to God. He made them, and He has set the right time to bring it all to pass. Yes, there will be seasons when you will walk through dark valleys. Your very soul will be tested to its core. These are the times when you must remain focused and trust God with all of your heart. Besides, you can't hurry God, so it's good to learn patience and wait on Him.

I used to live in Lawrenceville, a suburb of Atlanta, Georgia. Times were not easy then. I was living strictly on faith, the Lord leading me every step of the way. Atlanta was so vast that I hard time figuring out where I wanted to live. I chose to reside in Lawrenceville because it was like being in the country.

I needed a job at the time, so I began asking the locals around town for leads. I was pointed to a salon way on the backside of the corner behind the trees. To the average person it was terribly unappealing on every level. But I saw a gold mine.

I began working, and word soon got around that there was a new stylist in town. As the folks say, "And she can do some hair!" After getting a feel for the area, I realized there wasn't an upscale hair salon in town for black women. Seeing the opportunity, I decided to open up my own shop. I delighted in serving people. I set a goal to give them top-of-the-line hair care, with complementary beverages and hors d'oeuvres on occasion.

Many of the ladies who frequented my salon weren't accustomed to good customer service; they were just good ole' country bumpkins. But as much as I enjoyed serving them, in retrospect, it was clear why they couldn't appreciate it.

People who have been in mental bondage all their lives have a hard time adapting to freedom. In their minds, they are still in chains—which causes them to constantly act out in survival mode. It was going to take more than opening up a salon and serving them to make a difference in their lives.

After a time of working with country po' folks, I learned how hard it was to please them. They have what I call "a po' man's mentality." Yes, I know I'm speaking Ebonics, but there is a difference between po' and poor.

When you're poor, you know it and try to work your way out of it somehow. But when you are po', you're proud and totally oblivious to the fact. Worse yet, the po' have the spirit of a crab—meaning po' folks will not rise to achieve success, but the moment *you* do, they will pull you down. They are ungrateful, and one can never do enough for them. They have a hard time accepting change, if they accept it at all. Po' folks have a tendency to blame everyone else for their problems, which they actually created themselves.

Anyway, I found a fixer-upper in a commercial district. Boy, did it need a lot of work. I moved in and started the repairs. Little did I know the house was currently occupied. I lived in the back of the salon and used the front for business. I began to hear strange noises, especially at night, but I would dismiss them.

I proceeded to work on the place, taking every penny I had to make my salon beautiful; and beautiful it was. When I opened for business, my present clients followed. Women came from far and near and my salon flourished!

After a few months of living in the rental property, the noises became more intense. A scurrying sound came out of the attic, along with drumbeat sounds on my backdoor window. I would get up to go see who it was, but no one would be there. I'd return to my bed and lie back down. It really got scary when I turned off the light and an eerie, ghostly force filled my room. As soon as I jumped up to turn the light on, it would leave.

To tell you the truth, I didn't know what I was dealing with, so I went into the kitchen and got the biggest butcher knife I had and hid behind my bedroom door. I guess I was going to cut me a devil that night.

Days passed as I kept working. The sounds only worsened, interrupting my sleep. Looking back, I realized my night prayers to the Lord had unintentionally stirred up a devil, and the booger was uncomfortable. One of us had to go, and I knew it wasn't going to be me.

Night after night I would have very intense devotional prayer sessions. One night after praying, I was particularly exhausted. I'd had a long, hard day's work in the salon. I fell into bed and went right to sleep. I don't know how long I had been asleep when I was awakened by the sound of massive footsteps on the housetop.

Strangely, with each step, I could feel a force of pressure over me, as if the roof was going to cave in at any moment. The steps come to the edge of the roof; then there was silence. The demon spirit left off with an audible *poof!* as if it just disappeared.

The house was peaceful from that night forward. I've encountered demons before, but not on this wise. I knew they possessed people, but this devil was hanging around, occupying space. Either way, we have power over the Devil.

The word of God declares that Jesus gave them power against unclean spirits, to cast them out (see Matthew 10:1). The same power exercised by Jesus' disciples is still accessible today. The amazing thing is, I wasn't targeting a demon per se. Prayer ushers in the very presence of God. He manifests His authority and rule in our environment. What a display of the power of God through prayer! It had become a lifestyle from the very beginning of my walk with Christ Jesus. Crying out to Him in my bedroom at night was a constant thing. I needed Him, and He was always there for me. Thank you, Lord!

After all my hard work, I was able to save some money and buy myself a decent car. It wasn't a brand-new one, but it was what I had always wanted—a Cadillac de Ville. I was happy about my car, so I thought everybody else would be, too. Boy, was I totally naive.

Slowly things began to take a turn. As the weeks progressed I noticed my business begin to drop off. A few months went by and my business had dwindled to just a few clients here and there. I mean, I was barely making it. *Wow, what happened to my customers?* I wondered.

After all, I was very good at my craft as a stylist. I always got over-the-top compliments from my clients. Women who didn't have hair before now had hair, and of the women who had hair, I made theirs better. Many drove across Atlanta because they wanted great hair care.

Not to mention, their children even chimed in with compliments as they marveled at the success of their mothers' new looks. We all know that children have a habit of speaking whatever crosses their minds—good, bad, or otherwise.

For example: A Georgia peach walked into my salon one day. She heard about me through her daughter and after much convincing she finally decided to call and make an appointment.

The moment she showed up, I could see she desperately needed some TLC. Her hair was a mess, not due to any fault of her own. Having been burned by previous stylists, she was noticeably nervous. Not really knowing what to expect, she reluctantly took a seat in my chair, politely accepted my consultations, and the styling process began.

She shared her not-so-pleasant prior salon encounters as I worked to get her hair to a state of perfection. Finally, the finished product. *It's stunning,* I said to myself.

To tell you the truth, for what I had to work with, I couldn't go anywhere but up. "Are you ready to see your hair?" I asked.

"Yes," she responded with doubt. Turning the chair around to the mirror, she gasped. Quite speechless, her eyes told the story. She finally spoke, saying, "It's beautiful—no one has ever done my hair like this. Oh, I can't wait to show it off!"

A few moments later, her son arrived to give her a lift back home. He stepped through the doorway, and at first glance, he expressively asked his mother, "Who put that miracle on yo' head?" Elated, she looked at me with a big smile and said, "I know it's beautiful if my son likes it."

From then on, the Georgia peach would call in for her appointments and say, "I'm ready for my miracle." It was incidents like this that had me puzzled. How was it that I went from cash flow to no-flow? I couldn't understand what was happening.

Thelma, a weekly regular, entered my salon and without any hesitation commenced telling me the scoop. She said, "You know, someone ask me, 'Why are you going over there to 'Nita's shop every week like that, helping her pay for her Cadillac?'" I was taken aback as my mouth hung open in dismay. I hadn't given it a second thought that people would react so negatively. But react they did, behind a used automobile.

Seething with pure envy, all the ladies got together and decided not to patronize my salon. Instead, they went home and tied up their hair with scarves. You can best believe it; I saw it with my own eyes. It was just as well, though, because God had a plan.

A few days passed. One morning I was standing in my salon looking out of the window, watching the cars go by, when something came over me. For a few moments it was as if I was outside, looking in at the world through a glass, as though I was detached from everything around me and I was seeing a vision.

I asked, "Dear God, what am I doing here?" It was the strangest feeling, as if *here* meant that I was from somewhere out there. It took me thirty-one years to ask God this relevant question, and because of the question, I believe I experienced eternity; there were no constraints on my life whatsoever. I felt a higher calling and that I had the power to be whatever I was being called to. I had always felt different growing up anyway, and this was the confirmation of that feeling.

Why am I sharing this experience? Because this was one of the times God visited me. This unusual experience showed me that my destiny wasn't determined by a group of people. Their choice to stay away from the salon was a sign that my season for being there was over. People come and go, but God remains faithful. No matter the circumstance, you must find the strength and begin to sense your own significance, as I did. If you don't, you will live your life dictated by people's opinions and circumstances. Let me give you a couple of examples.

In Arizona, there are lots of woodpeckers. I was on my usual three-mile walk through the neighborhood early one morning. A woodpecker was perched on the telephone pole. He pecked on the metal box at rapid speed, like the sound of a drummer in a regimental band. It was plenty noisy.

He pecked time after time, obviously getting nowhere. The woodpecker didn't realize he was out of his element. His beak was not designed to peck on metal, but rather on wood or cacti. What had happened to cause the woodpeckers to do something so unnatural? These birds had slowly adapted to an environment that was hardly conducive to them.

Then there's the cat I saw as she crouched, ready to attack her little feathered prey. The moment the cat attempted to pounce, the birds flew away. She tried time after time, but no matter how persistent she was, she could never succeed. Her master had put a bell around her neck that announced her arrival, and this alerted the birds to her presence. She would find it impossible to live up to her fullest potential. This feline had to live her days bound by what her master wanted her to be instead of what she was created to be.

These are simple examples, but even so, they can be applied to our lives. You see, if you don't know your own significance and purpose, you will get sucked into a vacuum, forced into something or someone that you were not intended to be.

A prime example is a woman who is drawn into prostitution, coerced and intimidated by her so-called lover, who is, in reality, a pimp. He doesn't care how she is affected at all. He beats her into submission until she no longer resists. Eventually she succumbs to a depraved lifestyle. His one chief goal is personal gain—money.

God has given us dominion, the power to reign in life, to rise above every demonic force that comes against us, through Jesus Christ (see Romans 5:17). How do we attain this essential way of life? The answer is that we must seek God. It is He who reveals to us His will for our lives so that we may know which path to take.

It is crucial that we grab ahold of this verse in the Psalms: *"And the son of man, that You visit him."* Throughout my life, the Lord would visit me. I didn't always understand it, but He looked in on me and showed me, in His awesome ways, that I had a divine purpose, one that was bigger than me. As much as I loved styling hair for the ladies, the calling of God on my life was far greater. Yet in order to know that divine purpose, I had to pursue my Creator, and I encourage you to do the same. No one can do it for you.

Myles Munroe delivered a great message to the Body of Christ entitled, *"Power of Purpose."* He said, *"If you want to know the purpose of a thing, don't ask the thing. Purpose is only found in the mind of the creator of a thing. Only the maker of the thing knows the true purpose."*

He was so right on. But who was I, that God was mindful of me? Only a broken little girl, rejected and abused by her mother and father. A misfit, if you will, all through her little life. Never did I fit in, not even in school. I wasn't the popular type, and I really didn't want to be.

In high school I had my first and only reefer encounter. As a sophomore at Tucson High, I hung out with my Aunt Fredricka, one of my mother's younger sisters. My aunt was a cutie, petite with dark ebony skin, and she enjoyed pushing my buttons.

Even though she was only a few months older than I, Fredricka was obsessed with the idea of being "Auntie" and made it known that I was her niece. Especially when introducing me to her friends, she made it a point to rub it in. "This is my niece!" she'd say, as she waved with a mischievous hand gesture. Fredricka would put emphasis on "-ece." I would give her this how-I-hate-you look, and she'd crack up laughing.

We were in the same grade and wore the same dress size. My mother taught me how to sew, and I made most of my own clothes. My aunt would help herself to them without my permission. I hated this terribly. Having to deal with her ongoing disrespect, I came up with a plan of recourse. I decided to hide my clothes so she couldn't find them. It didn't help. Every morning I got dressed and left for school before she did, unaware that lagging behind was her plan all along. A few moments later she would arrive at school, dressed in my newly made garments, wearing them as if she had bought the fabric and made them herself! She would walk boldly up to me with a grin on her face, knowing I couldn't do anything about it.

Back to my reefer experience, Fredricka was invited to join some fellows who supplied a bag of weed. My aunt was no novice when it came to smoking reefer. With enticing words, she convinced me to come along, and we decided to leave the school grounds at lunchtime. We all walked to an underpass a few blocks from the high school. Everyone positioned themselves on whatever makeshift seating they could find. We'd soon come to know the real reason for the invitation.

Everyone watched while one fellow in the group rolled this funny looking cigarette. He ran it under his nose and took a deep whiff. He lit the thing up and took a long drag, then passed the reefer around.

When it came to my turn, I puffed and puffed, but I never did get high, not even a buzz. All I got was an aching throat from the smoke. My aunt, on the other hand, was wasted. She acted like a complete clown, giggling hysterically. You know what I mean—she was out of her head. She appeared to enjoy the effects of it. And all the while, the boys were running their hands all over her body. Poor auntie fell victim to their fiendish scheme. Unfortunately, this was only the beginning of her drug use. It wasn't until later on when we became adults that she revealed to me a shameful and painful secret she had been hiding for years, which had led her down this path in the first place. I knew that getting high was not for me, ever! I never liked the idea of sneaking around, even as a child. It took the fun out of it. Like the one day I elected to play hooky from school…

My first attempt was in middle school, I believe. Usually one skips school to go do something fun and exciting, right? Well, in my case, I had no fixed plans. I got up that morning for school as usual, but when I left home, I walked around the neighborhood a while. I knew I had to get somewhere out of sight, so I came to an alley and found a big box. It was just big enough to hide away inside, and so I climbed in and closed the top over my head. I stayed there for about an hour and grew very tired.

As I look back, it felt like being grounded and sent to your room for a week, except worse. After staying inside the box as long as I could, I got out of the box and went to school. That was my first and only attempt to skip class. I was so square that I didn't even know how to play hooky . . .

MY PATH WAS PLANNED BY GOD

As I came to understand that my path was planned by God, I began to consider the timing of my own birth. I made my entrance in December of 1959, a time in which the women's movement had been growing and strengthening since way back in 1848. American women wanted rights, the same rights as men. Female pioneers arose and began to fight for them.

These were ordinary women who had persevered through struggles, and who wanted to make a difference in the world. As a result, women began to enter higher government positions. They realized they didn't have to get married to have a good life. They could go to college, become educated, and choose their own careers. While I don't agree with everything women's rights stand for, I do believe that women have the capability of being great leaders, and are just as capable as men—in some cases, even more so.

Yes, America was changing due to the women who made historical strides to accomplish it. The same began to happen with women and the call of God to preach the gospel. The church taught that women should not teach or preach the word of God. Women were certainly not allowed to pastor congregations, let alone stand in the pulpit. It was not accepted by denominations for years. If by chance a woman was permitted to speak or talk (they didn't classify it as preaching), she had to ask permission.

According to history, in 1820 Mrs. Jarena Lee was the first black woman preacher in the AME church—born into slavery and separated from her parents at the age of seven years. Nevertheless, God called and anointed her to preach the gospel. Although full of the Holy Ghost, she was bound by the ignorance of erroneous teaching. Yet, God opened doors for her to preach, and preach she did. Many sects today struggle with the fact that God calls women. Yet God used women in both secular and spiritual roles to pave the way for women like me.

I must mention Deborah, the Prophetess, a female warrior, who God raised to be a judge over Israel in the Old Testament (see Judges 4–5). Little did I know, He would call me to preach the gospel too—to be a pastor, one of God's gifts to the Body of Christ. Yes, He did. I was shaking in my boots. I struggled with it for many years, feeling totally insignificant and wondering, *why me*?

Today, I find it an honor and a privilege, so . . . why not me? You see, long before I came on the scene, God was already at work in the earth, raising up women to be strong leaders that would help shape our world right along with the men. Many years earlier in my walk with Christ, I began seeing female evangelists for the first time, preaching in the church I attended. Even though they were greatly anointed, I saw their struggles, and I'd say to myself, *I'm glad that's not me.* But God was calling women out. He is no respecter of persons—no, God wants a willing vessel.

Speaking of calling, I was only nineteen years old when I heard the audible voice of God. One evening I had come home from a powerful church meeting, and I was high on the Lord. I lived with my Aunt Lou at the time and her, um, common law husband, George. Thank God, that night no one was home. Still in worship mode, I lay down across my bed and began to feel the Spirit of God as He filled my room. With my head on the pillow, all I could do was weep. His presence was strong.

"Anita, Anita"—someone was calling my name. Then I heard it again, a second time. In amazement, I rose and began to look around. *Who's calling me*, I wondered. Where is this voice coming from? I listened intently and heard it a third time. *"Anita, Anita."* Not knowing it was God, I lay back down and went off to sleep in a peace I'd never known before. I couldn't wait to tell my bishop about my experience.

Sunday morning rolled around, and as soon as I got to church, I ran into my bishop's office. I told him about my experience as his face tuned in with such intensity. With a smile he said to me, "Next time you hear it, say, 'Yes, Lord." I walked away, thinking, *the God of heaven was calling me*? If you'd asked me what it sounded like, all I could tell you is that it was the sweetest, most peaceful-sounding voice I had ever heard.

Yes, my path was planned by God. You can't forget an experience like that. It penetrates your very being and leaves you in a state of continual awe. Looking back, I wish my bishop would have been much more explanatory. I mean, the God of heaven came down to talk to *me*. This was the most pivotal moment of my entire life! We can read how the Lord did this very thing to others throughout the scriptures. The story of Samuel is one example. It is an awe-inspiring story of a little boy who was dedicated to God by his mother Hannah. She had been barren for many years and desperately wanted a child. Hannah promised God that if He gave her a son, she would give him back to Him, and God honored her prayer. Here's her story.

HANNAH'S PRAYER: GOD'S DIVINE PURPOSE

> *And she was in bitterness of soul, and prayed to the Lord and wept in anguish. Then she made a vow and said, "O Lord of hosts, if You will indeed look on the affliction of Your maidservant and remember me, and not forget Your*

maidservant, but will give Your maidservant a male child, then I will give him to the Lord all the days of his life, and no razor shall come upon his head."

So it came to pass in the process of time that Hannah conceived and bore a son, and called his name Samuel, saying, "Because I have asked for him from the Lord." Now the boy Samuel ministered to the Lord before Eli. And it came to pass at the time while Eli was lying down in his place, and when his eyes had begun to grow so dim that he could not see, and while Samuel was lying down, that the Lord called Samuel. And he answered, "Here I am!" So he ran to Eli and said, "Here I am, for you called me." And he said, "I did not call; lie down again." And the Lord called Samuel again the third time. So he arose and went to Eli and said, "Here I am, for you did call me." Then Eli perceived that the Lord had called the boy. Therefore Eli said to Samuel, "Go, lie down; and it shall be, if He calls you, that you must say, 'Speak, Lord for your servant hears.'" Now the Lord came and stood and called as at other times, "Samuel! Samuel!" And Samuel answered, "Speak, Lord for your servant hears.

—1Samuel 1:10–11, 20; 3:1–5, 8–10

What did God do?

He used a woman, who prayed a prayer, to have a baby boy,
Who made a vow, to give him back, whom God would then employ,
To be a prophet, who became a priest, while he was yet a lad.
Indeed, God's word would surely come to pass
The Lord came down to visit him as He called his name so clear,
"Samuel! Samuel! Samuel!"
"Speak, Lord, for your servant hears."

—Poem by Anita Joe

A TIME TO SPEAK

As I meditated on Ecclesiastes 3, the Lord revealed something to me that I hadn't noticed before. That is, every season comes with a sound. When there is war, it comes as a sound of marching soldiers with confused noises of battle.

When stones are gathered together, we hear the sound of a rumbling thud. Laughter brings a sound of joy and high-pitched giggles. If you take the time to think about the four seasons, you'll notice they too come with a sound.

Wintertime is a cold, dreary season, with hoot owls sounding off in the darkness of night—and the soft pitter-patter of snowflakes falling on windowsills. The crackling of icicles can be heard as they hang from crisp, dry leaves on the trees. Like the changing of the guards, springtime arrives. We anticipate the budding of trees and new flowers as their sweet aroma fills the air. Birds sing aloud their lovely melodies of praise, and the sound of thunder booms and rolls. The season of summer arrives with bright blue sunny skies. Thousands of bees buzz about their hives. One hears the rumbling sound of the monsoon rains that leave behind rushing waters that fill the arroyos, bringing to life

God's little creatures. The intrepid bullfrog leaps on the scene unafraid with an echoing mating call. A company of June beetles wearing green camouflage—with their sharp raspy sounds in simultaneous competition. During autumn, nature settles in and slowly drifts off for a long nightcap. Geese honk as they fly southward, and fall winds rustle through the leaves. Once green, their crisp textures of orange, brown, and red touch down on the ground with ease.

Every season has its own sound. Your birth was also a season, and brought the sound of your courageous cry—a herald, if you will—that said to the world, "I am here. I am alive." Yes, even in infancy, you made a cry that was heard by both God and men.

Perhaps, somewhere along life's journey, you have become silent. Someone or something stole the voice you had that could cry out and declare your God-given purpose.

What is it that has been lost? It is a mighty man or woman of valor. It is the sound of a king or queen on a quest to conquer every enemy that has oppressed you—that enemy who bound you and made you think living beneath your privilege was acceptable, simply because you didn't know who you were. I challenge you to arise and take courage. Make the same cry that you made in the beginning. Declare with a loud voice, "I AM HERE. I AM ALIVE!"

WHO'S YO' DADDY?

WHO'S YO' DADDY?

They answered and said unto Him, Abraham is our father. —John 8:39

One day while I meditated on the Word of God, the Spirit of the Lord spoke to me. He told me that three fathers are described in scripture, and all three have a plan for your life. First is your biological father. You were born into a particular family, and had no choice in the matter. You were given by God as a gift to your father.

Your father's plans for you may have been to cherish and love you. To stick around and watch you grow and develop into a beautiful adult. To protect you from danger and be there when you fell down, and then to pick you up again. He was there giving you fatherly kisses that made you feel special. He was a father who pushed you to get a higher education, so he sent you to college.

Perhaps you had a father whose plans were to never claim you as his own, or even worse, to abandon you, leaving the scene long before you could get acquainted with him. It could be that you had a father who disliked you and abused you right from the start, speaking cruel words over you that penetrated your very being, saying repeatedly that you were worthless and would never amount to anything good. He may never have shown any patience, so your slightest mistakes might cause him to beat you unmercifully.

It is possible that you had a father who would even sexually abuse you, threatening your life if you revealed his secret, leaving you fearful and full of pain.

Perhaps you had the kind of father who was present in your home. He took care of you and was a hardworking man, but he didn't know how to express his love. Rather, his emotions were cold and non-affectionate toward you, leaving you feeling unloved and rejected. Or maybe Mama had a few one-night stands and she doesn't even know who yo' daddy is.

My Aunt Lora asked me during a phone conversation one time, "'Nita, I've been meaning to ask you something," she said. "The other day I was talking with my sister, and the subject of Meadowlark Lemon (the famous American basketball player) came up. My sister said to me, 'You know that's 'Nita's daddy?'" Then my aunt asked me, with much surprise in her voice, "Did you know that he was your daddy?" I replied, "Oh, no. I didn't know." She said, "Seems everybody knew about it except me."

All I could do was to crack up laughing. It sounded so far-fetched that it was hard to believe. Although at times I wondered whether the man who raised me was my real father, being that he was so abusive. Nevertheless, he was the only father I knew. I don't know if it's true or not; my mother is dead, so I can't ask her. Plus, it's something that I wouldn't be willing to pursue.

Beloved, whether you had a favorable childhood or not, your father was to be responsible for you until you reached adulthood. Listen and know, "to everything there is a season." Just as your birth was a season, so it is with your childhood. Whatever your experience, life comes with options of suitable choices for the betterment.

Some years ago I looked into becoming a foster parent. After doing my research, I discovered a lack of foster parents in the system, especially good ones. I decided to sign up for night classes.

My then-husband and I were only too glad to step up to the plate and help. It didn't take long before serious troubles became apparent concerning the foster kids. I read books and saw films about the horrific stories of parental mistreatment of the children. You've heard the saying, "There is always someone else worse off than you." This was that.

One specific story stuck in my mind. It was a little boy whose parents were strung out on drugs. They used their son to support their habit by selling him for sex to anyone who came by the house. It didn't matter if they were male or female. Every night this little boy was forced to perform sex acts with adults—total strangers who were no doubt druggies themselves. The child was so traumatized that even years after he was rescued his memories haunted him, so much so that the very onset of nightfall became his worst enemy. At a time when most would welcome nighttime to get a good rest, he would wail and cry out in fits because the scars of the heinous activity went deep, always so fresh in his mind. It was as if he was reliving it all over again at that very moment. Oh, how that father totally misused and abused his fatherly duties.

There were many unforgettable stories. The only thing I could say at that time was, LORD, have mercy! I would oftentimes dare to say that once children go into the foster care system, their lives are no better. In fact, some are even worse off. There are, however, good foster parents out there who genuinely love these foster children as their own. We can thank God for them.

Initially, it was a system set up by ungodly people motivated by money. Why else would a child placed in a good foster home be uprooted because he or she reached a certain age, only to be placed in another foster situation requiring him to readapt, for reasons only God knows? How tragic.

As much as I wanted to take on being a foster parent, the Lord spoke to me in a dream that foster care was not His will for me. In the dream, it was made known to me that after pouring myself into a child and loving him or her back to wholeness, I wouldn't be able to handle the separation when the time came. Following the leading of the Lord, I relinquished the idea.

WHAT IS A FATHER?

Fatherhood is one of the greatest roles under the sun, although the task may appear daunting for some. According to *Strong's Concordance*, the Greek word for father is PATER, meaning "a male parent or ancestor," and by extension, "an honorific title, leader." It also denotes an archetype, which is the original pattern or model, of which all things of the same type are representations or copies. Hence, we get the expression "like father like son." Most often, children are a depiction of their parents, whether good or bad—all the more reason men should strive to be godly fathers.

The *Macmillan Dictionary* says a father is a man who acts or is thought of as a male parent, guardian, or provider. With that understanding, if a male parent is a guardian, it is his responsibility to watch over and protect his children. A father is one whom a child should be able to trust and depend on. It's just that simple; that's what my then-husband used to say.

Why, then, are so many neglecting their responsibilities? I'm inclined to believe there are two main reasons. The first obvious answer is because of a lack of love. It is what the Bible calls "unnatural affection." Loving a child is supposed to come naturally, but this is not always true in today's world.

The second reason is because many men do not choose to include God the Father and to make Him the head of their lives, allowing Him to direct their thoughts and behaviors. As a result, fatherlessness has become an epidemic across America. Scripture uses the metaphor of an ostrich to describe the callous heart of the daughters of Israel (see Lamentations 4:3). Though it speaks of the daughters, it can be applied to the sons as well.

After the female in an ostrich colony lays her eggs, her treatment of her offspring can be very cruel, to say the least. If by chance the eggs escape the dangers from neglect, the newly hatched young are subject to abandonment. The cocks walk away, leaving their young behind. The young that can't keep up are left to die in the wilderness. There are countless men who, like the ostrich, have walked away from their responsibilities as fathers, leaving their young children to fend for themselves.

Another atrocity that causes fatherlessness in the home is the diabolical scheme created by our judicial system that unjustly incarcerates multiple thousands of fathers, causing a breakdown in the family unit. You probably won't read much about this subject, but if we are going to tackle fatherlessness, we must be made aware of all the culprits involved.

An episode of *The Animal Kingdom* covered the lives of elephants in Africa. As I finished watching, the scenes left a lasting imprint on my mind. The narrator mentioned that the park rangers felt the elephants posed a problem because they were becoming overpopulated. They devised a plan and commenced removing the bulls (male elephants) to another part of the continent.

It appeared to have been successful, or so they thought. While doing a routine drive through the park, they began to notice dead rhinos on the jungle floor. As this continued and increased they were puzzled as to what—or who—was responsible.

While on a daily routine, they noticed a few teenage bull elephants bullying a rhino. The young elephants would tear branches from a tree and, with great force, throw them at the rhino to provoke him to anger. As a consequence, the rhino would charge the young bulls only to be stomped to death.

The rangers realized that they had made a big mistake. They gathered up the bulls and brought them back to their families. Herein is the amazing part—the violence stopped immediately!

The bulls play a significant role in the lives of their offspring, especially in the areas of training and discipline. How much more so for humans? Consider how drastic our society has shifted from well-mannered children to producing angry, violent teenagers, ranging from gang leaders to individuals committing random shooting sprees. The ramifications are no different than the young bulls. A father's involvement with his sons and daughters is the key to a well-developed child. There is no substitute.

 I pray:

> *May the God of heaven have mercy and bring wholeness to fathers and their families across this nation. May He heal broken fathers and bring them back to the home. May He put a hedge of protection round about them. May He overturn every wicked plan from the enemy devised against them. In the mighty name of Jesus!*

To reiterate, the definition of a father is an honorific title, which means it is an esteemed, respectful role. Dropping a seed to produce a child doesn't automatically earn a man the honor of being a father. A man must take it upon himself and assume his responsibility.

We can look around us and see men who have several "baby mamas," not willing to settle down with any one of them, but looking to move on to the next relationship. If and when they finally decide to commit to a marriage, there's a good chance more children will be produced, thus, making childcare extremely difficult.

If the shoe fits and you are not married, I don't recommend seeking new relationships. What I do recommend and pray is that you would be willing to make an about-face from ungodly attitudes toward women, which led you down this path. Perhaps your father was the epitome of sperm donors throughout his life, never taking on the responsibility to father his children. With that said, I challenge you to raise the bar. Submit yourself to the Lord and become that son who will make a difference.

There is a saying that in order to go forward, sometimes you have to go backward. Allow the Lord to lead you back to "the one" of your past relations and make it work! In my opinion this is the responsible thing. Notice I said, "allow the Lord to lead you." You will need divine direction, and the Father knows just the right woman for you. I'm not speaking of a forced relationship. I'm suggesting that you work with the woman who can receive your love and is willing give it back. If it is God's will, it will happen naturally.

Go in with the understanding that great relationships require hard work. Remember, you have already put the cart before the horse, but eventually things will smooth out. Again, you will have to back up to move forward. How admirable would it be in the eyes of the Father if you transcend old habits and make room for a God-union made in heaven, not to mention the much-needed examples of good wholesome relationships.

Apostle Paul says the man is head of the woman (speaking of marriage, see 1 Corinthians 11:3). Any father who turns from the unprofitable ways of the world, makes significant character changes, and consistently walks with God—ninety percent of the time, the woman will follow. Thus, the relationship can develop into a harmonious, godly union. Why do I feel so confident in this? Because the Bible is the blueprint for success. When the biblical injunction is followed, the Lord will honor the marriage (Hebrews 13:4). Anything He honors, He will bless.

The Lord is aware of your mistakes and weaknesses. He is able to make you complete in every good work to do His will through Christ Jesus (Hebrews 13:21). The Lord will equip you and cause you to rise up by His divine instruction to live a life of honor. Honor and respect for others is greatly lacking in our relationships today, all the more reason for unhealthy relationships altogether. A good dose of old-fashioned respect is the cure.

What do I mean by living a life of honor? It is conducting yourself in a manner worthy of Christ and living a lifestyle of pleasing God. As father, your chief goal is to honor God (reverence Him); honor yourself (self-respect); honor your wife as the weaker vessel (love her with understanding); and honor your role as father (give your children a name and be involved in their lives).

Beloved father, herein lies your blessings for life. Show me a father that honors God with his life, and I'll show you a man whose life is blessed. The Lord declares, *"Those who honor me I will honor."* His prayers are answered (2 Peter 3:7) and wealth and riches are in his house—the descendants reap the blessings of the father (Psalm 112:1).

Let's look at God's standard for a father in the Old Testament. According to *The Complete Word Study Old Testament*, the Hebrew word for Father is "AV"; it is closely related to the Greek meaning—begetter, creator, guardian; a benefactor. It is said to be the first word a baby vocalizes without having been taught.

In the book of Genesis we read the unique story of Abraham, whose name means "the father is exalted." God's intent was to raise Abram to Abraham, make a covenant with him that would change Jewish history, and this spoken promise would spill over to the gentiles. Through Abraham all nations would be blessed. Genesis reveals the Lord's remarkable relationship with him:

> *"For I know him, that he will command his children and his household after him, and they shall keep the way of the Lord, to do justice and judgment. That the Lord may bring upon Abraham that which He has spoken of him."*
>
> —Genesis 18:19

Abraham was seventy-five years old and married to Sarah, who was barren. His family background consisted of idol worship, yet, the Lord chose him to be "father of many nations." Why? It wasn't because Abraham was good looking and had a swagger in his step.

We know from this passage that the Lord made a personal declaration concerning Abraham, saying, "I know him." What a grand statement. Ever wonder what God is saying about you as a father? In other words, Abraham was co-laborer *with* God. The Lord knew that he would assume responsibility as a father and obey the divine commandments spoken to him. God deemed him trustworthy and dependable, as we can see from the verse that follows: *"that he will command his children and his household after him, and they shall keep the way of the Lord."* Herein lies the first thing that makes a good father.

Abraham did not mince words; the "shall keep" is the key. He adamantly enforced righteous conduct and justice into the life of his offspring, and the Lord saw it. As a result, his obedience brought upon him the blessings of life. There's no question why God was so certain about him. This father of faith understood the truths of his God. Thus, he passed them on through generations. In this, Abraham was a true father in God's eyes. His life was—and is—a prime example for every father today.

What does God want today's fathers to learn from Abraham? He was an ordinary man who simply believed God. He had a divine purpose, wrapped in his name. Abraham lived out this tall order by faith, making him extraordinary.

Herein is the most incredible part. Throughout biblical history the Lord is known as the God of Abraham, Isaac, and Jacob. The covenant line was expanded all because of the "shall" in verse 19 ("they *shall* keep the way of the Lord"). In other words, the teachings of God were so ingrained in Abraham's offspring that they were a natural part of life. They didn't know anything else to live by. How wonderful is that! It's equally wonderful to see in today's families, in third- and fourth-generation pastors on fire for God. I want to commend these faithful fathers who have impacted their children's lives. They have taught them to love Jesus with all their hearts and have given stern warnings against following after the ways of the world.

Establishing the principles of godliness in the children is God's commandment to every father. It is not to be taken lightly. I think it's fair to say that few men instruct their children in the ways of God as they should. Take a look at church attendance. The church is mostly filled with mothers, with their children sitting beside them. Fathers are watching sports or off playing golf. Sadly, they are more interested in sports than in the spiritual upbringing of their own children. Many feel it's the mother's responsibility to teach these principles to the children, but scripture doesn't say, "I know Sarah, that she will command her children." No, God said, "For I know him [Abraham] that he will command his children and his household after him."

It amazes me that so many men want to be the head of everything except when it comes to spiritual matters. But God has a plan. He is able to bring about a mighty awakening in the soul. Malachi declares,

> *"Behold, I will send you Elijah the prophet before the coming of the great and dreadful day of the Lord, and he will turn the hearts of the fathers to the children, and the hearts of the children to the fathers. Lest I come and strike the earth with a curse."*
>
> —Malachi 3:6

It is through the preaching of the gospel that men will come to love and cherish their children once again. Precious fathers, God will have family order.

My prayer is:

> *Through God and our Lord Jesus Christ, "the father will once again be exalted," in the mighty name of JESUS, amen.*

The second thing that makes for a good father is that he shoots his children like arrows in the right direction in life. The psalmist says,

> *Lo, children are an heritage of the Lord and the fruit of the womb is his reward, As arrows are in the hand of the mighty man; so are children of the youth. Happy is the man that hath his quiver full of them: they shall not be ashamed, but they shall speak with the enemies in the gate.*
>
> —Psalm 127:3–5

Verse four clearly addresses the responsibility of the father, for an arrow cannot shoot itself. It takes the hand of a mighty man and a trained eye—in other words, a skillful and wise father—who recognizes his child's potential. Then he cultivates it until that child has developed the things that will make him or her successful throughout life.

Some fathers struggle with children who have different ideas from his own. Nevertheless, through the father's wisdom, he directs his children to become the best they can be in a career, and to live out their own dreams and wishes. This will take sacrifice—that is, love, patience, and time.

FIGHTS AND PROTECTS

Fighting and protecting is the third thing that makes a good father. Let's read the story concerning David and his family in 1 Samuel:

> *So David and his men came to the city, and there it was, burned with fire; and their wives, their sons, and their daughters had been taken captive. Then David and the people who were with him lifted up their voices and wept, until they had no more power to weep. And David's two wives, Ahinoam the Jezreelitess, and Abigail, the widow of Nabal the Carmelite, had been taken captive.*
>
> *So David inquired of the Lord, saying, "Shall I pursue this troop? Shall I overtake them?" And He answered him, "Pursue, for you shall surely overtake them and without fail recover all." So David went, he and the six hundred men who were with him, and came to the brook Besor, where those stayed who were left behind. But David pursued, he and four hundred men; Then David attacked them from twilight until the evening of the next day. Not a man of them escaped, except four hundred young men who rode on camels and fled.*

> *...and David rescued his two wives. And nothing of theirs was lacking, either small or great, sons or daughters, spoil or anything which they had taken from them; David recovered all.*
> *—1 Samuel 30:3–5; 8-10; 17–18*

David was a hero in the eyes of his family. I can imagine that his wives probably loved him even more after this. You can well believe, if my man came and rescued me from a savage enemy, when I got home he would get a special head rub and hot vittles every night! His whole family knew without any doubt that they could depend upon him no matter the circumstance, because that's what fathers do.

Last, earthly fathers are givers. They look ahead and consider their children's futures. Proverbs 13:22 says, *"A good man leaveth an inheritance to his children's children."* Jesus compares earthly fathers to God when it comes to giving gifts and declares, *"If ye then, being evil, know how to give good gifts to your children, how much more shall your heavenly Father give."* —Luke 11:13

The word "good" in the Greek is AGATHOS. This Greek word contains both a physical and moral meaning in which the "good" produces benefits—good things such as leaving a legacy for their children; good things like being "the" role model in their lives; and good things that benefit, such as having a good name.

My then-husband George, who was seventeen years my senior, told me a fascinating story of his younger days. His father paved the way for him to enter into a very profitable career in the electrical field. He got a job at an Electrical company here in Tucson, a place where his father worked after he retired from the army. Previously, George attended the University of Arizona and was doing very well in his studies as a history major.

Along the way, he met a young lady who became pregnant with his child, and there went George's college education out the window. His parents, Dorothy and George Sr., made him marry, and he took on the responsibility of a father. You see, they didn't allow young men to walk away and be irresponsible back in those days. If you got a girl pregnant, you married her and gave the baby a name.

It's still the moral thing to do even today. After all, the girl didn't get pregnant by herself. I'm sorry to say that many men aren't worth marrying today simply because they have not been trained up to be responsible.

After dropping out of college, George looked for a job—any job. He started out with menial positions. That was in the fifties; black folks were struggling to get decent jobs, even with an education. He finally landed a job as a trash collector for the city of Tucson.

While at work, George ran into his father's boss. In conversation, the man spoke very highly of his father and invited him to drop by the office and see him. George was clueless as to what "dropping by the office" meant.

After running into the boss a second time, he realized the gentleman was offering him a new job. Finally deciding to pay him a visit, the rest is history. George was hired right on the spot and began to work for the Tucson Electric Supply Co.

In the beginning, George's boss wanted him to mimic his father. One day the boss approached George about his hair. George sported a big afro when he started with the company. "George," he said, "you know, your father used to wear a very short, conservative haircut." George replied, "Yeah, it looked real nice on my father," and he walked away. And that was the end of that. George proved himself to be dependable. He worked for the company for over thirty-five years as a sales manager.

Here is the amazing part. George's father died when he was a seventeen-year-old boy, but he left him something that would give him an advantage in life—a good name. That's what fathers do.

FATHER OF LIES

After the biological father, the second father described by the Lord Jesus in the scripture is the father of lies, because he is the author, or the originator, of deception. In other words, lying is one of his chief traits. He too has a plan for you.

His name in the Greek is *SATANAS*, meaning "hostile opponent." He is in direct conflict with Father God and everything and everyone that has to do with Him. Satan, who is also called the devil, is not to be taken lightly or dismissed as a figment of the imagination. The Lord Jesus, who knows Satan all too well, declares,

> *He was a murder from the beginning, and abode not in the truth, because there is no truth in him. When he speaketh a lie, he speaketh of his own: for he is a liar, and the father of it."*—John 8:44

These two recorded illustrations concerning Satan's character should have every human being on alert. First, he is a murderer; and second, a liar. Our parents used to say, "If you lie, you will steal; and if you steal, you will kill." Well, Satan the devil will do all of the above; there is no doubt about it.

The first lie recorded in scripture is in Genesis 3:1–7. Satan used a serpent, who was cunning by nature, to deceive the woman, Eve. Dispensing his mode of attack, he painted a deceptive picture with a brush of lies, causing Eve to doubt the Father and disobey Him. Satan is still swaying men today. His tactics have not changed. I will expound more in depth on this subject later in the story.

We know that in order to be a father, there must be offspring. So then who are Satan's children? This may come as a shock, but they are anyone who is not born of God and who does not confesses Jesus Christ as Lord. You see, anyone who is not born again will automatically be hostile toward God and His word. And we all were at one time. Listen to what the Gospel of John declares:

> *"I speak that which I have seen with my Father: and ye do that which ye have seen with your father." They answered and said unto Him, "Abraham is our father." Jesus said unto them, "If ye were Abraham's children, ye would do*

> *the works of Abraham. But now ye seek to kill me, a man that hath told you the truth, which I have heard of God: this did not Abraham. You do the deeds of your father." They said unto Him, "We be not born of fornication; we have one Father, even God." Jesus said unto them, "If God were your Father, ye would love me: for I proceeded forth and came from God; neither came I of myself, but He sent me. Why do you not understand my speech? Even because you cannot hear my words. Ye are of your father the Devil, and the lusts of your father you will do."* —John 8:38–44

These passages reveal that there is a spirit behind every action and reaction. Either it is a good spirit, which is of God, or an evil spirit, which is of the Devil. Satan will always be hostile toward things that are good. Seeking to kill the Christ was hostility at its highest degree.

Let's look at the scene. The Lord Jesus is speaking to the Jewish people of His day. They were rulers of the synagogue, called Pharisees and Sadducees, and were very religious. Their outer appearance seemed upright and godly. These religious rulers had perfect church attendance and were well versed in the scriptures. Yet they were devilish. To put it in layman's terms, with all of their religious activity, their true allegiance was to Satan. Listen to Jesus' words again: "If you were Abraham's children . . . if God were your Father . . ." In other words, you say that Abraham is your father, but you don't act like him. You say God is your Father, but you don't act like Him. I don't know about you, but I've been in churches full of people who don't act like the Father they claim. They haven't a clue about the ways of God. They are mean as rattlesnakes.

Like the Pharisees, they have a form of godliness (see 2 Timothy 3:5); they might read the scriptures daily, but they do not obey them. They are ingnorant of knowledge of the true Father. Worse yet, they have no heart to know Him.

One of the Ten Commandments, for example, declares, *"Thou shalt not kill"* —Exodus 20:13. Yet murder was in the hearts of these so-called religious leaders. Why? Because they were Satan's children. They did the bidding of their father because they were slaves to him.

This is not a man-made idea of enslavement. It goes way beyond that. It's demonic possession, which controls the thoughts and actions of an individual. Though all may not be possessed, many are under direct influence of evil. And when their father the devil puts the pressure on, his children will succumb. Let's look at it for a moment. The Scribes and Pharisees were moved with envy because of the good deeds Jesus did in their midst, and for that, they wanted to murder Him. They hated the Son of God. *"For he [Pontius Pilate] knew that for envy, they had delivered Him."* —Matthew 27:18

The spirit of envy drove the Jewish people to murder. *"And the lust of your father you will do; he was a murder from the beginning."* We read that the first murder is recorded in Genesis 3:8. Cain violently slew his brother Abel for the same reason. Again, Satan's tactics have not changed.

The children of Satan are in our midst today, and they are everywhere. Jeremiah 5:26 declares, *"For among my people are found wicked men."* They pose as clergymen, government officials, police officers, doctors, lawyers, and as we just read, church folk. They look moral or godly on the surface, but they are sent to trap godly men and women, the innocent, and the poor.

We see them at work in the hospitals; they are behind the alarming numbers of death rates because of unnecessary surgeries and chemically based prescription drugs. Among the death rate are the abortions that take place in the name of women's rights.

Police officers shoot and kill our children in the streets of America. Lawyers and judges put the innocent behind bars, only to find out thirty years later they were falsely accused, and release them. And it's only by chance that their story gets to the ears of someone who gives a care. Many lives are stolen away by wicked men. "How can they sleep at night?" you ask. That's just it; the devil doesn't sleep. You might be wondering, *what is this lady talking about?*

Many are blind to the reality of Satan's spawn, which leads to the reason that in America, crimes are classified by one's collar, rather than by the criminal deed. For example, white-collar crimes are considered nonviolent, motivated by money and committed by business and government professionals.

Because these persons have respectability and high social status, quite often there is little or no punishment carried out. Yet victims are left devastated and hurt by their criminal actions. This, my friend, is called corruption, and corruption always leads to violence—always.

Listen. It doesn't matter what color of collar they wear. As if a white collar is less devilish than a blue one. My goodness, what does it mean if you haven't a collar? It's absolutely outrageous!

In the eyes of the spirit, actions are either of God or of Satan—good or evil. According to the Holy Scriptures, officials are supposed to be ministers of God to the citizens for good (see Romans 13:4). But again, I say, unless they are God's children, they are children of Satan.

We read in the Holy Scriptures what Jesus and the Apostles declared concerning the children of the devil.

1. They are the counterfeit of the real.

They are called seeds of Satan: *"But while men slept, his enemy came and sowed tares among the wheat, and went his way"* (Matthew 13:25). Who is the enemy? Satan. The mastermind behind the tares (a counterfeit) among God's children.

2. They are planted by Satan.

The children of the wicked one: *"The field is the world; the good seed are the children of the kingdom; but the tares are the children of the wicked one"* (Matthew 13:38).

3. They are disobedient.

The children of disobedience: *"Wherein in time past ye walked according to the course of this world, according to the prince of the power of the air, the spirit that now worketh in the children of disobedience"* (Ephesians 2:2).

IT STARTS WITH JUST ONE LIE

Christians and non-Christians alike have been deceived, all because they listened to a lie from the enemy. Hence the reason drug houses are filled up with addicts, liquor joints are overflowing with alcoholics, and the list goes on. *It starts with just one lie.*

A while ago my then-husband told me a story of a certain person he saw while walking into the casino here in Tucson. He noticed that this man was talking to himself—out loud. When they passed each other, he heard the man saying, "Stupid, stupid, stupid! You are so stupid. Why did you spend all of your money? You idiot, why!" All the while, this man was hitting himself upside the head. He apparently listened to the voice of the father of lies, having wasted all his money. I don't know if he had to face a wife and kids when he got home, but one thing was for sure—he was left completely broke.

The voice we choose to obey affects our offspring. Humanity died because of one lie. One lie! And all became damaged goods. This brings to mind the time my father defended his perverted ways. "I think I was a good father except for that one thing I did," he said (meaning that he raped his own daughters). He wished it were only one thing! This statement disturbed me greatly. It was clear that my father was in denial about his true demented character. My first thought was, *Is my father out of his cotton-pickin' mind?* Even if that were true, how many times does it take to destroy a person's life? The Bible says, *"For in Adam all died."* Because of one man's sin, all died! Do you see what I am conveying here?

Thanks be unto God; we are not without remedy, for the scripture goes on to say, *"Even so in Christ shall all be made alive.* Alleluia!" (see 1 Corinthians 15:22).

The voice you choose to listen to is the voice you will obey. So I ask you, who's yo' daddy?

THE HEAVENLY FATHER

God is Love —1 John 4:16

Our heavenly Father can be summed up in one word, and that is *love*. God is love. According to *Strong's Concordance*, the Greek word for "love" is AGAPE. The translation of this word is "charitable," and the meaning is "benevolent—unselfish and deliberate." Agape love can only be known from the actions it prompts. Because of His great love for us, His plan far exceeds that of our earthly father's, and trumps Satan's schemes a thousand times over.

I am awed to have an opportunity to expound on what I feel is my Father's greatest character quality. His love so impacted my life that I feel compelled to speak from the heart concerning Him.

I find it an honor and a privilege to call Him Father. When I say the word "Father" I feel a deep inner peace and the joy of heaven that fills my heart. The Father's love is so amazingly indescribable that at times one may feel totally undeserving. It has left me asking the question, "How could this God love me so?" But when I understood His Divine character, it became clearer as to why. God's agape love is a Divine gift to all humanity. It would behoove all to be recipients and enjoy the great benefits of His love. When I think about the unbiased aspect of the Father's love, I marvel at how he extends it to all His children at the same time and yet makes each one feel as though they are the only one.

One day in my sewing studio I began to ponder His acts of love. The scripture declares,

> *For when we were yet without strength, in due time Christ died for the ungodly. For scarcely for a righteous man will one die: yet peradventure for a good man some would even*

> *dare to die. But God commendeth his love toward us, in that, while we were yet sinners, Christ died for us.* — Romans 5:6-8

This text shows a profound act by Father God that changed the course of history forever. When I read verse 8, I put my name in it. I made it personal, because had He not commended His love toward Anita, I would have perished. When I tell my story of brokenness, I have to end it with the words "but God."

Yes, it left me with struggles and heartache. And yes, I was broken by those who should have loved me. I was a castoff. Along the way, I sinned and fell short of the glory, *but God.*

You see, when Father God floods your soul with love, it won't matter what you did or who did what to you. You can't make a mess big enough that the Father can't clean up. It doesn't matter if your earthly father abandoned you or if you never knew him. It doesn't matter if you were raped, beaten, or left for dead in some alley. It doesn't matter how cruelly the hand of life has dealt you. You too will say, "But God!"

Listen to what Apostle Paul declares in Ephesians 2:4: *"But God, who is rich in mercy…* Here it is again. You see, these are the advantages and benefits of having God as Father. His mercies are not only rich, but according to Jeremiah, they are new every morning (see Lamentations 3:23).

I came to a place of understanding that helped me to move forward. Father God is full of compassion—no one can love you like the Father. He loved me and showed me kindness so that I could turn around and love others, no matter who they were. Because love is not partial.

EVERYTHING I NEEDED

When Love came in, it did two things for me. For the first time, at the age of nineteen, I felt like I belonged and was accepted. Second, His love began to erase the bad feelings of the past.

Beloved, don't be one of those Christians who are still bellyaching over past hurts because you refuse to accept the wonderful healing love of the Father. The saying is, "You can lead a horse to water, but you can't make him drink." But if you should decide to drink from His fountain (and I fervently pray that you do), know that you will never find a truer Father.

From personal experience, my heavenly Father was everything my biological father wasn't. As the song goes, "He looked beyond my faults and saw my needs." Father God is everything you will ever need and more.

Many today blame God for how their parents mistreated them. They ask, "If God is love, why did He allow this to happen to me?" I don't hold God responsible for my father's actions; no, that was his doing. But what I do hold God responsible for is how He wonderfully interposed Himself on my behalf, and who purely and undeniably ministered the solace I so desperately needed.

The Bible declares that *He is the God of all comfort* (see 2 Corinthians 1:3-4). The Bible also declares that *His merciful kindness is great towards us* (see Psalm 117:2). Ah, the awesome kindness of Father God. He can't help it; it's in His DNA. He is kindness.

Let's examine the word "kindness." The Hebrew word is *HESED.* It means "unfailing love, loyal love, devotion." Unfailing love? Pause and think about that!

Because the Father is a covenant God, He is faithful, He is loyal, and He never changes. These characteristics are lacking in our society, but not so with the Father; this is why we should look only to God to fill our deepest needs.

Listen to what David says in Psalm 27:10: *"When my mother and father forsake me, then the Lord will take me up."* I like the way the NLT says it: *"Even if my mother and father abandon me the Lord will hold me close."*

That's what LOVE does; it takes you up from despair and holds you close. Charles Spurgeon[1] says it on this wise:

> *These dear relations will be the last to desert me, but if the milk of human kindness should dry up, even from their breasts, there is a Father who never forgets.*

How I delight in the opening passage of scripture, *God is love.* My Father took me up, carried me in his bosom, held me close, and rocked me in His tender arms. He called me daughter and hushed my whimpers. Yet that was only the beginning of His kindness to me. I needed more. As David declared, *"Teach me how to live O Lord. Lead me along the right path."*—Psalm 27:11

He is a wonderful teacher; a wise instructor is He! With love, Father God taught me how to live—in other words, he taught me how to be holy, how to behave righteously, and how to carry myself like the queen that I am. He taught me that I belong to Him –I am the apple of His eye and everything about me is beautiful. The psalmist declares, *"For the Lord takes pleasure in His people: He will beautify the meek with his salvation."*—Psalm 149:4

The Hebrew word for beautify is PAAR; it means "to gleam, to embellish, and to boast." Father God embellishes the meek with the goodness of Himself. He takes pleasure in us. How condescending for the High and Lofty One, yet He beautifies us with the beauty of His own holiness. I was afflicted and broken, and now I am made a gleaming light of salvation.

FATHER GOD WAS MY PROTECTOR

> *He shall cover thee with His feathers and under His wings shalt thou trust.*
>
> —Psalm 91:4

When I was in my early twenties I resided in Houston, Texas. I lived in subsidized housing. The apartments were divided into sections—families on one end and singles on the other. Unfortunately, it was not a safe environment. There were drugs and violent crimes of rape. At the time it was all I could afford, making two dollars and thirty cents an hour.

The theft crimes had gotten so bad that they began stealing air-conditioning units from the apartments. One night I was in my bedroom watching TV when I heard the sound of sparks flying outside my window. My unit was gone, stolen right from under me, just like that. That was bad news for me, because it was in the midst of summer's sweltering heat. God knows I couldn't open any windows; it was too dangerous. I was already dealing with strange men knocking on my door in the night. "Hey, open up! I want to talk to you!" they'd shout.

Management did their best to take care of things around the complex, but there was a long line ahead of me. So I had to figure out the best way to stay cool. Some nights I would stand at the refrigerator door to get some relief.

One Friday night after church service ended, I was dropped off at my apartment home by one of the saints. I walked up to my apartment as usual, unlocked the door, and went in. I closed the door behind me, immediately locked it, and began preparing for work the next day. I soon retired for bed. Just as I lay down, the Lord spoke to me. He said, "Get up and go check the door." I answered back and said, "Okay." I got up and walked into the living room to check my door. *Hmm, it's locked,* I said to myself. I turned around to go back to bed. At that instant, the Spirit spoke to me again and said, "It is the Lord who watches over you even when you think you're locked in." Not understanding what that meant, I said, "Thank you, Lord," and went to bed for the night.

The next morning I got dressed for work. I was ready to walk out of the door, but I couldn't find my house key. Immediately, the Spirit directed my attention to the front door. I walked over, unlocked it, and opened the door. There my keys were, on the outside, stuck in the keyhole. His words came back to me. "It is the Lord who watches over you even when you think you're locked in."

What more could I express about the goodness of the Father's love and care? I would have to write another book. All of these virtues—mercy, kindness and tender care—are wrapped up in His love, and I have experienced every one of them.

I asked my Father to give me some insight into His love for His children, and this is what He showed me. His love is like a couture designer who goes through the process of designing and making beautiful garments. First, the designer, called a couturier, determines what category the design will be—in other words, the purpose of the garment, as he or she already has a finished picture in mind. Then the image is sketched out on paper. From there, the designer chooses specialty fabrics, silk threads, and beading for added beauty.

The pattern is then made, after which a mock-up of the design is created in the exact replica of the sketch. Because couture fabrics are of the highest quality and very expensive, they do what is called "trueing the lines"—double-checking for any potential flaws.

After the mock-up has been perfected, the couturier moves on to the chosen fabric for the grand finish. This is the most exciting part. The couturier, with his or her impeccable craftsmanship, painstakingly brings the garment to an incredible beauty. This takes hour upon hour to finish. Before the garment is completed, the name of the designer goes on the inside as a seal of authenticity.

The garment is then put on display for everyone to see and marvel at its beauty. The first question people ask is who the designer is. Some of the garments I painstakingly designed took months to make and were stunning. I bedazzled them with precious stones and embroidery. But when I finished them, I found that I couldn't let them go. They became my special keepsake, my one-of-a-kind.

You see, the more time and energy I invested, the more attached I became. Figuratively speaking, it is also this way with Father God. He created you and therefore He can't let you go. Your Father loves you and has placed His name of authenticity in you.

Hence, we get to strut about with the stamp of His magnificent image. You and I are His one-of-a-kind, unique and beloved.

All of this came about because of the sacrificial Lamb of God. The Bible declares in Revelation 13:8, *"The Lamb slain from the foundation of the world."* We don't know how long it took to prepare Jesus for the task, nor the depth of the investment. But we do know it was planned before the foundation of the earth was laid.

The Father sent His only Son, Jesus, to shed His blood and die on the cross. Herein lies another great benefit—God has given Him a name above every name, that at the name of Jesus, every knee should bow, of the things in heaven and the things in the earth; and every tongue should confess that Jesus is Lord to the glory of God the Father (Philippians 2:9–10).

That means the knee of sickness and disease, the knee of poverty and lack, the knee of fear and rejection, and yes, the knee of brokenness, must all bow. We too have been blessed with a good name, a mighty name, the only name given that we may have an advantage in life, and in the life to come—the wonderful name of Jesus!

And that, only the Father can do.

BORN IN OBSCURITY

BORN IN OBSCURITY

And there went a man of the house of Levi, and took to wife a daughter of Levi. And the woman conceived, and bare a son.
—Exodus 2:2

There are times when everyone reflects back over their childhood, pondering the different events that took place. Some look back on good times, but others, not so much. It is unfortunate that so many lives were filled with painful memories because of some kind of abuse—physical, verbal, mental, sexual, or all the above.

When individuals, especially children are forced to live in arduous circumstances, it becomes very destructive to every part of their being. They grow up with a stigma of little or no self-esteem, along with lacking confidence and self-worth. Thus, creating a need for approval making them vulnerable to the outside world. Usually, there's no one to intervene. As a result, the constant mistreatment creates one big ball of confusion. I can speak from personal experience, having come from a very dysfunctional family.

My childhood was not a pleasant one. Born one of six children, my father, a widower, brought two more, a girl and a boy, and I was thrown in the middle of the eight. Yet we were raised like one big family. Things were different in the '50s. We were not considered stepsisters and stepbrothers. The family blended in, and we were expected to treat each other like full-blooded siblings. For the most part, my parents got that one right. I can commend them for it. Today's merged families, in contrast, are bombarded with difficulties, not to mention the higher divorce rate among them.

The abuse I would inevitably encounter started long before my birth. My parents were full of issues of their own, passed on from their parents and their parents' parents. Blended with their problems, what do you have? Complete chaos. Which is why I chose the title "Born in Obscurity," meaning this: a person can be born into dark and horrific situations that are entirely beyond their control.

Before I continue with my story, I want to set the stage by expounding on a few great patriarchs of the Old Testament, the first being a Hebrew by the name of Moses.

Moses's life did not start out favorably either, to say the least. Nevertheless, God, in His sovereignty, who is always working behind the scenes to intervene using the appropriate means, protected the child Moses and brought about His purpose for the boy's life. Let's examine all the events surrounding his beginnings.

THE BIRTH OF MOSES

And the woman conceived, and bare a son. —Exodus 2:2

The "son" in this text refers to Moses, a descendant of Levi, part of the tribe of the Hebrew people known as the children of Israel. They were God's chosen people. Through them He would display His righteousness in the earth. God would in turn fulfill His promises to them, which He made to their forefathers.

Unbeknown to Moses, he would not have a normal childhood. He would grow up to see the undue cruelty afflicted on his people by wicked slave masters. For those who are not familiar with the story, the Bible reveals that the king of Egypt saw that the Hebrew people had greatly multiplied in the land. This made the Egyptians nervous and a plan was conspired against Israel to enslave them.

Born during a time of slavery, it appeared as if Moses and his people would have little or no future. The Egyptian Pharaoh devised a plan of rigorous slavery to stop the children of Israel from multiplying. The plan backfired and the nation of Israel increased the more. The Bible declares, *"The more they afflicted them the more they increased."* —Exodus 1:12

The Egyptians went further and devised a more fiendish scheme. Since putting the Hebrews in bondage had not been enough, the king gave orders to kill all the male infants, snuffing out their lives as soon as they were born. This diabolical device was the work of an unseen evil force to abort God's promise to His people. This is always the case when there is a spoken prophecy over the lives of individuals.

When we look into this story, it is easy to see that no one can help what they are born into or to whom they are born. I, like Moses, did not have a normal childhood. The difference in our suffering is that his was impacted from an outside source and mine came from inside my family.

I was born to a pedophile father who was also a bully, and to a verbally abusive mother. Both were blatantly partial, which would prove to backfire in the years to come. What was designed to destroy me turned to work in my favor.

In my toddler years, I lived with my Grandma Dorothy in Little Rock, Arkansas. Grandma Dorothy was my mother's mother. Everyone called her Dot. Mother's side of the family had little money and not have much education. She gave birth to eleven girls and four boys. Her last six came along later. Grandma Dorothy had a sweet, gentle voice when she spoke. She spent much of the time lying in bed. At my young age, I was unaware that she was terminally ill.

One day I was out playing in our backyard when I notice my mother walking rather hastily from the house. She wore a white dress with matching high heels, and a wide brim floppy hat. Mother glanced over her shoulder at me as she appeared to have been sneaking away. Unable to comprehend her odd behavior, I watched until she disappeared out of sight.

Looking back, I wasn't quite sure why they left me with my grandmother in the first place; perhaps it had something to do with my father being in the air force, I thought. It was my birth certificate that would shed some light as to why.

My parent's hadn't married at the time of my birth. I guess they needed time to work out the details. Perhaps that might explain Mother's white attire that day. I was too young to recount how long I spent in Arkansas, but I do remember bits and pieces of my life. Dot, along with all of her eleven children, lived in a very small shack, and I mean a real hut in every sense of the word. Back in the day, they called them shotgun houses because of the narrow rectangular shape with doors at each end.

The house had a wood planked porch leading out to the front yard, where a few hogs and chickens grazed. A pile of trash burned out front, which most people had in the country. I guess that was the only means of discarding their non-recyclable waste. One morning my curiosity got the best of me when I decided to see what this heap of sparkling, smoky mound was all about.

I walked over and laid my little foot on top of the amber-colored ashes. I quickly learned as every child does; play with fire and you'll get burned. I dared not try that again. I don't remember crying much afterward, but my toes sure hurt a lot. I was a tough little girl.

There was no running water, so to use the bathroom the family utilized an old-fashion outhouse on the back. I never saw any toilet paper. For me, it was not easily accessible. I had to do a little climbing to sit up on the seat. As I grew into my teenage years, I used to wonder why they built the bench so high. Shinning up to sit and then doing your business on the ground seemed ridiculous to me, then. After giving it some thought, I answered my question. I was only a little tot at the time, and at that age, everything is more prominent.

When it came to bath time, my auntie Phene, who looked after me often, would place me in a big metal trough filled with warm, sudsy water. I had fun splashing around until my bath was over.

I slept with Auntie in a twin-size bed. She was plump and a bit stout for a young lady. Sleeping arrangements were in her favor, she'd always hog the covers, pushing me off the edge of the bed. By early morning I'd be hanging halfway off the mattress, I had no choice but to get up and wander out onto the porch.

As I said, I didn't recall much at that age. Next thing I knew, I was living with my parents—a place where an unprecedented evil would invade my peace, and my world turns upside down. There I encountered the ultimate betrayal by a culprit with abusive practices—an assailant who committed unremitting crimes of incest against me. With my innocence slowly being stripped away, I'd have to grow up with a dark secret for years to come.

Shortly after moving away, Grandma Dot died of a rare case of leukemia, leaving behind her last eight babies, who were raised by my Grandfather Roberts and the older brothers and sisters. The last time I saw her was when Mommy and Daddy took a short trip to Little Rock on behalf of her illness. Mother led us up a tiny hallway towards grandma's bedroom. After a polite knock and brief pause, Mother leaned in and pushed her way through a rickety door that dragged across the wood floor. We walked in to see her sitting upright on her bed with an orange in her hand. She was peeling off the hull and asked me if I wanted a piece, in that sweet voice of hers. She handed me a segment as I reached with my little hands. I took a bite, and boy, that was the sweetest orange ever.

While I was eating, I noticed her plump body and her uncombed hair standing up on her head. She had beautiful cheekbones and smooth ebony skin. My mother had the same features and she passed them on to me. I'll never forget the sweet sound of her voice.

During the summers, our parents would pack up the station wagon that seated our family of ten and head toward Texas and Arkansas. For our travel, Mommy would fry up some chickens and pork chops along with her famous pound cakes. My mother knew her way around the kitchen, and for that reason we always had good-tasting food to eat. When we got hungry, my father would pull off to the side of the road. This was our chance to eat and stretch our legs. Most of the time, black families had to assemble in rural areas during the '50s before the desegregation laws were passed. Even though it was the '60s, there were still public restaurants down south that were not too accepting of black folks. I guess Daddy just played it safe.

We appreciated traveling to Little Rock. For us children, there were many benefits. Grandma Dot had her last eight children while my mother had hers. As a result, we enjoyed hanging out in the country together. We didn't seem to mind the humid late nights of summer, swatting at fierce insects as we ran and played in the rural neighborhood. There was no way Mother would allow us to remain outside so late at home. Most of the townspeople sat out on their front porches waving hello to everyone who passed by. My siblings and I got a kick out of the southern accents and would tease our aunts and uncles about their speech.

It was different when we went to Texas to visit Daddy's people. For one thing, it was very boring, and I didn't see any girls to play with. Everyone mostly lingered in Ma Dear's house. It didn't feel much like a vacation for me. Whenever there were chores to do, Mother was always calling my name, as usual. "Get in here and do those dishes" or "Come in here and fold the clothes," she'd say. Trust me, it was never ending. Mind you, everyone else was out playing while I helped.

We called my father's mother "Ma Dear" even though we weren't at all close to her. I never experienced any kind of affection from her; perhaps I didn't expect it, either. My mother would complain about how her mother-in-law disrespected her. "I don't know why she keeps calling me Agnes," she'd say, which was my father's first wife. "My name ain't no Agnes. My name is Jonnye!" Boy, she was furious! Of course, after becoming an adult, I certainly can understand that one.

My father's side of the family seemed to be a bit more civil and perhaps a bit more educated. He had a younger brother who took pleasure in rubbing his accomplishments in my father's face. Yes, this uncle thought he was the cake and the punch for the party.

Every chance he got, he would make pompous comments. That behavior came from the way they were both brought up. My grandfather Carey was also partial, favoring my uncle, who was the baby boy. Grandfather physically and verbally abused my father all of his young life.

My father was nearing the end of his air force career at the time my parents came to take me to live with them. There were only four children then. Soon the others came along, making eight children all together, four boys and four girls.

They put us in two categories, four big ones and the four little ones. Whenever something went down in the house, they would address the children, saying, "You four big ones are responsible for cleaning and carrying out other duties in the house" or "You all make sure the four little ones get their bath." Mind you, some of us were stair step, but the four older children were responsible for the smaller ones.

My brother Craig and I were what I consider the middle children. I was the end of the four big ones, and he was the beginning of the four little ones. You know how it's said that the middle child strives for attention? Well, it's true, especially in our case. Of course, we didn't realize what we were doing at the time. The older I got, the harder I worked at it. I think we both felt left out and ignored a lot of the time.

When it came to discipline, Mother was the chief enforcer. Whatever she said went, and my father backed her up. When it came to whipping our behinds, she didn't hesitate. It was overkill, in my opinion. We used to say, "Mommy loves to give woopin's!" She wasn't the kind that would say, "This is going to hurt me more than it's going to hurt you." Not even close.

Speaking of discipline, the four older children were treated vastly different than the younger children, and not in a good way. This wasn't solely because of age. As I mentioned before, my parents were very partial, and I mean it was blatant.

Ms. Jonnye was what we called our mother at times. She had a dark complexion and with her long hair, she was beautiful. Grady was a very fair-skinned man, thickly built and handsome. Their children came out in a rainbow of different skin tones. I, along with two brothers, were dark skinned like Mother. Ms. Jonnye was partial to light skin and a slender build, and I was neither. Needless to say, the rest of us did not get the motherly affection every child needs and longs for, especially the four oldest.

Yet, my elder sister and I got the brunt of my parents' wrath. I often wondered if Jonnye's seemingly callous disposition toward her oldest girls gave opportunity for Grady Ray to so easily move in and rape his own daughters. I would always ask myself, "Where was Mother when our father would come into our bedroom in the middle of the night?" After all, we lived in a very small three-bedroom house, with our bedroom being right next to theirs. How is it that she never came to look in on her daughters? When I say never, I mean never! At least not to my recollection. One would think, the way my father was carrying on, anyone could have stumbled in and caught him in the act.

Mother was not the affectionate type, but when she did show it, it was with her two main favorites. Let me give you an example of what I mean. I was in the fifth grade. Seated on my bedside, I needed Mother's advice about a childhood issue I was facing. So I walked into her bedroom and saw she was in the bathroom with the door closed. I knocked lightly on the door. "Yes?" she replied. I started talking. To my amazement, she answered back with a very gentle tone. Oh, how warm her words felt, I thought. Well, that was short-lived; she mistook me for her favorite daughter, calling me by her name. I corrected her. "No, Mommy, this is 'Nita." Immediately her voice switched to harsh mode, and she shouted, "Well, whoever the HELL it is!" Her coarse words cut deeply. I walked back to my bedroom to nurse my wounds.

Another time, during the winter, I'd caught a cold as all kids do, coughing uncontrollably, sore throat, etc. By nightfall, everyone was in bed asleep, except me. I had a terrible cough, and it kept me awake. A normal mother would get up and tend to her child, giving them cold medicine, feeling their little forehead to see if there was a temperature—you know the drill. Not my mother. I coughed and coughed through the night. The next thing I heard was her loud voice ringing out through the house: "Stop that coughing in there!" You can rest assured I did my darnedest to hold it in. I think that was my last cough, too, scared that I might get a whipping if I was to let out the slightest whimper.

No, Ms. Jonnye didn't play, and she wasn't merciful, either, especially if you weren't the favorite. It seems as though she was out of touch with feeling. Growing up, I didn't go to her much in times of pain and distress because I was too afraid. Either I held it in or dealt with it the best I could. So again, I ask, where was she? With our bedroom being two steps away from my parents and no doors on our room to speak of, this was my mother's choice. "This is going to be 'Nita's and Rhonda's room," she'd said, as the family walked through our new home.

Looking back, I wondered why Mother suggested this specific room for her oldest daughters. It wasn't a bedroom at all. Undoubtedly, the initial design was for a dining area. There was a clear passageway on both ends of the room. But Mother had it in her mind to convert it into a bedroom.

Needless to say, we never had any privacy. Anyone could walk through at any time. As a matter of fact, everybody did. They had to walk through because the bedroom was connected to the kitchen. I suspect this was Mother's intention. She was privy to what had been going on all along and perhaps she hoped that giving us a room without doors might curtail my father's incestuous cravings. Well, it didn't. For years, Ms. Jonnye acted as if everything was normal. Although, I was a child, I could see there was something off about Mother. On occasion my father would act out overt sexual misconduct toward her daughters and women friends, and she'd only blink at the situation, when she should have spoken up. Mother was weak, unapologetically so.

Let me pause right here and say that it was the plan of Satan to attack me early before I could get a good start in life, before I came to know my divine purpose. Despite the attacks, God's plan was already fixed from the beginning. He had a plan for Moses and His people Israel, so He had a plan for me. Hebrews 11:23–28 confirms God's divine intervention. Let's look at how God showed up for Moses in the midst of extreme circumstances.

Jochebed, Moses's mother, stepped up to the plate to defend and protect her son. Her name in the Hebrew is Yowkebed, meaning "Jehovah is glorified." I classify her as a one of the Bible heroes. Here's her story:

> *So the woman conceived and bore a son.*
>
> —Exodus 2:2

Conception is both physical and mental. The moment a woman knows she's pregnant, her response is usually "I'm expecting" or "I'm having a baby." She makes this declaration before ever seeing a physical child. She mentally conceives an image of her baby in the now, along with the physical conception in her womb. After having a mental picture for nine months, the first glimpse of her baby in her arms is the confirmed picture in her mind. What am I saying? A woman bonds with her baby long before she sees the child's physical features. Which is why, miscarriages are so emotionally painful. This bond between mother and infant is so strong that a mother will risk her life to save the child. At least that's the natural response.

> *And when she saw him that he was a goodly child, she hid him three months.*
>
> —Exodus 2:2

Jochebed displayed what every mother on the planet should do in the face of danger regarding her own children. She is an example for all generations to come. Not only did she live up to true motherhood, she also lived up to her name—Jehovah is gloried! Little did she know that from this one courageous act, the history of the Hebrew people would be greatly affected, and God would be glorified for the whole earth to see.

Let's look at this short passage of scripture concerning her. *"And when she saw him… that he was a goodly child."* The moment she looked at her son, something immediately happened within that took over her whole being. As she beheld the beauty of her baby boy, she deemed him priceless, and the mama bear came alive. I can hear her saying to herself, "Look at this beautiful being that came forth from me. He is so precious. I will rise and protect him, even if I should die in the process. The enemy will have to go through me!" There is no doubt her faith had a lot to do with her courage.

Jochebed was so courageous that she is written in the hall-mark of faith. The Hebrew writer declares, *"By faith Moses, when he was born, was hid three months of his parents, because they saw he was a proper child; and they were not afraid of the king's commandment."* —Hebrews 11:23

Jochebed had every reason to be afraid and could have easily decided to give in to the conditions surrounding her. The penalty for anyone who disobeyed the king's commands was sure death, and coupled with the fact she was a slave, there wasn't a snowball's chance in hell that she and her family would be shown any kind of mercy.

Unlike today, there were no social services such as welfare or women's shelters to help her transition out of danger. My goodness, women in those days had no rights. Jochebed had to deal with hardships that no human should ever have to undergo. Her world was full of devastation of the highest degree. How very sad that many mothers today will not stand up and protect their children, and offer the weakest excuses—fear, lack of money, or perhaps the weakest of all: "I don't know what to do." Find out!

As much as I understand that there are legitimate reasons why women become overwhelmed with fear and feel trapped, the focus must not be on how they feel, but on saving the child, your child. The young have no one but you to protect them.

Ask Jochebed. If she were here today, she'd say, "There is not much to fear in the world that would keep me from protecting my son. It was a mother's love that made me rise and fight." So here's the point I want to make. Just because you find yourself in a seemingly helpless situation, it doesn't mean you should roll over and let things happen.

Read the story, my friend, and put your faith to work. Look at the hand of God working behind the scenes protecting and directing Jochebed and her son from death. I want you to be encouraged and know that your life is important to God, as everyone's life is. If it were not, the devil wouldn't fight to try to destroy it.

Moses was born into an obscure and seemingly helpless situation, but it was not hopeless. God was on the side of that little bitty baby boy. God divinely protected him in the midst of cruelty. Yes, it was difficult, but it all played right into the plan of God.

As time went by, Jochebed was faced with another dilemma. As her child grew, Jochebed had another decision to make. She had to act, and what an act. Her decision to rise would prove to pay off greatly in the end. The Bible says that through her courageous efforts she saved her son's life for three whole months. I'm sure you are familiar with the story of Moses, but let's recount it: *"And when she could no longer hide him, she took for him an ark of bulrushes, and daubed it with slime and with pitch, and put the child therein; and she laid it in the flags by the river's brink."*—Exodus 2:3

How Jochebed must have felt after doing all that she could to protect her son, and yet it was not enough, or so she thought. For three months she had the joys of holding, feeding, and watching her baby son grow. The Bible says, *"She could hide him no more."* Moses's mother had exhausted all of her efforts. She did all that a poor slave could do within her own power, and now she was faced with an impending quandary. She probably cried for days, wondering, "Lord, what to do? Please help me!"

In spite of all of her efforts, she found herself saying, "I don't want to, but now I have to let my baby go." This is where the drama begins, because the God of heaven was watching in the wings all the time. He saw Jochebed when she first decided in her heart and said, "I can't let my son die. He's my gift from God." No doubt, downcast by this difficult decision, she places little Moses in a basket. As he floats along the river's brink, the Lord steps in so wittingly that his mother didn't miss a beat. Not only did God spare little Moses, Jochebed was paid wages by the Queen of Egypt to babysit her own son—pause and think about that!

How often do we hear today of mothers making bad decisions concerning their children? It has become so prevalent that the moment you turn on your TV, there are reports of neglect and abuse. Women leave their little children with a boyfriend they barely know, only to return to find their baby's life destroyed. The reason often given is that the babies would not stop crying, so out of frustration, they shook the infant to death.

Another sad story that made national news was a young Caucasian mother of three who reported her children had been kidnapped by a black man. She gave a random description to the police, and the hunt was on. Every black man in the United States was under suspicion. Let me say for the record that black folks knew the story was a hoax from the beginning. It's not within a black man's nature to kidnap someone else's kids. As the investigation unfolded, it proved that this young mother had killed her own children. The reason being she wanted to start her life over with a new boyfriend. When it hits close to home, the effects are different.

Here's my story . . .

Years ago, my aunt and her common-law husband were looking to relocate their family from New York to Atlanta. In conversation, I mentioned Atlanta would be a great place to raise her children. After a few weeks, my aunt and her tribe arrived. I was delighted to see her again. She still looked the same, except that she now had five children.

But auntie wasn't finished; she still had a bun in the oven and would go on to have one more. Life for me was busy. Managing my salon and pastoring a small church took much effort. When it came to church business, half the time I didn't know what I was doing. Despite it all, the Lord was with me. The power of God was evident. Souls were saved, bodies were healed, and devils were cast out.

My aunt and I began discussing plans for her employment. She expressed her passion for the medical field and was an exceptional caretaker. So I suggested a few nursing facilities in the area. Eager for employment, she went looking for work and was happy that she'd successfully landed a job rather quickly. However, the next step was to secure a childcare provider. In all of my aunt's six children, five of them were between the ages one and six years old. Consequently, childcare costs would be a financial hurdle to cross, especially beginning a new job. Moreover, she approached me. "Nita, can you care for my children while I work?" she asked. You can probably guess what my answer was. "Uh, no, that's not possible, Auntie. I have too much on my plate to watch children during the day," I replied.

Trying to come up with a solution, she says to me, "I know, I'll take them to work with me and leave them in the car." She goes on to say, "I have some blankets and food for them, and I can check on them when I take my break." I came unglued. I yelled at the top of my lungs, "Girl, are you crazy! There's no job in the world worth putting your children's lives in jeopardy! Not to mention the fact you could wind up in jail!" I don't think auntie even gave a second thought to the danger she'd place her children in. Thank God, she listened.

I have a sibling who courted a certain gentleman she met some years ago. He came from a decent family and appeared to be the family-man type, having a stable job and all. She fell in love, got married and gave birth to three beautiful children. Over time, she and her husband separated and eventually divorced. Well, it can happen to the best of us. I'm sure she never thought it would be her experience.

Unfortunately, as the marriage goes, so go the children. With a decision motivated by selfishness, this mother of three packed her bags, moved away, and started a new life without them. In her own words she said, "I have to be happy. These kids are going to grow up and make their own lives."

This is a true statement; children do indeed grow up. But how will they grow up and what kind of life will they have? What damages will they acquire? What will they be left to cipher through in life in order to find normality? Abandonment? That is not an easy pill to swallow.

Nonetheless, my sibling felt her decision was justified. In her mind she was determined to erase everything and everyone that reminded her of the marriage. I'm sure there are times we all wish we could sit down with a #2 pencil, erase, and rewrite certain events out of our past. When it comes to children, once they arrive there is no erasing them. It's not until years later we look back with regrets over missed opportunities. Her ex-husband was a dope-smoking-every-evening type of guy, and into his children about as much as I am into football. I hate football. She left him to raise them all alone. My niece, heartbroken by the ordeal, spoke to me with a deep sadness. "Auntie, I miss my mom. I want her to come back." Unfortunately, she never did. As I look back, I have to give the man some respect for being there and providing for them.

Another courageous mother is found in 1 Kings 3:16–26. Her name is not mentioned; only that she was a harlot. When we read these passages of scripture, we see two women fighting over a baby so contentiously that the dispute had to be brought before the king:

> *Then came there two women, that were harlots, unto the king and stood before him. And the one woman said, "O my Lord, I and this woman dwell in one house; and I was delivered of a child with her in the house. And it came to pass on the third day after that I was delivered, that this woman was delivered also: and we were together; there was no stranger with us in the house, save we two in the house. And this woman's child died in the night; because she overlaid it. And she arose at midnight, and took my son*

> *from beside me, while thine handmaid slept, and laid it in her bosom, and laid her dead child in my bosom. And when I rose in the morning to give my child suck, behold it was dead: but when I had considered it in the morning, behold, it was not my son, which I did bear." And the other women said, "Nay; but the living is my son, and the dead is thy son." And this said, "No; but the dead is thy son, and the living is my son." Thus they spake before the king. Then said the king, "The one saith, 'This is my son that liveth, and thy son is the dead': and the other saith, 'Nay; but thy son is the dead, and my son is the living.'" And the king said, "Bring me a sword". And they brought a sword before the king. And the king said, "Divide the living child in two, and give half to the one, and half to the other". Then spake the woman whose the living child was unto the king, for her bowels yearned upon her son, and she said, "O my lord, give her the living child, and in no wise slay it."*

Now, let's examine the women in these scriptures. I will call them birth mother (has the living child) and grieving mother (has the dead child). Grieving mother lost her son during the night by way of suffocation. I suppose she rolled over on him in her sleep. No doubt, it was an accident. After discovering her baby's fate, grieving mother was grief-stricken. Instantly her mind became warped and thoroughly deluded. In a desperate attempt, she committed a heinous crime against birth mother by stealing away her infant son, which is called kidnapping, by the way.

Nonetheless, she came up with a fiendish plot to deceive birth mother into thinking the dead baby was hers. Okay, you lost your bundle of joy – that would be enough to make you lose your mind. But stealing away another as a replacement is criminal. The thought of it is incomprehensible. Besides, any woman who has given birth surely knows her own baby from another. Listen to what she says in verse 19:

"But when I considered it in the morning, behold, it was not my son, which I did bear."

The word "consider" is BIN in Hebrew, meaning "to discern, perceive, pay attention to, understand." Unless the birth mother was deaf and blind, there was no way she could have mistaken the dead child for her own. But this didn't stop the grieving mother from doing the unthinkable—she switched the babies, hoping she would get away with the evil plot.

Reading on further, birth mother took courage, certainly the mother bear rose in her too. She fought for her son's life and for his return. She is an example of courage in two ways. First, she chose not to keep silent, and second, she took the matter before the king. Out of love for her baby, she found a resource that she knew could help her get him back. But she could hardly have guessed how it would happen.

Let's recap. *"Then came there two women that were harlots, unto the king and stood before him."* Though birth mother's lifestyle was not an honorable one, she did not let it keep her from the presence of the king. She was desperate to save her baby. After hearing their full-blown arguments, King Solomon made a wise decision concerning the two women—to slay the child with a sword, dividing it in half so each could have a piece of his body (the king's ancient day version of a DNA testing). Well, that's when birth mother cried out. No!

The scripture goes on to say, "For her bowels yearned upon her son." In other words, she had so much compassion and pity that she could not bear to see her child suffer. This mother willingly gave up her son that he might live. We can see the correlation between Jochebed and birth mother. Neither of them were of any influence. Nevertheless, God intervened on their behalf. Birth mother's child was saved and returned to her, all because of her decision to rise and fight.

PERSONAL REFLECTIONS

- Ecclesiastes 3 mentions three pertinent things by which God plans. What are they?

- Being that God planned the season and timing of your birth, what world events surrounded it? How has this affected your life today?

- With the understanding that God has planned out your life, in the grand scheme of things, where do you feel you fit in?

- Explain the season you are experiencing right now. How is it affecting your spiritual walk?

- According to Psalm 8:4 God is mindful of us. Describe three ways God has been mindful of you.

- God had a purpose for every individual. According to Jeremiah 1:5 it is established before we are born. How does this passage of scripture apply today?

    A. How do we discover our divine purpose?

    B. How are we expected to live it out and why?

    C. How does fulfilling our purpose benefit others?

- Write a short paragraph telling how this chapter impacted your life.

NOTES

NOTES

CHAPTER II

FROM BROKENNESS TO WHOLENESS

I am forgotten as a dead
man out of mind:
I am like a broken vessel.
—Psalm 31:12
Broken
Promises
Acceptance
Sadness
Trust
FEAR
Happy
Unforgiveness
Joy
Love
Peace

I am like a broken vessel...

When David wrote this psalm, he had reached adulthood some time ago and was serving as king over Israel. With these words he expresses the personal inner turmoil of being forgotten and broken. These were times David felt dishonored and overlooked as a king and a man. To make matters worse, he suffered this negative treatment from loved ones.

No doubt a spirit of rejection from the past haunted him. Yet in the midst of mental conflict, David had to appear authoritative. With all the demands that accompany leadership, he was expected to perform his daily routine, functioning without fail.

An individual's position in life, no matter how influential, does not ease the effects of brokenness. Many in our world today secretly suffer as David did—broken, yet functioning. They work with a smile by day, then cry tears of sorrow in the night shadows.

Let's examine the psalmist's two words: "Forgotten" in Hebrew is SHAKACH (shaw-kay-akh), meaning "to mislay, i.e. to be oblivious of, from want of memory or attention." The *Macmillan Dictionary* definition of "forget" is "to fail to think of or do, especially through carelessness or thoughtlessness; neglect."

"Brokenness" in Hebrew is AVADH, meaning "destroy, destruction, or perish." *Webster's Ninth Collegiate Dictionary (Webster)* defines it as "violently separated into parts: **shattered**; crushed."

I believe David struggled throughout his life because of the mistreatment stemming from his childhood. I can relate to him on many levels. Perhaps that's the reason he's one of my favorite Old Testament patriarchs. There's no doubt that being forgotten or ignored leaves one feeling like a broken bottle. I know this from experience all too well.

If my memory serves me right, I was a teenager when the eve of Christmas was approaching with all the festivities and expectations. I felt the usual excitement in the air, anticipating what this Christmas might bring as I reflected on the gifts from last season.

In my elementary years, my classmates would make holiday chains out of green and red construction paper. I couldn't wait to get mine home. I'd run straight to my bedroom and drape the chain over the window. Each day I plucked off a piece—a red one, then a green one, until at last it was Christmas day! Everyone knows children look forward to this season all year, but something was about to transpire for me and my three older siblings that would change everything about the season.

One afternoon during Christmas break my siblings and I were lounging in the living room when our parents walked in with an announcement. "You four big kids won't be getting any gifts for Christmas anymore. You're old enough now, and uh, you don't need any gifts" said Mother. As she spoke our father stood by silently. They offered no reason for their decision.

"What, no gifts!" I said to myself. I couldn't believe my ears. This was shocking, a blow to my heart. I observed the faces of my other three siblings and saw how much it affected them as well. Talk about major disappointment. None of us ever expressed our feelings about it.

Perhaps over the years we had gotten used to such mistreatment. But what could we say? It was clear that our feelings didn't matter. Nonetheless, it didn't stop me from wishing they'd change their minds.

Christmas morning rolled around and everyone entered the living room. Sure enough, the four younger siblings ran to the tree and started pulling out their gifts while the four elder children had nothing with their names on it. We sat around and watched. The noise of tearing wrapping paper blended with the excitement in the younger voices as they said, “Look what I got!”

As each one discovered their gifts, I battled hurt feelings. I was so hoping way deep down in my heart that something would be under the tree for us, but there wasn't. I fought back the tears while I sat perched on the sofa in silence that morning.

Afterward, as my mother would have it every year, I had to take down the Christmas decorations and clean up all the mess left behind. It was the saddest Christmas ever. We four older siblings left the living room with long faces.

My father saw our hurt and spoke up and said, “Ya' Momma could have gotten y'awl something.” Perhaps he was feeling guilty about their decision and shifting the blame made him appear innocent. His attempt was in vain; it didn't help matters. What was this I felt? It was the feeling of being forgotten.

These feelings were only perpetuated over time, coupled with embarrassment. It involved Mother's friends when they came to the house for a visit. They compared her children's looks—out loud. “Jonnye, you know, your daughter (my younger sister) is so cute, she looks just like you,” they'd say. Mother would get the biggest smile. She loved it when her friends compared us. Seeing that I too wanted a compliment, they'd look over at me and say with a different tone of voice, “'Nita, you look just like yo' daddy.” As if something was wrong with that.

In that instant, Mother would give me that quick glare of distaste, written on her face, as if she gloated proudly that I'd been made to feel ugly. What they were really seeing was a terribly abused child. Again, my feelings didn't matter. I so wanted to hear my mother say, “Nita's beautiful, too. All my daughters are beautiful.” But that never happened. When you grew up in my household, where partiality was the blatant norm, there were plenty of times I felt forgotten.

One Saturday morning the family was sitting around the table eating breakfast. We had bacon, which everybody enjoyed. Mother used to buy it by the box load.

The baby brother, who always got what he wanted, asked, "Mommy, can I have some more bacon?" She followed with a very tender voice. "Yeah, man (that's what she would called him), you can have some." So I thought I'd ask. After all, I wanted more bacon, too. "Mommy, can I have some more meat?" I said. "I'll meat you around the corner!" she replied. That was her sarcastic way of saying no. It was as though she resented my asking.

After a few times of that, you just knew not to ask. Well, unless it was beans and rice. Again, what was this? The feeling of being forgotten. The consistent partial treatment began to make me feel as though I wasn't good enough, although I didn't realize the full impact at the time.

You see, the people in your life who have significant influence over you, especially your parents, can either make you or break you. In my case, I was broken…forgotten, like a broken bottle. In spite of all that, I had to function as an obedient child, performing all of my duties without fail.

OFFENSES WILL COME…

Being that we live in a pretty messed up world, no one can go through life without experiencing brokenness on some level. It comes through the acts of offense. As a matter of fact, St. Luke records Jesus' words, saying, *"It is impossible but that offenses will come; but woe unto him, through whom they come!*—Luke 17:1. In other words, it's not *if*, but *when* they come.

No matter the culture, social status, or race, offenses are everywhere. It is like a glass jar that falls to the floor, whether by accident or intentional it shatters into multiple intimidating pieces. Uncertain as to where it all scatters, hiding in places that one wouldn't expect—the making of a potential danger zone. Even with taking careful steps, you're subject to injury. The same goes for our world; it is full of them. They are happening at this very moment.

Across town, up the street, even next door. In my case, it was happening in my own bed, right next to me. My father would come into his daughters' bedroom in the night to sexually abuse us. If he wasn't molesting me, he was having his way with my elder sister. This went on for years.

At the age of ten I lay on the floor in the family room one evening, watching television. Popular shows during this time were Perry Mason and The Twilight Zone, viewed by many households. My father entered, sat in his recliner, and started watching as well. I must have been feeling the need for fatherly attention so I got up and went over to sit on his lap. The moment I rested on his knee he went for my breasts and begin fondling them. Immediately, I threw his hand off, then quickly jumped up and resumed my position on the floor. I dare not even share his verbal response. Oh, the anger I felt! *You nasty man,* I thought. From then on, this is what I called him. I didn't have a daughterly respect for my father because he didn't behave like one.

So then, being that offenses are everywhere, so is brokenness. Broken people are hurting people, and when people hurt, they usually hurt other people. But did my father know he was hurting his children? Did he care? I'll let you be the judge of that.

Whether he realized it would or not, this kind of behavior and his participation in it will always repulse me. How a man finds a child, his own child, sexually attractive is beyond me. I take that back—it is a demon.

After reaching womanhood, I pondered my father's actions. I came to the realization that he didn't have a fatherly affection toward his daughters. In his eyes, we were but sex objects.

There were times he would purposely make opportunities to see us naked. Talk about completely out-of-control perversity (sigh). And most people will carry on with ungodly lifestyles if there is no one to challenge them.

In the fifth grade I had a teacher named Mrs. Nichols who was loving but strict. She was known to administer a good scolding to whomever stepped out of line in her class. No one was exempted, not even me. She turned out to be the best teacher I ever had. One day she caught me misbehaving. Mrs. Nichols gave her usual piercing glare, as she looked over the top of her glasses. Then she'd speak with a stern voice, "Anita! You're being rude, crude, and unattractive!" Trust me, after that, my conduct quickly shifted to an A-1 student.

If only someone had stepped up and said to my father, "Look, man, your behavior is wicked, unacceptable and ungodly! You need to get yourself some help!" No one ever did. Instead, my folks were in denial, perhaps even hoping it would just go away!

In the reality of life it doesn't work like that. Issues don't just go away, especially devils. Because these issues are deep-seated and demonically driven, there must be a confrontation. The more deviant the behavior, the more reason to confront it.

The spirit of incest is an inflamed lust that is never quenched. The longer it is it allowed to operate, the more it will persist. This is not a simple household chore that has been overlooked. "Oops, I'm sorry, I accidentally forgot to take out the stinky trash and now it has to hang around for another week."

Let me reiterate, pedophilia is sexual perversion, a demonic spirit that feeds on garbage in the form of pornographic materials and vile music. In the United States of America, there is plenty of it! According to the Growthtrac website, pornography is said to be an eight-billion-dollar-a-year industry with close ties to organized crime. Pornography is the doorway to this wickedness, and every time an individual engages in these sensual images, it feeds and stimulates this perversion, causing it to grow.

My father used to hate cats. If a stray came into the yard, he'd say, "Don't feed it and it will go away!" This couldn't be truer when it comes to this addiction. We must understand that we live in evil times. Having said that, pornography has become normal, accepted entertainment, but acceptance doesn't make it right or good. Anyone who chooses to delve into porn will pay a hefty price they're unable to handle. Like being caught in a spider's web—the more a person engages, the more entangled they become, until everything spirals out of control.

This is an addiction, tied to the emotions; whenever a negative emotion rears up its ugly head, the flesh will act out. Any addiction linked to the emotions is very hard to break, but it is not impossible. Clinically speaking, they are called "emotional disorders." The Bible calls them "the lust of the flesh" (see Galatians 5:19-21). They become strongholds that can only be broken by the power of the gospel.

I don't believe anyone grows up desiring to be a pedophile. There are demon spirits roaming the earth, although we can't see them. They look to possess the souls of individuals. Once possessed, victims are under their control, causing them to carry out deviant acts in the dark and undercover.

When a person is possessed, they can do little to help themselves. Nevertheless, they know the behavior is wrong. The sooner it is acknowledged, the sooner they can receive deliverance.

I watched a documentary on TV of psychiatrists trying to understand the mind of a pedophile. They interviewed different individuals, then proceeded with extensive counseling sessions. When the men were asked why they carried out their perversity, they responded with answers that would provoke a sane person to want to reach through the television, pull their heads out through the screen, and give them a really good boxing job. Of course, beating a person certainly wouldn't help, although it might make one feel better.

It was obvious that the doctors were getting nowhere with their patients—it was a waste of time. With an understanding of the scriptures, I'd say to myself, "If only those doctors knew the Bible's way of handling foul spirits. Listen. You can't counsel demons away. They must be cast out." I can envision hell's minions laughing behind the scenes, because they know the feeble attempts of psychiatry will allow them to remain safely housed.

I've heard stories of women whose fathers were church pastors, so-called ministers of the gospel. These men enter the pulpit to preach on Sunday morning, then sexually molest their daughters during the week. How they were able to carry on this ungodliness with absolutely no conviction of its sinfulness is proof of sheer demonic activity. The Bible, in Romans 13:13, calls it lewdness: vile, total debauchery; unbridled lust; unashamed indecency.

It angers me when I hear in the news of the human sex trafficking of defenseless, innocent little girls and boys. Some are sold into slavery by family members in exchange for small amounts of money. Children are forced into the world of unspeakable evil of twisted-minded individuals in order to satisfy their sick pleasures. This is a crisis! It's at epidemic proportions and it must be stopped!

My anger was stirred, once again,
when I heard these precious little ones now have AIDS to their end
This has taken my anger to a higher dimension
and so I turned to pray
Lord, kill these monsters, take them out –recompense their misery
I know, I know, what a harsh prayer to pray
Perhaps I'll change it someday
But for now, today, I have absolutely no other words to say.
– Anita Joe

May the face of the Lord be against those who do evil, To cut off the remembrance of them from the earth – Psalm 34:1

Peter, Paul and Mary's 1962 hit song entitled "*If I Had a Hammer*" has lyrics that seem entirely appropriate in regard to this wickedness. This book is my "hammer." It is a way for me to hammer out the danger of sexual and physical abuse. To hammer out a warning to every spirit-filled believer to rise up and fight for the innocent and the vulnerable. And if America is truly "The Beautiful," we need to lead the way. We must begin hammering out the dangerous works of darkness like never before, in the authority of Jesus' name and by the power of the gospel.

So I ask, what do we have as a result of porn? Rape and murder on our streets. I must say this: America, we can't have it both ways. If you want the raping of women and children to cease or at least drop dramatically in this country, pornography will have to be outlawed—it is a must.

CHARACTERISTICS OF BROKENNESS

Brokenness takes on many forms—insignificance, emptiness, excessive anxiety, bitterness, fear, rejection, depression, addictions, shame, melancholy, obsessive thoughts, compulsive behaviors, and perfectionism.

Many perfectionists suffer double simply because they can't live up to their own expectations; this takes depression to a new low. I met a very unhappy airman many years ago who was a perfectionist. She was a born-again believer and very intelligent, to boot. Her struggles were obvious. I noticed them one day when I was asked to perform a wedding. Prior to the ceremony, she had volunteered to cut the wedding cake for the few attendees.

She proudly proceeded, picking up the knife, and oh boy, it was rocket science from then on. The airman must have turned the cake every way but loose before she was through. Every slice was measured and cut just so; as if her life was under strict surveillance by the Air Force commander, who could be ready to strike at any moment. I'm talking about your regular sheet cake with a bride and groom on top.

This lady made a major project out of a no-brainer, as perfectionists often do. In reality, individuals of this caliber feel diminished in their own minds. It's what I call a "self-inflicted imaginary competition." The constant need to prove one's self, one's worth - cross every "T" and dot every "I," or else I'm a failure. With that, this unhealthy state of being will keep an individual from treasuring present achievements. Thanks be to God, there is a remedy for these obsessions through our Lord Jesus Christ.

The scripture declares, *"Come unto me all ye that labor and are heavy laden, and I will give you rest."*—Matthew 11:28

In the Greek, "rest" is the word ANAPAUO; it means "be refreshed, take ease," from *ana*, "up," and from *pauo*, "to make to cease." The word describes a final ceasing; or to stop, to ease up. Jesus has the power to give us rest so we no longer have to struggle with obsessions. Isaiah 53:5 takes it further: *"He was wounded for our transgressions, He was bruised for our iniquities; the chastisement of our peace was upon Him."*

What a wonderful display of exchange made by our lowly Savior. He took the punishment that we deserved, that we might experience what He deserved—peace. This is not a worldly peace (meaning temporary). Jesus said, *"My peace I leave with you."* Therefore, it is a deep, sustaining, inner peace.

The Hebrew meaning of peace is wholeness, in body and mind. In other words, Christ's punishment was sufficient to meet our every need. We no longer have to suffer the effects of brokenness because Jesus has already done so. But we must come to Him, trusting and accepting His ways, and He will give us rest.

Broken
Promises
Acceptance
Sadness
Happy
pain
Trust
FEAR
Unforgiveness
Joy
Love
Peace

LIVING IN BROKENNESS

I have already stated that many have been broken on some level. I, too, have certainly had my struggles. I was laden with inner turmoil. Making matters worse, I backslid from my childhood teachings of God and headed down the wrong path, looking for love in all the wrong places.

So, how do I continue on with my story? Gosh . . . it began so long ago.

SETTING THE STAGE

Before I proceed, I want to set the stage by giving few examples of what it is like to live in brokenness. First, living in brokenness is tough, because it is a state of mind. Proverbs 23:7 tells us, *"As a man thinketh, so is he."* Second, one experiences the feeling of inferiority; the notion that one is unable to measure up. Third, rejection: the feeling that something is wrong with you or that you must be bad. Fourth, insignificance; feeling unimportant or worthless. And fifth, shame: the feeling of humiliation.

It is a known fact that everyone on the planet needs to be accepted and loved—everyone. We are wired that way. When people don't experience genuine love and affection, nothing is stopping negative feelings from wreaking havoc in the soul.

Looking back, I thank God that all these negative emotions were merely feelings. This meant that *I wasn't any of those things*—I was only made to feel that way. My mind had been conditioned over the years to think in a certain pattern. Let me give you a positive example.

Early in my beauty career, I met a pleasant young lady. She was striking in appearance, but not too much. I observed her mannerisms. Pardon me for saying, but they were the total opposite of her appearance. She carried herself in a queenly fashion, highborn, if you will. I was trying to figure out where all this high esteem was coming from. I almost couldn't believe my eyes. The woman detected my facial expression, addressing it as she said, "I know I'm not beautiful, but my father called me his beautiful baby girl all my life; that's all I know. This is why I act this way." Her statement left its mark.

My point being that you only look as beautiful as you feel. This woman felt beautiful, in contrast to what she saw of herself. Her mind had been conditioned. As we thinketh, so we are. The same result occurs when the opposite message is enforced, when our self-esteem has been beaten into the ground. Until this is dealt with, an individual can be mentally and spiritually tormented, which causes them to act out in unhealthy ways.

The mistreatment I experienced chipped away at my self-esteem. It absolutely affected my behavior and how I felt about myself. For example, I was the kind of person who would always give my all, even overcompensating in many instances. But I didn't expect it in return. King David also displayed this kind of behavior. Let's read:

> *Then Saul said to David, "Here is my older daughter Merab; I will give her to you as a wife. Only be valiant for me, and fight the Lord's battles." For Saul thought, "Let my hand not be against him, but let the hand of the Philistines be against him." So David said to Saul, "Who am I, and what is my life or my father's family in Israel, that I should be son-in-law to the king?"*—1 Samuel 18:17–18

David didn't feel worthy to marry the king's daughter, let alone be the son-in-law to a king. Although in verse 17 we see it was not a sincere gesture on King Saul's part. Because of the mistreatment David experienced in his childhood, he deemed himself unworthy to have close ties to a king.

Who am I? asked the young lad after fighting a battle with a ten-foot-tall giant and winning. He did not see himself as a hero. David took the humble approach, and because of that, Saul took full advantage.

Herein is the most troubling part. Saul began to resent David, making life very uncomfortable for him. Saul was overtaken by a spirit of jealousy. Speaking of jealousy, this is the worst thing to experience from those to whom you look up. In my case, it was the same scenario, except in a mother-daughter relationship—resentment followed by jealousy followed by rejection. Although there are cases when a child may be jealous of the mother. Nevertheless, both seem abnormal and are detrimental.

As it was with Saul, my mother was used to getting all the attention. She loved being waited on. And so that is how she raised her children, teaching us very well how to cater to her every need.

As I grew older and began to perform for myself the very things I was taught, it did not go over well. It left me feeling confused. I wasn't sure what to do. For any child, it is difficult growing up under such treatment because it sends mixed messages: Do I do well or do I not? Either way I suffer punishment.

Here's my story . . .

In the summer of '78 I graduated from high school and beauty college in the same year. I was so excited! Somehow, I had stumbled upon one of my passions in life. I've always been the creative type, so cosmetology was right up my alley.

I doubled up on my high school classes so I could finish the year early. This allowed me to go to beauty college full time. I studied hard and made even better grades in college than in high school. With my training completed, the only thing left was to take the state board exam.

The Board of Cosmetology was in Phoenix, our state's capital, a little over a hundred miles from Tucson. So I was dependent upon my parents to get me there. I was only seventeen years old, and certainly didn't have a car to speak of. I walked through the house looking for my mother, thinking how proud she would be of me and my accomplishments.

As I entered her bedroom, I saw Mother lying on the bed. Being a thrifty shopper, she was searching the newspaper for coupons; this she did frequently because we had a big family. "Ma, I have my state board exam in Phoenix in a few weeks and I need a ride. Will you take me?" I asked. I stood in the doorway waiting for a response. Mother continued flipping through the paper as if I wasn't there.

I left her presence in tears, feeling terribly let down. I thought, What am I going to do? My career is gone. If they don't take me, how will I get there? I was already feeling overwhelmed with life, having moved into adulthood. This was the time I really needed positive direction. Instead, I still had to deal continually with Mother's evasiveness. It was frustrating to have to suffer under the hands of a mama who was mean as the dickens and just didn't care. Overcome with hopelessness, I cried for days.

Shortly thereafter, my father saw my sadness and said, "What's wrong with you?" I told him the story, and to my surprise, he comforted me. "Don't cry, we'll get you there," he said. That certainly made me feel better. But God was already working on my behalf.

A few days later, the phone rang. "'Nita, telephone!" they said. To my surprise, it was one of my schoolmates wanting to know if I had a ride to Phoenix. "No," I replied. She politely invited me to ride with her group.

Everything was set, and I was on my way to becoming a licensed cosmetologist. *Ah,* I thought, *I'm going after all.* I was excited all over again, flooded with joyous emotions. It was a great day for me. It goes without saying that this was not a coincidence. God is always for the underdog. The trip up to Phoenix felt like a reward for all my hard work. I wasn't nervous about anything. My confidence level soared through the roof.

It was the middle of summer when examination day came. I packed all of my cosmetology supplies early on and double-checked everything to make sure I was ready for the trip. I had a few dollars to take with me that I'd gotten from tips and babysitting the neighbor's kids. My ride arrived early that morning in hope of beating the desert heat. This was a good thing, because after climbing aboard the car, the only air conditioning was the old-fashioned manual kind—roll-down-zee-vindow. But I didn't dare complain, because I knew the Lord had made a way for me.

After driving for over an hour we arrived at our hotel. I was whipped! The Arizona sun had drained all my energy. I've never been a fan of the summers out West for this reason—it was just too hot. I could barely rise to walk to the building. Once I made my entry, the air-conditioned lobby was my saving grace. It was as if I'd stepped out of a towering inferno into an ice chamber. Straightaway, we all dotted over to the hotel's restaurant counter and ordered the tallest cold drink on the menu. Everyone was leaning toward frozen daiquiris, so I order the strawberry flavor for myself. The first sip was tasty, sweet, and oh-so-satisfying.

The group settled in the lounge area a few feet away. We reflected on all the hard work we'd put in and were happy to have made it to State Board. There were plenty of students that didn't. For some reason, they either dropped out or couldn't pass the pre-college exam.

We also confessed our apprehensions while indulging in our icy drinks. It didn't take long before I devoured mine. My next move would reveal a sneaky surprise. I leaned forward to pick up my suitcase when my head started spinning. Whoo! What's happening? I thought. I didn't know that this tantalizing tropical invention was a disguise for a mixed drink, and being that I don't drink, I should have asked for the "virgin" version. It was a good thing that the State Board exam was the following morning. There was no way I would've been able to function under the influence. Thank goodness, I had the rest of the night to sleep off the effects.

Awakened by the alarm, I stepped out of bed refreshed, then quickly dressed. I was eager to get underway. Our group met in the hotel lobby, then loaded up in the car once again and headed downtown to the Capitol Building. We drove up to a mammoth historical structure, parked, and made our way inside.

Everyone entered the designated room dressed in white uniforms, not fully knowing what to anticipate. The space was a bit tight with a setup identical to our beauty college. The cosmetology instructors were cordial, and this I found comforting. We took our seats as they handed out the written exam with only a hundred questions. The college pretest consisted of three hundred and fifty questions. "This was going to be a breeze!" I thought. The practical examination followed. It entailed working on a live model and answering questions that the instructors threw at us. We soon completed all of the tests. The time seemed to fly by. A few hours turned into a few minutes, and voila, it was over. With the examination now behind us, we gathered up our belongings and parted, with goodbyes. Again, we loaded up the car and headed back to Tucson. Thirty days later I received a notice that I had passed with flying colors. It was official; I was a board-certified cosmetologist!

The next thing for me was to find a job. I looked for a stylist position at a few salons, only to be confronted with rejections. This was my first experience of real prejudice. Nevertheless, I kept looking and finally landed my first job at the Guys and Gals Salon on Grant road. It wasn't a fancy salon, but the people were nice.

The owner loved my work and was happy that I had come on board. It was a commission-based salon, and after one week I'd made my first 150-dollar paycheck. The next day I went out to cash my check and returned home. I owed my mother seventy-five dollars for a pair of contact lenses she bought for me prior to getting my job. I'd promised Mother that if she bought them for me, I'd pay her back. I was more than happy to fulfill my obligation.

As soon as I arrived home, I entered her bedroom. She was preparing to go out. Mother leaned toward the mirror to put on her mascara as I approached her. "Ma, here's the money I owe you," I said. She continued looking in the mirror, then quickly turned to take the money out of my hand, without a thank-you. The look in Mother's eyes told a not-so-pleasant story. With unmistakable anger, she said, "What about some gas money for driving your big ole' blankety-blank around!" Woo! I was blindsided, confused, and hurt all at the same time. I didn't understand her reaction. After all, I was taking the bus to and from both schools. Did she mean I had to start paying for a ride to church on Sundays?

The hate that spewed from her mouth stunned me so much that I felt very discouraged when I left her presence. I thought I had done a good thing—the right thing. She might as well have spit in my face. What good is it to keep working? I was too naïve to connect the dots. Mother had compared herself with me and had become enraged with jealousy.

In retrospect, I understood that nothing I had done or could ever do would make my mother appreciate me. Her mistreatment of me only increased; it was obvious this woman didn't like me at all. But why? Just as Saul saw greatness in David and became jealous, so it was with my mother. I never saw her show any signs of happiness no matter what I did. Now at the time I didn't know it was jealousy, and I didn't understand it until years later.

It was hurtful, but at least now I knew what I was dealing with. It has been distressing to come to grips with the person who trained me to be excellent, scolded me for anything less, and then refused such a treasure as I. Much of the time I felt like a useless and unappreciated child.

WHO AM I?

Broken people cannot answer this question because they don't know who they are. There is a loss of one's self; there is no clear concept of being, direction, or goals. An individual may often feel a lack of control over their circumstances. They have a generic idea that when bad things happen to them they must deserve it, but when good things happen, they don't deserve it.

Another reason broken people don't know who they are is summed up in one word, "undone": Webster's definition of brokenness. Undone defined is "open," which is exactly what one becomes when broken. These two underlying characteristics are what makes broken individuals susceptible. To what, you might ask. To more of the same abuse; physical or emotional harm. This is called "revictimization."

Let me give you an example. By the time I became a young adult, my home life was so unpleasant it was as if I had become the target for verbal and physical bullet practice minute by minute. Finally, I decided that I had to move away. I quit the salon, packed my belongings, and moved to Houston, Texas, to live with my Aunt Lou, one of Mother's older sisters. She seemed fond of me. Aunt Lou stood up for me when my mother aggressively demeaned me in front of the family. I was timid about making my journey into the world. I had just turned eighteen and was pretty naïve about life. After all, I didn't have the kind of parents who would sit me down and teach life's essentials. I needed to learn these important skills, like what a true friend is and how to go about choosing one. Like what type of person would make a good spouse. How to be confident and set goals. How to avoid certain pitfalls and how to solve problems if I should encounter a pitfall. You know, just good ole' information for life's journey. I had to figure it all out on my own, although that's not always a bad thing, because by these one learns to be independent. But, you can be sure that in my venture to figure things out came with a lot of bumps and stumps along the way. When I thought about it, I guess my parents couldn't teach on such matters, because then they would expose their own negative characters.

One can't really know a person's character until you've lived with them. My love for Aunt Lou grew, along with the attention she gave me. After a few months stay, I discovered that she too displayed abusive traits. But, the difference was, she favored me. I was the daughter she never had, and the affection she gave was somewhat emotionally fortifying.

The damage I sustained from my parents was deep. For that reason, developing relationships, whether male or female, all seemed to contain the same abusive traits of my parents. Most meaningful associations were one-sided. By the time I married, my relationships were no different.

As a result of my childhood experiences, I displayed the people-pleaser syndrome. I felt the need to work for love and affection—how sad is that? Of course, I had no idea I was doing it. It was a mindset. Getting emotionally involved with people who had no intention of doing the right thing was a behavior that would take a long time to undo, simply because I had no idea who I was. You see, if I had been a whole person, I would have never allowed myself to enter most of the relationships in my past. Looking back on some of the stuff I put up with makes me chuckle, which is a sign that I have definitely moved on.

It goes without saying, clarity of one's self is very important. There is a connection between knowing who you are and what you want in life. I'm not talking about being self-centered or selfish. I'm talking about values like your self-worth, self-respect, your personal and social standards, and principles and morals that you've set to live by. These are priceless treasures that only come by learning; therefore, someone needs to teach them to you.

There are several ways they can be taught: by verbal instruction, by observation, and by how one is treated. Let me explain further. In Proverbs 31:10–31, King Lemuel describes a beautiful picture of the virtuous woman.

He starts off by saying, *"Who can find a virtuous woman? For her price is far above rubies."*

The virtuous woman has a price—a high price. For this reason, she is rare. What is the price and how did she acquire it? There is no amount of wealth that can compare to her worth. Are you getting this, ladies? Knowing your worth will keep you from selling yourself cheap.

If you notice, the scripture is not talking about physical beauty, although she may have it. But the inner beauty of a woman is what makes her priceless. Her loyalty, strength, honor, talent, loving care for her family, and most of all, her reverential fear of God—this, beloved, is real beauty—beauty that will not fade away with time.

All of these inner qualities have to be taught—developed—made. No one is born with them. And, might I add, they can only be appreciated in others by those who themselves possess and are acquainted with such knowledge, by others who are willing to take the time to get to know a person, to look inside and discover an individual.

Here's my example: Near the end of my third-grade year, my classmates and I sat at our desks without any particular assignment. Earlier that year my teacher, Mrs. McConoughey, allowed me to read the first book I had ever written in front of the class. After I had completed the story, she asked the classmates to give me applause. Along with all the students, she seemed to be very proud of me that day.

So here it was, the last day of school, and my teacher was sitting behind me at one of the classroom desks grading papers. Mrs. McConoughey wore gold-rimmed glasses, which complimented her teased-up blond cascaded French roll. It was always neatly in place and full of hairspray. Most teachers at that time had some kind of fixed style to their hair.

She spoke behind me in her usual stern tone. "Anita, you may have one of those dictionaries." She pointed toward the window. Her voice startled me at times, but I was happy that she was giving me a gift of sorts. All the schoolbooks and materials lined the built-in shelves along the wall beneath a huge window that looked out to the playgrounds. I rose from my seat and walked slowly toward the dictionaries on the top shelf, wondering which one I should choose. Taking a glance at both books, I opened one of them to observe the content. "That's right," she spoke sternly as I jolted inside. "You should always look inside a book before you choose it." That statement left me with a good feeling about the choice I made.

The point here is that Mrs. McConoughey's intuitiveness taught me that I had value. She gave me a reason that I could feel good about myself. She looked inside me that year and discovered talent, strength, and beauty that would develop over time.

This step shows how one comes to know their worth, whether it comes from a patient, loving parent or a guardian. Or, in my case, a schoolteacher.

Another way we can learn who we are is for Father God Himself to teach us. This is good news. King David said it like this: *"I will instruct thee and teach thee in the way which thou shalt go: I will guide thee with mine eyes."*—Psalm 32:8

One cannot put a finger on how God will intervene in a life to bring about wholeness. But without His help, the hope of becoming completely whole is unattainable. Though my life started out with a mountainous terrain of dysfunction, the Lord found me in the nick of time, put me in a spiritual cast, and began molding me for my success. He was and is working in His own special way to bring it about. The same goes for you, beloved. We cannot determine what our life will be just yet. God's instructions are mystical, if you will. They're not a simple "do this" or "do that" regimen. For example, the book of Genesis reveals the life of a little boy named Joseph who had quite a spectacular dream of the stars bowing down to him. (see Genesis 37-50). He decided to share this phenomenon with his family. It seemed so outlandish that they despised him for it. Thus, would begin a chain reaction of the unforeseen. But, why would a child have such a dream as this? Or, how would it come to pass, is the greater question. Only the Lord knew that, after being driven away because of a dream, purpose would ultimately arrive at destiny's door.

Beyond human thought, a little boy, so loved by his father, is plucked up from his family by divine providence. God was his instructor, guiding him with His eyes and teaching him in the way he should go. A path so cruel and filled with hardship it would hardly seem fair. Leaving one perplexed, perhaps even to ask, "Where is God in all of this?" He was there, working with a heavy hand, developing just the right character to fulfill His divine plan. A little Joseph boy, now a man, came up the rough side of the mountain as a means to become a great leader who would sustain a nation.

WHAT IS BROKKENNESS? THE OPPORTUNITY FOR DIVINE PROVIDENCE

Before I close this portion of the chapter, I want to talk to you, the real and unique you. The beautiful, smart, talented, and gifted you.

Consider the vastest mountain range in the world with all its grandeur. The terrain stretches as far as the eyes can see—the mountains are impressive and overwhelming all together. A massive work they are, created without lifting a finger—spoken into being by the voice of many waters. And yet, a Mount Everest will melt like snow at the presence of its Maker.

Perhaps for you, too, life is one massive emotional terrain with no end in sight. You may be wondering, "Will I ever get through this? When will this mountain ever come down?" Let me point you to the One who knows how to cut to the chase. He is not intimidated by your foes. He will show up on your behalf. And at His presence every mountain will melt like snow, that He may make His name known to your enemies.

 *Dear beloved, my prayer for you:*

May the God of heaven show up and show Himself strong on your behalf. May He bring down every high mountain, may He make every crooked way straight. In the name of Jesus the Christ.

Worry no longer about where you came from and who did what to you. *What is brokenness? The opportunity for divine providence.*

FIRST THINGS FIRST

FIRST THINGS FIRST

FORGIVENESS

> *"For if ye forgive men their trespasses, your Heavenly Father will also forgive you."*
>
> —Matthew 6:14

For most people, forgiveness is a subject that is difficult to swallow. Reason being, it is not a natural inclination. The flesh wants revenge for the pain it suffers. The thought of excusing a crime committed against oneself by a perpetrator causes unpleasant emotions in some, and frustration in others. I think it's safe to say we've all felt constrained when it comes to the practice of forgiving others. Although many may be uncomfortable with the idea, we are commanded by the Father to forgive trespasses. Matthew 6:14 makes it crystal clear; if you don't forgive, you will not be forgiven. Last time I checked, humanity will always need the Father's forgiveness.

Here's my story . . .

After I became a born-again believer, I so wanted my family to experience the new birth as well. Sharing my testimony of how Jesus washed me of my sins and brought me into the light did not go over well. My family could not understand. I prayed continually that the Lord would save them. Unfortunately, my relationship with my family wasn't any better than the time I first left home. In fact, it had gotten worse. I thought my parents would have been happy about my accomplishments—first and foremost, that I was living a Christian life. Second, having opened my own hair salon without any assistance from them—not that they would have offered. It all seemed to go unnoticed.

Perhaps I missed it. I mean, could they have been proud of me and I didn't see it? If by chance they were, they had a strange way of showing it. Even the few times my father mentioned being proud of me, I never trusted his compliments. I always suspected some hidden agenda.

This discredit was another thing added to my hurtful past that I held against them. After years of combating insults, my soul was beset with resentment. How vividly I remember during my childhood being provoked beyond irritation. I wanted to lash out to avenge myself. But they were my parents, so I held it in. Plus, if I wanted to live, I knew better than to confront them.

I had been walking with the Lord for several years now, and He had begun to deal with me in a way I never expected. I was living in Atlanta, and I called home to talk with my parents frequently. They rarely called me; if we talked, I had to do the calling. Oftentimes, the conversation left me with hurt feelings. On this occasion, after speaking with them, I hung up the phone in tears. I fell down on my knees and began to cry out to God—again.

When the person or persons responsible for your brokenness are mistreating you, everything that they ever did comes back to your mind. It's not what they've done at that moment that hurts. It's all the other hurts compiled with the present hurt. The wounds get deeper.

So there I was, telling the Lord all about my parents' mistreatment of me, with crocodile tears. After a few moments of sobbing, God spoke to me. His words were shocking. In response to my whining, He spoke with a loving but stern voice and said, "What about you?" I immediately stopped sobbing—every tear dried up. I was absolutely stunned at this. I felt as though someone had poured a bucket of ice-cold water in my face—splash!

I couldn't and didn't understand what the Lord was saying. "What about me? What did I do, Lord?" He replied, "You will not forgive." I'll never forget His words. The thought had never crossed my mind that I was bearing unforgiveness in my heart. Oftentimes the light of truth can be cumbersome. Perhaps this is because humans mainly see only one side of a situation, their side.

I thought those who were responsible for my brokenness owed me recompense. Certainly it would have helped matters, but unfortunately, I couldn't bank on it. Would the lofty parent bow in admission to their offspring for any wrongdoing? Years passed with hopes they would. In vain, I waited for an apology. In vain, I waited to see a change. There was no attempt. Like a ball and chain, I held on to the offenses.

God's commandment to forgive is not based on whether the individuals change or not. Oft times a person may continue to act foolish, but you can rest assured, *"VENGEANCE IS MINE, I WILL REPAY," says the Lord* (see Romans 12:19-18).

Here's the deal: nobody, and I do mean nobody, has the right to hold grudges. We all have sinned and have come short of the glory of God. How often do we seem to overlook offenses that we've committed? According to Romans 3:23, *"Not one is innocent before Him."* That day, I learned how offensive unforgiveness is to God. Not only so, but it's a hindrance to me, both naturally and spiritually. How so? If you don't forgive, you become stopped-up like a drainpipe, nothing coming in and nothing going out. You know what that looks like, don't you? Green and black slimy gook with an overwhelming stench. Listen to what Jesus says to us in Mark 11:25–26: *But if you forgive not men their trespasses, neither will your Father forgive your trespasses.*

The word of God is clear why it is of highest importance to forgive. In Matthew 18: 23–35, Jesus addresses it again in the parable of the unforgiving servant. This parable conveys that there is a consequence to harboring unforgiveness that is meant to be delivered to the tormentors. In other words, is very dangerous—potentially detrimental to one's own soul.

I know that in American churches we don't want to identify with this truth. Understand this scripture text. If you don't forgive, you can't be forgiven, and if you can't be forgiven, sin lies at the door; which in turn will cause your soul to be lost for eternity. Beloved, I reiterate; the Father's forgiveness is conditioned upon your willingness to forgive others. And we all need the Father's forgiveness. Don't we? Therefore, we must forgive.

We can be grateful to the Lord for his longsuffering toward us. In His patience, He gives us time to come clean. That day, I confessed and repented of the sin of unforgiveness. I forgave all the offenses that were committed against me. This is the first step to freedom. At first it was kind of bittersweet. Part of me was glad, and the other part wasn't feeling it. I'll just tell you the truth. I was really upset with those folks. I could come up with a whole lot of reasons to remain upset. Especially knowing they would continue their abuse. Although I must say I did begin to feel better—lighter—in my spirit.

So then, what was the Lord really conveying to me when He said, "You won't forgive?" Simply this. As Jesus was dying on the cross, He was being ridiculed and mocked by the heartless crowd. He cried out, "Father, forgive them, for they know not what they do. Yes, they did horrible things to me, but Father, I will not hold this against them. Please forgive them" (author's paraphrase). In layman's terms, Jesus was saying, "Forgive them because they are truly stupid." We are not above Christ; we too must let it all go and move forward. Do you recall my opening scripture of Ecclesiastes 3:5? *"There's a time to get, and a time to lose, a time to keep and a time to cast away."*

My friend, this is your time to loose yourself by casting away all the bitterness.

The question you have to ask is this: what do I have to gain by dragging around a ball and chain of miserable memories? OH, dear beloved, how often we need God to move for us but we are unable to receive His unlimited blessings simply because we are bound. This is not to diminish anyone's hurts. They are real, and yes, being mistreated is harrowing. But if you are going to be healed from your brokenness, you must be willing to forgive. First things first. Nothing will change until it is dealt with.

What does it really take to forgive? Some might say time; perhaps so. If that were the only thing required, why are so many stuck in their past? Fifty years later they talk about their abuse as if it happened yesterday. What's the answer? It's simple; a determined will. There has to be a wholehearted willingness. A person has to *want* to forgive.

Here's my story . . .

I was experiencing a new level of joy and peace, and it was growing! The things that had me bound had lost their grip. The chains of the enemy were broken by the power of the Holy Ghost. The more I yielded myself to the will of God, the more His work in me began to manifest.

Reflecting on my upbringing, I couldn't help but see the silver lining, how it helped shape me into who I am today. One Christmas holiday I went home for a vacation. Mother and I were sitting at the dining table having a conversation. I mentioned how glad I was that she didn't give me the partial favor that she gave my other siblings.

You see, the two siblings my parents held in high regard didn't turn out so well. Her baby son started out in life with great potential. His parents were proud of him. By and by he succumbed to the popular drug, crack cocaine. His habit became so extreme that our parents had to take extra measures to hide their valuables. They thought it would protect them from being stolen. It was to no avail. Their own son ripped them off. Worse yet, their belongings were sold on the street for little to nothing. The family home became an uneasy place to dwell. As sure as you'd put something down, it was gone. Even guests were warned to safeguard their belongings. My sister grew up with a lack of initiative and was unable to think for herself. Looking to men for support, she was in and out of different relationships, and finally married a man she didn't love. At least she thought she didn't love him. They have since reconciled with each other.

All in all, I came to terms with it, because if my siblings' messed-up lives were the result of Mother and Father loving them so much, I was glad that they hated me so much. I was hoping to get some kind of response, but there was none. Mother usually kept her feelings inside. If you think about it, what could she say to that except, "I'm so sorry for the way I treated you"? That wasn't gonna happen, not in a million years.

Yes, the Lord was changing me for the good. But for me to get to that state of mind, I had to learn to forgive offenses. Let's examine the word forgiveness. It is the Greek word APIEMI. Primarily, it means "to send forth, send away." A few more definitions from *Vine's Complete Expository Dictionary* that are important to mention are "to pardon, to leave, abandon; to tolerate."

Peter struggled with the idea of forgiveness. He presented a question to the Lord "How many times shall I forgive my brother, up to seven times? Jesus replied "Nay, but up to seven-times- seventy. This is where tolerance comes in. It's easier said than done…I know. The Lord's grace is sufficient.

Perhaps you have been walking around with unforgiveness for a long time. You might be saying to yourself, *I really do want to forgive because I know it's right. But I can't. I don't have the strength.* Beloved, God will help you. As I stated before, all you have to do is be willing, from your heart.

Unfortunately, circumstances do happen in life that can cripple to the point of sheer anguish and despair, causing many to fall into bitter resentment, trapped for years on end. Which reminds me of the lame man at the pool of Bethesda. The Bible says he lay there thirty-eight years. That is a long time to be in the same predicament. Let's read his story:

> *After this there was a feast of the Jews, and Jesus went up to Jerusalem. Now there is in Jerusalem by the Sheep Gate a pool, which is called in Hebrew, Bethesda, having five porches. In these lay a great multitude of sick people, blind, lame, paralyzed, waiting for the moving of the water. For an angel went down at a certain time into the pool and stirred up the water; then whoever stepped in first, after the stirring of the water, was made well of whatever disease he had. Now a certain man was there who had an infirmity thirty-eight years. When Jesus saw him lying there, and knew that he already had been in that condition a long time, He said to him, "Do you want to be made whole?" The impotent man answered him, Sir, I have no man, when the water is troubled, to put me into the pool: but while I am coming, another steppeth down before me. Jesus said unto him, "Rise, take up thy bed, and walk." And immediately the man was made whole.* —John 5:1–9

This passage shows the compassion of Jesus. It's a fascinating story to me because in the midst of all the sick people around the pool, Jesus saw one man, in particular. He saw his struggles, his heart, and his future. When Jesus perceived that he'd been there a long time, He said to the man, "Do you want to be made whole?" Why would Jesus ask such a question knowing the man's condition? After all, he remained at the pool in hopes that someday his turn might come. He began to explain to Jesus his tedious efforts: "I have no man" and "No matter how hard I tried, I couldn't reach the pool fast enough."

Revelation: The man had two things working against him. One, he was looking to an inferior source for help. Two, he was relying on his own strength. With that, he would most certainly remain crippled.

We have a tendency to make this common mistake because we look to men to solve what only God can.

The Bible described the man as being impotent. In the Greek this word is ASTHENEO; it means "to be without strength, diseased, to be weak; ill." I compare the struggles of the impotent man to unforgiveness. Like him, we do not have the strength within ourselves to forgive. We must look to the source for our help, Jesus the Christ. He will give us the power to forgive all offenses. I speak of power because the bitterness of unforgiveness is a spiritual bondage; chains must be supernaturally broken.

The power of God is stronger than resentment—it overrides animosity. And by the power of the Spirit, one simple act of forgiveness will break its chains. The scripture declares,

> *If the Son therefore shall make you free, ye are free indeed.*
> —John 8:36

It is Christ's ultimate intent to make you free, to loose you from all that binds. He knows what you've been through already; you don't have to keep rehearsing it. Listen. In the midst of explaining his issues, the Lord looks at him and says, "RISE." Let's examine the word "rise" in the Greek. It is the word EGEIRO, meaning "to arise, to stand from a prone or sleeping position." From the base meaning there are several, but these are the meanings I want to emphasize: "to restore from a dead or damaged state: to heal, to raise to life; to cause something to exist." Jesus spoke the power of His word and the man's entire life was changed immediately! Oh, what good news. The believer does not have to continue in a self-imposed prison. Through the Son you can be made free!

I can't express enough the crippling effects of unforgiveness. Many are unable to rise to the joys of life because they are sick and afflicted with various diseases. You've heard the saying, "You either get better or bitter." I encourage you to choose the former. Jesus declared, *"I have come that they might have life, and that they might have it more abundantly."*—John 10:10

The blows of life may have damaged you, but this same Jesus is asking you today, "Will you be made whole?"

THE PROCESS

THE PROCESS

When an individual has experienced brokenness, it must be understood that becoming whole is a process—a journey, if you will. But what is needed for the journey? The answer is, *faith*. That said, in this next section I will allow the Father to speak a personal word of encouragement to your heart:

> *I will always require faith on your part. Your faith in response to the process will determine your outcome. I will do what you believe me for. My Word declares, "But without faith it is impossible to please Him, for he who comes to me must believe that I am He."*
>
> *Understand that my ultimate goal is to transform you into the image of my dear Son. You are my children and I am concerned with everything about you. I want every part of you, brokenness and all. Know that in My eyes you are a finished product. That is the reason I started the work in you in the first place. I always finish what I start. My word declares, "being confident of this very thing, that He who begun a good work in you will complete it until the day of*

Christ."—Philippians 1:6. *Therefore, it is important for you to see yourself as My "good work" in process.*

I'm taking you to a place you have never been; it's a new journey. Heretofore I will prepare you. Your first step is to receive My direction; I will be your map-My peace shall be your compass-My word shall be your guide.

Dear children you must be teachable, reachable, and receptive. The walls you have built up will have to come down, which I know is not always easy. But don't worry, I am very good at pulling off layers of brick. I know how to take the stony heart and make it into a heart of flesh. At times you won't understand the "how" and the "what" of My hand. But hear My words;

"Fear thou not; for I am with thee: be not dismayed, for I am thy God: I will strengthen thee; yea, I will help thee; yea, I will uphold thee with the right hand of my righteousness."—Isaiah 41:10

It is important for believers to know that we have been bought with a price, that we are no longer our own. The Father does to us and for us what pleases him.

Let's examine the word "process." *Webster* defines it as, "progressive advance: a natural phenomenon made by gradual changes, that leads toward a particular result; the process of growth."

Here's my story . . .

My process began when I became born again. Accepting Christ as Lord and Savior was the most wonderful experience I have ever encountered. I'll never forget. It was a Monday night in the year 1980. A Christian lady I met at Houston Community College invited me to church. "My church is having Women's Mission Service tonight, come and go with me," she said. I was accustomed to going to church, so without hesitation, I gladly accepted. She offered me a ride, and once class was over we got in her car and drove off.

I had no idea we were headed to a "holiness" church. I'm sure that was God's plan. Upon arrival, we stepped out of the car and walked toward the stone-front building. Right away I noticed the unpaved parking lot. That was a little strange.

When we walked into the church, the décor was the typical burgundy color throughout, accented with gold and brass. Most churches had the same layout design back then. I observed a handful of ladies standing in a circle near the back of the church. To tell you the truth, I didn't really understand what was going on. One lady was crying, the other lifting her hands as if she was under arrest. Suddenly, one of them fell to the floor—now that was really strange, I thought. I stood there looking as a spectator when Eleanor, the mission president, laid her hands on my head and prayed silently. At that moment I didn't feel anything to speak of. But after returning home later that evening, the unexpected happened. Just about the time I laid down, I felt compelled to kneel at my bedside and pray. That's when the Spirit of the Lord came over me. I began to experience a purging, as though my very soul was being washed. I continued crying out to God, confessing my sins. Jesus came in and changed my heart; my life was no longer the same. I knew I had been born again (although I hadn't known the term). That night I slept peacefully, like a newborn baby, no pun intended. When I rose that morning, I knew that I had to go back to that same church. Little did I know that I would receive more of what God had done in me. His work had only begun. The following Sunday morning I entered the church house, and the Spirit was strong. The word was preached under the anointing. My mind was captured as the tears began to fall. The next thing I knew, my hands went up, and the praises of God flowed freely out of my mouth. That had never happened before. I wasn't used to that kind of praise. Everything happened spontaneously, as if it had always been a part of me.

The power of God was evident, like electricity flowing through my body. All of this was beyond me. A new creation in Christ had emerged. I'd hold my hands out in front of me and say to myself, "Wow, even my hands look new!" I was so full of joy and excitement! I was deeply in love with Jesus from the very start, and I couldn't wait to tell someone, anyone, what my Lord had done for me, how He took a broken sinner and washed her with His blood until she became white like snow. Immediately after the Lord made His abode in my heart, I felt so many emotions at once: joy, peace, freedom, acceptance, and Ah . . . *love*. I experienced real love for the very first time in my whole entire life. I hadn't known this "Jesus" kind of love, purely unconditional and impartial. In my childhood I had to work to earn my affection. But this . . . this was *true* love. I didn't have to do anything to earn it. His love made me hold fast to Him.

I sought the Lord diligently; oh, how I longed to be close to Jesus. Yes, He was my Lord and Savior, and I cherished everything about Him then and even more today. In this very moment while I write, I feel the very same joy in my heart. It doesn't go away, you know? This was the beginning of my born-again experience, and I will always be grateful to the Lord. Now the real battle had begun, the battle of light against darkness.

Before I continue, please note that the journey entails drama, if you will. Though it's positive, there is an unexpected series of events that will take place. In other words, it may not feel positive at the time, but trust me—it will work toward a better you. It's like the preparations of a delicious pot of stew cooking on the stovetop. It may boil over a few times, but an experienced cook wipes up the mess and continues until the finish.

During my process of healing, I began to see the abuse I suffered in a different light, simply because I didn't realize some of what I encountered was abusive. I thought it was merely a part of my upbringing experience. I learned differently after hearing about other people's early life. Their stories were of parents who loved unconditionally. The comparison was astounding. I couldn't help but wish I'd had that for myself. You see, that too is something I have to process.

Let me give you an example. I was invited to a women's networking club. Upon arrival, everyone introduced themselves. Afterwards we were given an assignment and divided into groups. Everyone was asked to tell the most unforgettable and exciting thing that had happened in their childhoods.

One woman told the story of her father surprising her with a pony she'd always wanted. I'm thinking to myself, *What! Fathers give their children ponies?* All the women had incredible stories of loving parents and wonderful events, all except me. On the flip side, you find that there are stories worse than your own, like the time I happened to turn on the TV and *The Dr. Phil Show* was on. He was talking with a young lady about nineteen or twenty years old. She had been sexually and physically abused by her mother and stepfather at the tender young age of five. Hearing her story brought tears to my eyes. This precious little girl was kept in a closet by her parents. They barely fed her and only let her out when they wanted sex. They would force her to perform all kinds of sex acts on them. She said that if she didn't perform like they wanted, they would beat her and make her do it again. Afterward, they would throw her back into the closet, leaving her to beg for food and water. She was severely underdeveloped for her age and no doubt slowly dying from starvation. The young lady told her story in tears. "One day my mother was giving me a bath. While standing in the tub, my mother pushed me backward into the water. I almost drowned," she said. Her malnourished little body fell into the water as her mother walked away laughing at the top of her lungs. "I struggled to get up," she said. "It was only by the mercy of God I pulled through."

The young lady, still sobbing, asked the age-old question. "Why? How could they [mother and father] do this to me?" During the interview, Dr. Phil stated that she was rescued at the age of nine. Then her picture was shown on the screen. She looked about the size of a five-year-old. It made me gasp. "Oh dear God!" I said. She was, of course, admitted to the hospital. After being examined by the doctors, they found pieces of plastic and other foreign objects in her stomach, as she was trying to feed on anything she could get her hands on. It was said that her female organs were destroyed. She'd never be able to have children. I am so thankful her story ended well. The young lady was adopted by a wonderful woman who loved and raised her as her own. Her adoptive mother explained all the fears the child wrestled with because of the trauma.

"When I first got her, she was so messed up emotionally. She could not be in a room with the door closed. I had to take all the doors off the hinges as a comfort to her," she said. The young lady hated doors. There were many other interventions the child's new mother had to manage. This young lady had begun her journey of healing and had many years ahead. The love from her adoptive mother definitely played a major role in her healing.

I need you to understand a couple of important points. One, you must acknowledge that you are broken in order for the process to begin, and two, you must be willing to go through the necessary steps. Receiving Jesus Christ as Lord and Savior is that first step. He will give you the grace to go through the process of healing. Some healings will come sooner than others; this is normal. I know there are a lot of self-help materials out there, but even with all of them put together they are still lacking. Nothing can compare to the power of the gospel to bring healing to a broken soul. My own wounds were so deep that only the power of Jesus could destroy the yoke of bondage from my life.

Even with all of my wonderful salvation experience, I was still broken. Just because a person gets saved, doesn't mean all is well in his or her soul. I was bound by my past; this I found strange. I really couldn't understand what was going on, and I surely didn't know how to deal with the bondages. One thing I knew, the devil had lost a soul to the kingdom of God, and I wasn't going back. The good news is, I learned that the issues I struggled with had names. I could recognize and identify them as strongholds. For your knowledge, there are three main strongholds. These are *fear*, *root of bitterness* (which we have already covered), and *rebellion* (rejection). From these stem every bondage known to man.

Now, back to my story. In the beginning of my Christian walk I was clueless as to how to handle the demonic world. All the spiritual bondages mentioned kept me broken. Consequently, I didn't know my identity in Christ. There wasn't much taught about the subject either. Talk about a steep uphill journey. Don't get me wrong, I understand at the age of nineteen you have a whole lot of growing up to do, but when you come from an abusive background it is more difficult. Loving myself was completely foreign. I spent my young adult days with little self-worth; I was pitiful!

One thing was clear, though; I knew Jesus loved me. In all of the chaos, He made me feel special. During my devotional time, I'd sing my favorite song, entitled "Jesus Loves Me." It gave me confirmation, especially when I was struggling with rejection.

No doubt, His love was what kept me. Even with all of my mistakes, Jesus never gave up on me. As you go through the process, you too may make mistakes. But His love for you is greater than your biggest mistakes. He will give you the grace to rise, repent, and move forward.

Once you have given your life to the Lord, you are saved and you get to go to heaven, a place where there is no more pain and suffering. This is the first step to the journey of being made whole. I call it "the born-again process." To know that you know you are saved is a victory in itself. The greatest miracle under the sun is salvation, the saving of one's soul. The love of Jesus is so strong that He went all the way to the cross, suffered, and died just for you and me. I think about how He shed His innocent blood that day, how He hung on the cross from the sixth to the ninth hour and said "It is finished" so that all of the pain that you would ever suffer in this life, whether big or small, was conquered. Jesus carried it on Calvary's cross. He made it possible for us to live again through His precious blood.

My dear friend, if you have not accepted Jesus Christ as Lord and Savior, I want to pause right here and invite you to accept Him into your heart.

Please pray this simple prayer:

> *Father, I acknowledge that I am a sinner. Please forgive me and wash me of all my sins. I believe that You sent Your Son, Jesus, to shed His blood and die on the cross for me. I believe in my heart and confess with my mouth that You, Father, raised Jesus from the dead on the third day, and He is now seated on the right hand of the Father. I ask you Jesus to come into my heart and make me your child. I give You my life freely to do what You will. By faith I believe I am saved, in the mighty name of Jesus, Amen.*

If you prayed this prayer sincerely with a penitent heart, the Father will hear your cry, wash away all your sins, and deliver you from the power of darkness. I personally welcome you to the family of God. I want to encourage you to go and share your born-again experience with someone. It is important to make your faith known. Jesus said,

> *"Also I say unto you, Whosoever shall confesses me before men, him shall the Son of man also confess before the angels of God.* —Luke 12:8

So, my dear friend, go and tell of the goodness the Lord.

RESTORATION

"He restores my soul." —Psalm 23

Restoration is another part of the process. I had a brand-spankin'-new spirit, but my soul needed to be restored. King David writes and declares, *"He restores my soul."* What did he mean? Let's look at the definition. *Webster* defines it as "bringing back to a former position or condition: something that is restored; esp: a representation or reconstruction of the original form."

Biblically speaking, to restore is to build up, to make stronger than before—how's that for starters? Restoration is pertinent to the life of the believer, which only God can bring. This fact speaks to our extreme need for God. Without the new birth process, restoration is not possible. There are institutions that may try to help some, but oftentimes you will walk away with a prescription for anxiety and depression. God's intention for every broken person who comes to Him is to restore. To make you better than you were before. No matter how shattered the soul, God can and will restore every part. As a matter of fact, the entire Bible is about restoration, from the entire universe to the nations, to people and to things. He is the God of restoration! If He can restore a universe that was in total chaos and darkness, surely He can restore your broken soul. The work that Jesus did on Calvary's cross is our guarantee. His shed blood bought the victory over two thousand years ago. Like a beautiful, ornate piece of antique furniture that had its beginnings displayed in someone's home, cast outside and left to become weather-beaten over time. As a result, it became unattractive and unsightly. Bear in mind that someone took the time to skillfully craft this fine piece of choice wood. It was a delight of the craftsman, and when completed, he stood back and admired his handiwork. I'm sure he even rejoiced over it the same way God does with you and me.

I love antiques because they have character. The unique structure of the carvings makes them outstanding. At times I would go on the hunt for a special piece, searching until I found it. Finally, there it would be! Worn and not looking like much, the piece of furniture would have totally lost its luster and be discolored and chipped. One might easily discard it as trash, but I saw the beauty of it. No matter how unattractive, I knew just what to do to bring it to the place of beauty. This is how God sees His children when they are broken. He searches and seeks us out, and when He finds us, we are in terrible need of His restoration power. Like Zacchaeus (see Luke 19:5–10) and the women at the well (see John 4:7–29), Jesus sought them until He found them and saw their beauty when others didn't. Because of life's mishaps, you too have become broken and chipped, with missing pieces.

Now here is the clincher. When it comes to the restoration process, it always gets uglier before it gets better. Like a piece of old used furniture, we have to go through a stripping before our beauty can be brought out, and yes, it hurts. I went through it and so can you. I call it a spiritual stripping; it's the next step after the new birth. I'm sure when Jesus revealed to the woman of Samaria her secret love affair, she said to herself, "Ouch!" But look at what took place; her soul was restored. Miraculously, the same restoration power spilled over to the townspeople after hearing her testimony. When He visited Zacchaeus in his home, the man's heart was exposed, and it was revealed he was a thief. Zacchaeus was willing to repay everything he'd stolen, plus some. What is my point? The truth hurts and heals all at the same time, regardless of our level of brokenness. Nonetheless, we still need restoration because of our sinful nature. Jesus didn't ask the woman or Zacchaeus how or why they arrived at such a condition, He knew why—and He had the power to restore their souls.

WHAT IS SPIRITUAL STRIPPING?

Spiritual stripping is the removal of destructive mindsets and habits by the Word and power of the Holy Ghost. We developed these negative characteristics of the old nature, knowingly and unknowingly, when experiencing past abuses. It is said that habits are hard to break. This is true. Mere human effort will not suffice. It is also said that habits are made to be broken.

Let me paint a simple metaphoric picture. In the natural, strong chemical solvent is used to strip away all the old layers of paint and lacquer. Once applied, the solvent has to sit a while until it breaks down the surface. After this, everything starts to bubble up—becoming one big mess. Are you feeling me, beloved? The same goes for you and me. The writer of Ecclesiastes declares that there is a time to break down. Yes, God does break us down to bring change to our lives. Though change is not always easy, it is a must. Another analogy is a house that has been carefully prepped and painted on the exterior. But for some reason, the interior of the house was left with very little cosmetic work. From a distance it looks great. Should you get up-close, you're inclined to see a shoddy attempt at a remodeling job slapped together to cover up its flaws. Now consider individuals who attend church. They may sing in the choir, they may be ushers, they may teach Sunday school or even preach from the pulpit. But don't follow them home, because up close they are not what they seem. I'm not saying these persons are not saved, not at all. What I am saying is that once a person has been born again, the nature of Christ (called the divine nature) has been imputed in the believer and must be developed over time. If we are going to remain in Christ, we must have a dire need to begin a spiritual stripping. Everything must be stripped away until there is only bare nakedness exposed. We must also understand that God is Omnipotent, Omnipresent, and Omniscient. These are not mere names; He has the ability to see the real you. How else could it be possible to bring healing to our souls except to have God be completely aware of all things concerning us? He knows our ins and outs; there is nothing about us that is hidden from Him (see Psalm 139:2).

For me, it wasn't always a comfortable state in the beginning, but it was a good thing. Let me repeat, we must allow the Spirit to come in and reveal all our negative behaviors so that we may deal with and correct them. For example, the need for revenge—she did it to me so I'm going to do it back to her. Or our propensity to bend the truth and then justify our lie, calling it a *little white* lie. Hmm...I don't think lies are white. This is called deception. What about hiding behind sarcasm because of resentment?

Truth be told, I didn't like what I saw about myself. But because we are children of God, He will confront us with a gentle hand without exposing us to the world. This He does because He loves us. At times it didn't feel like love. The internal struggles were frustrating, to say the least. But as I have already mentioned, it gets better.

"A time to build up"—Ecclesiastes 3:3

Ahhh, herein lies a reason for the believer to rejoice. After looking back, the pain of being broken down is deemed worthwhile, leading toward a "built up you" in Christ Jesus. The Hebrew meaning for "build up" needs exploring. This word has several dictionary descriptions: "begin to build; repair; to set up."

The study of the life of Jesus reveals the heart of God—compassion in action. His compassion for the broken and downtrodden only proves His capability of handling all human need. The Bible declares: *"He raises the poor out of the dust and lifts the needy out of the ash heap, that he may seat him with princes"*—Psalm 113:7. Our Lord will never do anything halfway. He is bent on making sure that we have honor and sit among the noble of the land. To do anything less would allow the enemy of our soul to rejoice. How does Jesus build us up in order to make us sit with princes? It begins with humility of heart. This is the kingdom of God. The Bible declares:

> *Therefore humble yourselves under the mighty hand of God that He may exalt you in due time.* —1Peter1:5

According to the principle of the kingdom, the way up is first to go down. In other words, we must become nothing before God, and then and only then will He make something of us. It is imperative that we get this, because humility is the key to our success. The preceding verse of 1 Peter 5 reads, *"for God resists the proud but gives grace to the humble."* You should know by now that I have a story to tell.

Years ago I received astonishing news that my bishop's wife had died in a terrible car accident. She, along with her sister, aunt, and grandbaby, were traveling to a funeral late that particular night. The aunt, at the wheel, fell asleep and the vehicle hurtled off the road into an embankment.

I'm not sure if any survived. Hearing the story was dreadful as I thought on the three generations that died in that crash. I couldn't help but reflect on the life of this woman. She was not the Christian one would suppose, being a bishop's wife. No, she was a hellion. She wanted the world at its finest, and being married to a man of God was hindering her lust for ever entering in. One could say she was acquainted with trouble. This went on for years. By the time she made up her mind that she was going to leave God and her husband for good, she began plotting to destroy one of the church sisters. I wasn't present during the time it all took place, but the story goes that the bishop's wife was so angry she attempted an assault with a hatchet. I won't go into the whole story. After she made her final exit, it was said that in conversation she made this statement: "I am free and now this mama is fixing to live!" I shuddered at the thought, for at the moment that we think not, Jesus will come and our soul will be required of us. Over the years of resisting the conviction of the Holy Ghost, pride had entered her heart, leaving her without remedy. This is not a light thing, because the scripture declares that God hates pride and arrogance (see Proverbs 6). There is no room in the kingdom for pride—none! Pride is the number one hindrance to God's people in every area of their lives.

I'm in no way judging this woman, because at the time, I was dealing with my own shortcomings. After falling into fornication, I had disgraced the name of my God. I had to do some soul-searching. Here is the reason for the story. With reverential fear, I confessed that I hadn't always lived righteously before the Lord and I probably deserved the same fate as she. I asked the Lord, "What was the difference between she and I?" The Lord spoke softly to my spirit, "I give grace to the lowly."

Ah…never more comforting words to my soul. You see beloved, God is looking at more than our actions; he is looking at our hearts as well. He sympathizes with us when we are humble, therefore pouring upon us more grace. This is all the more reason to understand why Jesus was chosen to be our example in the first place. Christ was tempted in all manner as we are. His intention is never to condemn us, for He knows our weaknesses. He also knows when we want to be weak. Grace, God's unmerited favor, is what He extends to the lowly believer. Understand beloved, grace is not a ticket to continue in our weaknesses, but by grace, through faith, we are strengthened to rise.

Another way the heavenly Father builds us up is in our minds. The bible declares:

> *But be ye transformed by the renewing of your mind.* —
> Romans 12:2

This passage implements change as well. There are a few words in the Holy Scriptures that speak to this: *re*new – *re*storation—*re*generate—*re*vive; all have one thing in common, the prefix *re*. It occurs originally in loanwords from Latin, used with the meaning "again" or "again and again" to indicate repetition. The other day I was visiting an elderly mother who'd suffered a stroke and had fallen. As with all stroke victims, she had to go through physical therapy to regain mobility and strength. I observed as she sat head downward, slouched in her wheel chair, appearing to be very tired. The therapist would instruct her to do exercises and repeat them several times. She spoke softly to her patient. "Lift up your head real nice and high for me, okay. Remember, where your head goes, your body will follow." This couldn't be a truer statement! Wherever the mind goes, so goes the body. Renewing our mind through the power of the Word destroys the old ways of thinking and builds us up so that we may obtain the mind of Christ Jesus (see Philippians 2) and "go" the way of righteousness. Like the repetition of physical therapy, we must immerse our mind in the Word—over and over again, until it permeates our entire being. I want to encourage you to yield your vessel totally to the will of God and have a strong desire to live a holy life.

As we yield, God, through His Word, has the power to bring inward change, when and where it is needed. The Bible declares:

> *The word of God is quick and powerful, and sharper than any two-edged sword.*
>
> —Hebrews 4: 12

The word of God is alive and active, cutting deep within our soul, spirit, and mind, removing all that is negative. Or better said, all that is ungodly. Before we can fulfill our true purpose in the earth, it is imperative that we allow the Word to work in us.

My prayer for you, beloved:

In this season of your life, may the Lord bring restoration to your soul and build you up that you may sit with princes in the land. In the mighty name of Jesus.

THE PITS OF LIFE

THE PITS OF LIFE

He brought me up also out of an horrible pit, out of the miry clay, and set my feet upon a rock, and established my goings. —Psalm 40:2

Throughout the Holy Scriptures, pits are mentioned, beginning in Genesis and ending in Revelation. Some are literal and others metaphoric. Some were of a spiritual nature, described as the inside of hell and death, while others were physical (i.e., man-made).

What do I mean by man-made pits? It is when someone becomes a victim of persons with abusive, twisted behavioral patterns, who inflict severe trauma, leaving their victims with the feeling of no way of escape. Usually they have control over their victims, and can be close family members, teachers, clergymen, coaches, babysitters, and the like. Perpetrators often shows signs of hatred, jealousy, resentment, or all the above toward their victims.

When these negative emotions are present, horrible mistreatment will inevitably follow. This, beloved, is an example of being in a horrible pit. In this psalm, David uses the pit as a metaphor to describe the horrific experiences he encountered in his life, which is what I will focus on in this part of the chapter. The Hebrew word for "pit" is BOR; the word that describes its meaning here is the word "dungeon." According to *Strong's Concordance*, dungeons were shafts in the ground, hewn out of soft stone, relating to the word "bore"—as one bores a tunnel or hole by digging.

In the Old Testament, pits were originally used as cisterns to catch rainwater in the winter for the upcoming harvest. When empty, they were intended for criminals—hence the reason they were called dungeons. These pits were different from ordinary prisons; they were described as deep, dark, and clammy. And if by chance someone was hating on you for no reason at all, you could also be thrown in a pit, and it was nothing nice (see Jeremiah 38:6). Once a person was cast in, there was no way out.

The only means of rescue was with the aid of someone who would let down a rope and pull you out. These pits were often muddy and wet from holding water, providing no solid foundation, thus making standing impossible. One could not live very long in such miry conditions. Speaking from personal experience, being in the pits is a time of insurmountable stress that causes agony and pain coupled with fear that can send you into a downward emotional spiral. It makes you feel as though you are all alone. In some instances there is the feeling of death itself.

There are different kinds of man-made pits, such as sexual and physical abuse, fear, and rejection, to name a few. David knew firsthand what it was like to suffer under those who were supposed to protect and love him. During his childhood he experienced emotional abuse, neglect, and severe rejection.

I often wondered what his family life was like, being that the Bible doesn't mention all the details. According to the Talmud, David was born to the illustrious family of Jesse, who served as the head of the Sanhedrin (the supreme court of Torah law). He was one of the most distinguished leaders of his generation.

David, the youngest of seven brothers, was said to have been mistaken for a bastard child; therefore, the family treated his birth with utter derision and contempt, as described in Psalm 69:8:

> *I am become a stranger to my brothers, and an alien unto my mother's children.*

The passage also states that David was kept separated from the family. He was not permitted to eat meals with them but was assigned to a table in the corner. Jessie gave him the task of shepherding the sheep, with deliberate intentions of sending him to pastures in dangerous areas where wild beasts roamed in hopes that little David would be attacked and killed while performing his duties.

I can only imagine the look on Jesse's face when his young son came running into the house with excitement, saying, "Papa, Papa, I killed a bear today with my bare hands, and yesterday, I killed a lion! I protected the sheep just like you told me, Papa. Did I do good, huh? Did I do good?" Whether the story has any validity or not, we are well familiar with how he tackled those ferocious beasts single-handedly (see 1 Samuel 17:34–37). David had accomplished something that neither his father nor his brothers could ever do.

Clearly, the odds were stacked against him, but God was with David. What was designed to kill him only made him strong.

A HORRIBLE PIT

I, too, was in a horrible pit, and it seemed unending. I couldn't even begin to process what was happening. Each day the aftermath of sexual abuse and rejection proved to be catastrophic, starting with my mother.

It was Saturday morning; my siblings were gathered in the kitchen watching Mother prepare breakfast when I walked in. I joined them and observed her whipping up the pancake batter while the bacon was frying.

Everyone was present except for two of my siblings, the oldest and youngest sister. While stirring in a bowl, Mother asked, "Where is my baby girl?" Mother didn't seem to be concerned about her eldest daughter. I knew where she was and I explained my baby sister's whereabouts. Using an incorrect word, I said, "Rhonda gots her!"

My mother came unglued! Her loud and coarse response was paralyzing; it shook me to my core. "It's not *gots*, it's *has*!" she screamed. The look in her eyes and the anger in her voice was like watching a volcano erupt. To a five-year-old, this was frightening. This was the first negative encounter coming from my mother. It only mounted from there.

Looking back, I realized that she was lashing out at me because of the sexual abuse I encountered, perpetrated by her husband, my father. How sad that my mother saw me as the problem—the other woman—instead of the helpless victim.

I didn't know how to process what I felt or heard. The best way I can describe it is like being hit by a fast-moving train out of nowhere, without warning. From that time forward, I lived under the stress of a man-made pit. A horrible pit indeed, set up by the enemy to destroy me. I was bullied and then molested at night by my father, rejected and verbally and physically abused by my mother during the day. To add to the horror, I was tormented by horrible nightmares, which gave the enemy another avenue to enter and wreak havoc in my little life.

I feel it is important to address the subject of nightmares and dreams because they are messages either from God or Satan. Through them we can receive warnings or instructions or, if from the enemy, lies, fear, depression, and oppression. How is this possible? Can dreams really come from Satan? The answer is an absolute yes. There is a realm of darkness that is real and active. Listen to what the scripture says in Ephesians 6:12:

> *We wrestle not against flesh and blood, but against principalities, against powers, against the rulers of the darkness of this world, against spiritual wickedness in high places.*

So then, biblically speaking, what are dreams? What effect do they have on an individual?

In the book of Job they are called "visions of the night." Eliphaz describes his experience, saying,

> *In thoughts from the visions from the night, when deep sleep falls on men, fear came upon me, and trembling, which made all my bones to shake.*
>
> *Then a spirit passed before my face; the hair on my flesh stood up:*
>
> *It stood still, but I could not discern the form thereof: an image was before my eyes, there was silence, and I heard a voice, saying, Shall mortal man be more just than God? Shall a man be more pure than his maker? Behold, he put no trust in his servants; and his angels he charged with folly: How much less in them that dwell in houses of clay, whose foundation is in the dust, which are crushed before the moth?*
> —Job 4:13–19

Elipaz, in his counsel to Job, included the telling of this nightmare. It is clear that the dream was straight from the pit of hell. The voice he heard was demonic. There was no biblical basis for such statements. It was a demon speaking lies, painting a false image of God being completely callous and unconcerned about His creation. Not only so, but it also invoked fear.

Listen how *Webster* describes nightmares: "a bad dream that causes feelings of great nervousness or fear." We know from the above passage that nightmares are real, and according to Ephesians 6:12, they come from Satan. He takes advantage of our vulnerable state of sleep with the sole purpose to deceive and inflict fear. If you don't know it by now, the devil does not fight fair.

I was in grade school when inundated with dreadful nightmares. They would consist of gloomy gray coloring, with pitch-black dark-

We wrestle not
against flesh and
blood, but against
principalities,
against powers,
against the rulers
of darkness of this
world, against
spiritual wickedness
in high places.
—Ephesians 6:12

ness all around. My dreams were always of hideous monsters made of rocks, having long fangs, chasing me through the streets in the night. The scene: Running, running, running, as fast as I can—I dared not look back—I felt it getting closer, with deep ferocious growls about my neck; suddenly, with one swoop, my feet now off the ground with my legs dangling, kicking and screaming "Mommy help me—h-e-l-p m-e! My voice dissipates into thin air—desperate for help, my heart pounding with fright, fighting with all my might to get free—but it was to no avail. Then the monster opens his mouth wide, slowly coming down for the kill with razor sharp teeth ready to devour. Just when they were about to tear into my little body, I'd suddenly wake in a panic. I'd find myself on my bed, in my house. I'm safe. Ah . . . it's only a bad dream. This was only the beginning of demonic invasions. I was a teenager when I encountered a demonic entity as described in the scripture text by Elipaz.

Here's the story . . .

My two oldest brothers were away one weekend, and I decided to sleep in their bedroom. I jumped into my pajamas and joined my younger brother Craig, who was already in bed. He slept on the top bunk and I made myself comfortable on the bottom. We talked and laughed, and before I knew it, I had fallen fast asleep. Suddenly, I felt the weight of someone or something on top of me. I tried to move but I couldn't. Fixed in, all I could do was look down around the bottom half of my body. I saw a creature-like being lying on top of me. Its appearance was like half man and half beast with hairy legs and feet like an animal's hoof. I felt its body moving on me, as though I was being violated. It was very strange.

The nightmare appeared very real—like being awake, yet I was asleep. Finally, opening my eyes, I was horrified and mortified at the same time. My spirit had been invaded by a lust demon—unauthorized sexual communication, if you will. Yet, it was as if I'd been harassed by a human being.

I slowly looked around the room. Although I couldn't see anyone, I felt as though a presence was lurking in the darkness. Somehow, I gathered myself together. A few moments passed and I shucked the experience off as a bad dream. Only this was not a bad dream.

Needless to say, I never slept in my brother's room again. I couldn't help but wonder what my brothers may have encountered in their young lives while sleeping in their bedroom.

Many years later when I mentioned this phenomenon to a friend, only to find out there were many others who'd had the same experience. After becoming an adult and having come to know Christ, I learned that demons are spirits and they do exist.

In my research I found that, according to *Webster*, there are names for this type of spirit. They are called incubus and succubus. These names are not mentioned in the Bible. The scripture calls them unclean spirits, or devils.

It was after that attack that I began to struggle with lust. Even though it was low-key at the time, the manifestations of the effects were well beyond my mental capacity. Let me explain. I'd feel unusual sensations within my body, acting out impulses. For example, I discovered the world of art at an early age. While most children were drawing a human silhouette in stick form, I had the ability to create actual images, I was talented beyond my years.

There were times I would sit down with pen and paper and start doodling, then find myself drawing nude pictures. As I grew older, I began to see visions of naked bodies flash in my head. I didn't plan this; it just happened. It was the demon of lust in operation.

Getting back to the nightmares, they were assailed against me by demons to invoke fear. Just as Elipaz described in Job 4:14, fear came upon me, and trembling, which made all my bones to shake. This kind of fear has torment . . . it does not come from God (see 1 John 4:18). Why this avenue? Dreams are a way into the soulish realm, into your emotions. The aim is to bind your mind by gaining control over your thoughts. If he (Satan) can control your mind, he can control your body, which in turn prevents you from doing the simplest tasks.

Many today have become incapacitated by fear. Fear of being alone, of crowds, of disease; fear of dying, of heights, of getting old; fear of failure. It is a spirit that deprives us of achieving our goals and living out our God-given purpose.

I spent my early adult years anticipating that at any given moment I might be viciously attacked and my life end in violence. Therefore, I was careful not to set goals or expect great things to happen in my life. Expressing joy was out of the question, because I knew something would come along and steal it. I operated in fear for a long time, until I realized I had been given power and authority over it. When we operate in our God-given authority in Jesus' name, every devil has to flee! Jesus declares:

> *Behold, I give unto you power to tread on serpents and scorpions and over all the power of the enemy . . .* —Luke 10:19

With that knowledge, I began to understand my weaponry and I shifted from defense mode to offense and declared war against the enemy of fear and all its kin. I say kin because fear does not operate alone. Who are these kin? Intimidation, fright and/or flight, doubt, accusation; condemnation; these are the biggies. But no matter how big they seem, when we utilize the name of Jesus, we activate the power of God and by His power we can overcome our roughest, toughest rival. According to 2 Corinthians 10:4 we have the ability to demolish the very fortress of the enemy. All the throes of hell are no match against the power *given* to us by Christ, who also declared that the spirits are subject to us because our names are written in heaven. This is a combination that is praiseworthy; blessed be the name of the Lord! So, instead of running from the enemy, we must put the enemy on the run.

> *For the weapons of our warfare are not carnal, but they are mighty through God to the pulling down of the strongholds* —2 Corinithians 10:4

If you are bound by fear, I pray that you will be set free today. As you place your hand on your head, repeat these words:

By the authority given to me by Christ, I come against the spirit of fear and call it out by name. I disannul the works of darkness assigned against me. The Word says, the Father has not given me a spirit of fear, but love, power and a sound mind. I declare that I have the mind of Christ from this day forward, therefore, fear can no longer operate in my life. I command you to lose my mind and let it go, now; in the mighty name of Jesus the Christ. Amen.

Those of us in the Christian world understand very well the satanic forces that fight against mankind, leading to bondage and possession. How does this happen, you might ask? All Satan needs is an open door; however small it may be, he can and will enter. Our family home was wide open for demonic activity. There were porno materials present in the house along with ungodly music, foul language, dirty jokes, and inappropriate touching. Demonic activity had it easy, simply because there were no boundaries set for unacceptable behaviors. Satan works through all of the above. The issue lies with these facts: most Christians are either ignorant or don't believe certain objects give demons access into their lives. I assure you, they do, and once demons enter, they will take full advantage. Let me note that my parents were not saved. Although both had a church background from their youth and insisted their own children attended every Sunday, they were not true born-again believers. For all Christians, God gives us stern warning:

> *Be sober, be vigilant, because your adversary the devil as a roaring lion walketh about seeking whom he may devour.*
>
> —1 Peter 5:8

Apostle Peter makes it very clear that you and I have an adversary. He is an invisible enemy. Whether you are saved or not, this devil is seeking to devour you! Let me put it in layman's terms. Satan is not your friend. He means you absolutely no good. He is the adversary of your soul, and he is on a relentless prowl to bring as many souls as he can down into the pits of hell for eternity right along with him. Let's examine the word devour. In Greek it is KATAPINO; it means "to eat up." In this passage of scripture it means "to destroy spiritually; to ruin the soul."

The devil's aim is to destroy and to ruin the souls of mankind, period! Simply because you are God's creation, and the devil hates God! I'm talking about major supernatural resentment. He was once God's chief angel in heaven, but because he chose to rebel against his Creator, he and the angels that followed were cast out by God without any chance of recovery. So yeah, Satan the devil hates anything that has to do with God and His purpose. That means you and me; believe me when I tell you. The metaphor used to describe him is so befitting. Just as a lion of the jungle has no pity on his prey, neither does Satan have pity. He is a bona-fide predator. What is he after? Your soul, that one precious, priceless, eternal part of you. But there is good news. Satan has already been defeated through the redemptive shed blood of Jesus on the cross. Satan's eternal destiny is the lake of fire, God's determined and ultimate destruction of His enemy.

 My prayer for you today is:

> *May the God of heaven have mercy on your soul and keep you from the hand of the enemy, in the mighty name of Jesus.*

Listen carefully to the definition again: to devour is "to destroy spiritually; to ruin the soul." The *Macmillan Dictionary* defines ruin to mean "destruction, decay or collapse" or "the remains of something destroyed or decayed: the ruins of a bombed city."

When something becomes decayed or destroyed, only fragments are left behind of what once was. In other words, though the devil may not be able to take you out physically, his aim is to ruin you emotionally and spiritually (i.e., to leave your soul fragmented). An individual may be alive physically, but because of severe brokenness he or she is incapable of functioning normally. This is a major hindrance to anyone's chance of knowing and developing an intimate relationship with their Creator and discovering the greatness within. And not to mention having normal, loving relationships with people.

Many people walk around bound in their own dysfunctional worlds today, again due to trauma. They have no clue about how to get free, or worse yet, may not even know they are dysfunctional and that the culprit (Satan) is behind it. With that being said, there is a good chance the abused will in turn become an abuser.

You more than likely work or even live with someone that is dysfunctional; or perhaps you are the abnormal one. What do I mean by dysfunctional? For example, people who are full of anger all the time, for absolutely no reason. They are out of control; violence is their middle name. Then you have the neurotic personality (which describes my father, by the way) who is happy with laughter one moment and five minutes later goes off the deep end. Being around these people is like walking on eggshells. How about those who can't tell a story without lying? They can't tell the truth if their lives depend upon it. Then there's the melancholic personality, living on pity for pity. I knew a young lady personally who displayed extreme melancholic depression. It was the saddest thing in the whole wide world. We will call her Mary, to tell the story. Mary had a sister who, according to their mother, was the pretty one. We'll call her Julie. It was blatantly clear that the mother preferred Julie over Mary. Even when it came to their children, she would show this ungodly partiality. The son-in-law made me privy to their unconventional yearly family gatherings. All the relatives would gather at Grandma's house for Christmas holiday dinners. When it came time for sharing gifts, the mother would buy gifts only for Julie's children.

Needless to say, exchanging gifts, for Mary's children, was a very sad experience. What happened to "If I can't buy a gift for all my grands, I won't buy any at all?" Mary's mother didn't have a clue of the true meaning of Christmas.

Mary suffered gravely because of the abusive treatment of her mother. She wanted the same affection her sister Julie received. No matter how hard she tried, it wasn't happening. Mary thought, *If I can play the sick card, perhaps I can get my mother's affection.*

Throughout her life she would act out melancholy behavior (which is a demon spirit). She was always sick and under duress. If it wasn't her head that was hurting, it was her back. If it wasn't her back, it was her stomach. As a grown woman, she grew worse. There were hospital stays, then surgeries, and on and on. Last I heard she was on her deathbed, all because she wanted her mother's love, which she NEVER got.

Children need their parents' love; it is a must-have. If they don't get it, they become victims of brokenness. As for Mary, she never recovered. Her mother will have to answer to God. Let's continue with more examples.

Perhaps as you drive down the street or take a stroll in the park, you happen to glance over and see a person looking up at a telephone pole holding a full-fledged conversation, shaking his fist and shouting vulgarity. What about people we've seen with a blank look on their faces, staring into space; their minds completely gone. All the above-mentioned are in a pit. When I think about it, I realize *these people are somebody's children*!

That ole' serpent the devil has entered through an open door, victim unaware, with the intent to completely destroy them. Children are at an even higher risk of these attacks from the enemy, particularly in today's society, where godlessness is widespread. They are weak and defenseless, making them easy targets. Remember, the devil is a predator, and predators don't fight fair. He seeks whom he may devour, and the earlier he can begin his attacks, the greater the damage. According to the scriptures the woman and her seed is constantly under attack. There is a reason for this ongoing war.

Revelations 12 reveals the outbreak of an epic battle taking place. When we think of battles, the last place to contemplate its happenings would be in heaven, God's personal domain. It was in this very place

Lucifer rose up with a takeover spirit and fought against the angels and his Creator. He was defeated, cast out of heaven and down to earth, having great wrath (see Revelations 12:7-12). From then on, this sore loser has been in a state of intense displeasure to the destruction of mankind, for this reason: God has put enmity between the seed of the serpent and the seed of the woman for the sole purpose of crushing his head (see Genesis 3:15). In other words, we are a constant threat to the kingdom of darkness, especially when we come to know who we are in Christ Jesus.

 If you are in a pit today, my prayer is:

> *That the God of heaven will intervene on your behalf and pull you out of the horrible pit, that you may come to know Christ in His fullness and grant you the knowledge of who you are in Him; in the Mighty name of Jesus, Amen.*

Before the abused gets to the place of knowing who they are in Christ, our Adversary is on a hot pursuit to derail us– working overtime, because he knows his time is short. How I was able to live through the trauma is beyond me. The damage and stress impaired me emotionally and mentally. It was an overload on my young mind and body.

It is said that children have a built-in-mechanism that helps them to cope with abuse. I would say so; I'd gotten used to living under the pressure without realizing it. There was no relief, ultimately, stress became my sister. When I became an adult, I felt life was supposed to be hard. Being under strain meant that I was accomplishing something. The more difficult the task, the more I delved in. It was all about having earned something. If it was too easy, then I was being lazy. You get my drift? Whether good or bad, I'm still that way. But at least it's for my benefit, and not others.

The stress I endured came with severe side effects. I developed ghastly breakouts of painful cold sores that covered my nose. At the age of five, I entered first grade struggling to learn. My emotions were in an upheaval. The smallest matter made me upset. I developed a mental block, unable to do what was common to first graders. The mental block left me unable to count numbers. At the age of five, counting is not only simple, but fun, right? Not for me. I couldn't grasp the concept. This made my mother very angry, being the parent that helped me learn my school lessons at home. She didn't practice much patience when it came to me, anyway.

If I couldn't grasp what she was trying to teach me in the time she thought I should, she would try and beat it into me. And I do mean beat. Imagine, at the age of five, I'm sitting at a little desk with my pencil in hand and paper before me. I'm already nervous because my mother is standing over me with a leather belt in her hand. I'm also having to deal with the harsh tone in her voice, coupled with the fact that I was molested by my father the night before.

I would proceed to count my numbers, but after a certain point my little mind couldn't comprehend, and I was unable to continue on. The next thing I'd feel was the leather belt coming down, striking my little body repeatedly. Now I'm crying from the pain of the beating and trying to understand my mother's instructions at the same time.

In a desperate attempt to escape the beatings, I found a book in my parents' bedroom and used it to copy numbers down for my homework. I crawled under the bed, hiding so no one would see me. What a relief, I thought to myself. The next thing I knew my eldest sister saw me and went to tell our mother. I can still hear her now as she walked up the hallway, saying, "Mommy, 'Nita's under the bed. She's got a book and she's copying her numbers!" That gained me another beating. Needless to say, first grade was rough. As a result, I was held back and had to repeat it. Yet Ms. Jonnye's mistreatment grew worse.

One day my elder brother was playing outside when he discovered a beehive. He ran into the house, saying, "Come and look what I found. There's a big bee's nest in the backyard!" My siblings and I all jumped up and flew out the front door, eager to see what all the excitement was about. I brought along my musical bear that my parents bought me. Everyone headed toward the backyard with my brother leading. We arrived at the shrub where the bees were nesting, looking with amazement as they moved in and out of their hive.

Shortly, all my siblings left. I stayed behind, playing with my new stuffed bear. I sat right in front of the beehive, winding and rewinding as children do, letting the music play. I was so engulfed in the sweetness of the melody that I had completely forgotten about the bees. I guess the tinkling sound got on their nerves. Next thing I knew, an army of bees attacked me with one fierce blow. I screamed in agony! Dropping my toy bear I ran to the front of the house. Mother met me at the door without any urgency to see about me. When I entered the house, everyone stood gazing as I cried out. Finally my father walked over, picked me up, and put me in the tub to soak. His intentions were not for my comfort, but for an opportunity to see my body. That was the sympathy I got for being stung by a host of bees that day. My little body was wracked with pain, not to mention the unsightly swelling from the beestings. You would think it couldn't get worse. Well, it did.

Shortly after, Mother tired of the kids being in the house. "I want all y'all to go outside," she said. I was hoping that didn't include me. I stood in front of her in fear, begging for a pardon with my eyes. I did not want to take my freshly bee-stung self back outside! But it didn't matter to her. With a stern gesture, she said, "You too, get on out there!" Of course I had to obey. Slowly I moved toward the door, whimpering, fearful that the bees would come back. As soon as I stepped outside, the bees attacked me again. This time, out of fear of punishment, I couldn't cry out. Nobody dared to care. The stresses began to mount, with no reprieve. As I grew older, I became depressed along with being stressed. What a combination.

I found an escape, though; sleep. Bless God for sleep! It brought me much relief from the cruel treatment. It gave me a break from family noise and from my name being called to do so many of the chores around the house. Trust me, if I was awake, I'd have to be doing some kind of work. Never mind that I was a child in school who had homework to complete or that Mother had other children who could have helped. It didn't seem to matter to my parents. They expected all chores to be done and done well. I'm not against chores. But Mama 'n'em didn't know when to stop.

I didn't have a clue that I was depressed; all I knew was that I felt like an unhappy little child that was always dumped on. In my day, if you were a black child growing up in America, there was no such thing as depression, which was probably a good thing, in many cases.

My parents had their uncommon way of handling depression. If I walked into their presence feeling down, perhaps because I had a bad day at school, they'd take one look at me and say, "What's wrong with you!?" in their usual harsh tones. I was too scared to say how I really felt, so I answered, "Nothing." They would follow with, "Well, straighten up that ugly face and get out of here!" I did what I was told for fear of a whipping. I straightened up my face and went on my way.

Excessive sleeping is said to be one of the signs of depression. Even though I was a child, my depression was real. I imagine in today's society, if I had been diagnosed by a doctor, I would have been on every medication under the sun. Unfortunately, the mentality is, "Give them a pill and everything will be well." Not so. Unless one's conditions are changed, the attempt to medicate is purely in vain. In my childish mind I handled it the best way I knew how, and that was to sleep. Yes, I would find myself asleep a lot, even in my school classrooms. When most kids would settle in for activities, I would settle in for a nap. I don't believe my teacher ever took the time to wake me—perhaps she did. Learning? Well, it was hard to concentrate. I was excited about school and learning new things, but I found the lessons nearly impossible.

Sleep was the only way to remove myself from the horror of being molested and the lack of love I would feel after I came home from school. It was hard for me to cope with living in my parents' house. So much so that there were a few times I'd even pretend to be in a deep sleep. And this is how it went. I'd lie in my bed with my eyes shut tight, breathing very heavy, almost snoring so that anyone who passed by could hear. Then sure enough, I'd hear my mother call my name. "'NITA!" I wouldn't answer. She'd call me a few more times and then say to one of my siblings, "Where's 'Nita?" Someone would come and look in on me and then respond saying, "She's asleep, Mommy!" Silence followed. I could feel my heart racing, hoping that Mother wouldn't come to my room and that she'd stop calling me. To my surprise, she did. *It worked!* I said to myself. From then on, sleep was something that I would use every chance I got.

Through all of my unhappy experiences, I understood my need for God at a young age. Although I didn't know, it was He who kept my mind intact all the while. I was broken emotionally, but my heavenly Father didn't allow the harsh treatment to break my spirit. This doesn't mean that I don't have struggles in some areas, because I do. The truth is, God is greater than our struggles.

ROBBED OF INNOCENCE

Webster defines innocence as "free from guilt or wrongdoing, free from or knowing nothing of sin or evil, pure."

1. When innocence is unlawfully taken away, a child becomes exposed to matters that they cannot handle, either mentally or emotionally.
2. The child begins to act out his or her experiences and is considered troublesome, which ofttimes leads to more abuse.

As I stated before, children are defenseless and fragile beings. That said, in this next section I will expound on the word PREDATOR. Webster says, "One that preys, destroys, or devours. An animal such as a wolf or lion that lives by preying on other animals." In the animal kingdom, preying upon a victim is simply instinctive behavior. Each species preys on another in order to survive in the wild. Unfortunately, humans fall under this animalistic behavior. Like a lion, fierce and strong, human predators show a disposition to injure or exploit for their own gain. Their victims are given to plundering, which means "to take illegally or by force and/or to rob." This is what commonly happens to children that are abused, especially sexually. Children don't have the capacity to consent or forbid in such cases. Because a child is vulnerable, he or she falls prey to the grip of a human predator, only to be savagely ripped of their innocence. A child's innocence is precious and it must be protected by any and every means. One cannot overestimate extra precautions. Reason being, human predators are bent on abusing their authority by forcing themselves upon their victims for their own twisted gratification. Yes, I say twisted, because a grown man who attempts to penetrate an infant is very disturbed. It is a sickening and repugnant act (women are guilty of incestuous conduct as well).

Listen to the Psalmist as he shares an experience with a predator.

> *I am surrounded by fierce lions who greedily devour human prey, whose teeth pierce like spears and arrows.* —Psalm 57:4

This was a time in David's life when he felt defenseless against men. I believe we can apply this passage to his encounter with King Saul. In the beginning of their relationship, it is noted that Saul loved David greatly; so much so that he made him his armor bearer, but something happened that would change his heart. The Lord gave David victory over the champion of the Philistines. Though David was only a young boy, he was courageous and knew the power of his God. He won a great victory for Israel. When all the people began to praise David, it did not set well with Saul. Driven to envy, the king's love for David became pure hatred. The boy's presence made the king's life most miserable. From then on, Saul attempts to murder David.

You see, as long as David was just the servant boy, Saul did not feel his manhood was threatened. But this great victory caused David to exceed Saul as both king and man. For he too was one among the soldiers, running scared. The story is found in 1 Samuel, chapters 16–19.

David looked up to Saul like a father, especially being that his biological father had rejected him. The young lad highly respected and honored Saul as king of Israel. He should have been the very person

David could trust most. How sad it was that the boy had to run for his life.

How many countless thousands of children in our society today have had to run for their lives because their homes became so unlivable, so scary? As a result, they are forced at an early age out onto the street to survive in an ungodly world.

Here's the clincher. As the story goes, David was a boy living at home, minding his father's sheep. King Saul asked his father, Jesse, for permission to let David stay and serve him in the palace. It wasn't David who asked to go. Ah, dear mothers and fathers, the same goes for you and your children today. They didn't ask to be born into this world. I want to drive this in for you parents who haven't grasped this yet. You gave birth to your children, not the other way around. You owe it to them to love and care for them. Without a price! This is God's commandment to you as guardians. So then, after they arrive, why would you want to mistreat them? God is not pleased.

We are not like the wild beasts of the fields whose reasoning and emotions are limited. We have the capacity to act with an intelligence that makes us different. What gives? Why is there so much violence toward our children today? While the saying, "broken people break people" is true, it's much deeper than that.

Here are two reasons. The first is a heart condition.

> *The heart is deceitful above all things, and desperately wicked.* —Jeremiah 17:9

Note the word "desperately"; in Hebrew it is ANAS; it means "to be ill, sickly; incurable, beyond cure; very sick, woeful." *Webster* defines it as "reckless because of hopelessness; ready or willing to take any risk; rash. Done without any regard to what happens afterward; irresponsible." If we combine these two definitions, it explains the actions and reasons behind the mindset of the human race apart from God.

Man's rash decision to disobey God's commandments brought on a world of evil that was unimaginable. A consequence that he was not prepared for. A changeover so rapid and radically wicked that mankind instantly became separated from God; thus, his heart was darkened.

An episode of Dateline proves this very fact. It revealed the police department of a notable town on a relentless pursuit to expose and catch as many pedophiles as they could. The host who interviewed the detective responsible for setting up the sting operations asked, "Why do these men commit this kind of crime, knowing there is a good chance they will get caught?" The detective explained, "When the urge comes over them to have sex with children, they can't help themselves. They are driven, desperate, and they are bent on carrying out this wickedness with little thought of being discovered, which is the reason they become reckless." The thought of getting caught didn't matter any longer. Neither did it matter how it would harm the victims, or the scars it would leave behind.

For years I would try and get into my father's head, asking myself, "What was he thinking?" In retrospect, his conduct exuded unethical practices. I came to my own conclusion that my father was a sick man. Getting his freak on any way and with anyone he could was only a symptom of a sick heart. He had a twisted, distorted sense of love. I am convinced he was and is sick (sin sick), mentally and spiritually. Let me tell you why I say so. My father had a temper also, and you didn't want to make him mad, ever. Not knowing the depth of his anger, he began telling me a story of a time he was traveling the highway. He and another driver got into an altercation. My father explained that he became very angry. He went on to say, "I passed the driver, pulled out my gun, and shot into the car." He seemed to be proud of what he had done. "What happened to the man?" I asked him in amazement. "I don't know," he replied. "All I know is the car went off the side of the road and came to a stop, and I kept going." Then I asked again, "What did the other man do? Was he dead?"

"Well, like I said, the car went off the side of the road, and I kept going. As far as I could see, the car didn't move," he replied. I couldn't believe my eyes or my ears. He was calm, with no remorse. No regret, no nothing! Herein is the reason why there are prisons.

Mankind is depraved without God. We've all experienced desperate and dark times when our actions were unsavory. For all have sinned and come short of the glory of God (see Romans 3:23). We dare not speak of them because they are shameful and disgraceful. If not for the redemptive work of Christ, we would all be doomed.

One never knows what's going on deep inside a person's heart. But, when they open their mouth the heart will surely reveal itself (see Mathew 12:34). Another story that my father told me was a real eye-opener. As I mentioned before, my father is a widower. According to him, his previous wife died in a fire in their trailer home. My father never mentioned how the fire started. He said, "After that, mentally I couldn't cope. I had nightmares every time I lay down to sleep. The doctors put me on medication to help manage my condition, which I've been on ever since." I was astonished, saying to myself, *Oh dear GOD! Is my father crazy? Have I been raised by a lunatic all my life?*

I feel it is important now to expound on the origin of mankind for the sake of laying a foundation. Originally, man was not a depraved creature. He lived in a beautiful garden full of fruitful trees and flowing rivers. It was a very simple beginning. Man was given an assignment, to tend the garden. And one commandment: *"but of the tree of the knowledge of good and evil you shall not eat."*

When God contemplated the creation of man, it seems to me that He conducted a counseling session. The Bible declares,

> *And God said, Let us make man in our image, after our likeness.* —Genesis 1:26

I mention a counseling session because the "us" in Genesis 1 is plural. The "And God said" plainly shows a dialogue. In this passage, we understand that the Creator decided to make the creature in the likeness of Himself, which means mankind was created special above all of His creations.

This reveals that man, like his Creator, has been blessed with an intellect, the ability to reason. He can love, nurture, and have relationships and has the ability to make sound, rational choices. Savor these words for a moment: "And God said, let us make man in our image, after our likeness."

I would say, "Only a father thinks like this." Because fathers want their children to be like them, look like them, and act like them.

> *And God blessed them, and God said unto them, Be fruitful, and multiply and replenish the earth, and subdue it: and have dominion over the fish of the sea, and over the fowl of the air and over every living thing that moveth upon the earth* —Genesis 1:28

What an awesome display of His sovereignty. He created man in His image and then blessed them. What does it mean to be made in His image and His likeness? First, it means that although we are the creature, we are akin to God. This knowledge is imperative because only through a proper relationship with Christ can we claim Him as our God. Herein, He makes our lives more meaningful. Second, God is holy and righteous; everything about Him is moral and ethical. Mankind is also morally and ethically responsible to make moral choices. This is where our conscience comes into play, Christians and non-Christians alike. This is also important because good conduct is what makes for a livable and peaceful society. Without being told lying and stealing is wrong or that murder is evil, our conscience tells us it is. Again, I say it is of great importance. If mankind is going to operate under the blessing of dominion here on earth, it will rest in our continued obedience to God. Third, God, through His Word, has revealed that He is a social being: God the Father, God the Son, and God the Holy Ghost. Man is also a social being who needs relationships with others. No matter how much an individual may say "I like being alone," everybody needs good, sound relationships. Besides, if we participate in the blessings of procreation, it's going to take two. The Holy Scripture declares,

> *And the Lord God said "It is not good that man should be alone."* —Genesis 2:18

When God created Adam, He had in mind to make the perfect mate for him. From Adam's rib, God formed the woman. They were male and female. From the beginning, man was created as a unit—a family, that is. God's earliest plan for humans was to live in perfect harmony with Him and each other on the earth all the days of their lives. I know this sounds surreal for today simply because many don't understand true relationship. But that subject is for another book. Let's continue. Listen to Genesis 2:25:

> *And they were both naked, the man and his wife, and were not ashamed.*

I don't know about you, but the more I read the Bible, the more questions I have. I asked the Lord, "Why did You make them naked?" The first thing that came to mind was that everything about them was pure—there was no sin, no shame. Therefore they had no need for a covering. Adam and Eve depicted the very image of God. We can see from these passages there was perfect union. They were innocent and unashamed. All they knew was God, and everything about them was godly. They could not live in the glorious presence or walk in harmony with their Maker otherwise. What sweet fellowship! Just the thought of the past, where there was once absolutely no strife between God and His creation, is over-the-top amazing.

Even though mankind became wicked and lost his place with God, he still has God-given ability and is responsible to God for making good moral choices if he so wills. Moral decisions governed by spiritual laws; ethics and proper behavior; that which is right and universal. Proper conduct is useful for harmony in relationships. One guideline that comes to mind is to do unto others as you would have them to do unto you. Call it the golden rule if you like, but it is a biblical statement (see Luke 6:31). This moral principle has proven trustworthy and is best practiced by all. This has been my moral compass throughout life. It has kept me on the straight and narrow. But unfortunately, our courthouses and jail cells are filled with persons who refuse to live this way. By law, then, they are made to obey what is commonly right. I mean, why would capable adults want to continually abandon their consciences and have to be forced into doing what is right? Again, this is the reason for prisons.

This leads to the second reason for violence against children, and that is, we have an adversary. I mentioned this earlier in the chapter, now I will expound more in depth.

THE TEMPTER

Satan is the tempter, so-called because of his subtlety and deceptive tactics, according to Luke 4. His motive is to test or tempt mankind, to trap and ultimately destroy him. So then, if the heart is wicked from the beginning, where does Satan come in? The answer is found in the book of Genesis, where the serpent is having a conversation with the woman. The serpent used deception, causing the woman to yield. Let's read:

> *And he said unto the woman, Yea, hath God said, ye shall not eat of every tree of the garden? And the woman said unto the serpent, We may eat of the fruit of the trees of the garden: But of the tree which is in the midst of the garden, God hath said, Ye shall not eat of it, neither shall ye touch it, lest ye die. And the serpent said unto the woman, Ye shall not surely die: for God knows that in the day ye eat thereof, then your eyes shall be opened, and ye shall be as gods, knowing good and evil. And when the woman saw that the tree was good for food, and that it was pleasant to the eye and a tree to be desired to make one wise, she took of*

the fruit thereof, and did eat and gave also to her husband with her. —Genesis 3:1–6

Eve's desire for wisdom caused her to heed the voice of the serpent and reason within her mind against the commandment of God. She did not understand that knowing evil would entail becoming a part of evil. Then her husband, Adam, followed and they died instantly. I speak of a spiritual death. I've often wondered why Adam followed his wife so easily. Who tempted him? Especially after God spoke to him directly. I received a revelation by the Spirit and he said to me: "Look at the scripture again. It says, *"She took the fruit thereof and did eat, and gave also unto her husband with her; and he did eat."* He directed me to the word "gave," which in Hebrew is NATAN; it means "to put or give over." Here's what the Spirit revealed—no one can put anything in a person's hand unless the individual is wide open to receive it.

We see absolutely no resistance from Adam, not even the slightest discussion about the matter. No, not even a question to his wife. For example, "Woman, didn't I tell you God said we would die if we ate of this tree? What are you doing?" Instead, Adam followed suit. He took the fruit and ate. What was the Lord showing me in this passage? Adam wanted it as much as his wife. Eve just happened to eat first, and when he saw that she didn't drop dead, he followed. Let's read it again. *"And gave to her husband with her . . . and he did eat."* You see, the word "with" also shows they were partners in crime until all hell broke loose.

This reminds me of a conversation I had with my father concerning his gambling habits. This is how it started. "You know, yo' Momma and me, we go to the casinos and we win money. She doesn't get out much, and uh, she asks me to take her, so I take her. Can't be nothing wrong with gambling. Shoot, God knows we need money, and I need money to pay my bills, so I asked God to help me. Can't be nothing wrong with that, is it?"

As I sat listening to all that mumbo-jumbo, I dared not make a comment, because I knew him. He was fishing for an answer to fit his logic, so telling him the truth would not go over well. When I did respond, I said, "Ask God for yourself. He'll tell you."

A few days later, my father was upset with his wife. All their winnings took a turn, and they started losing money. I mean, come on, people—the gambling industry's intent is not to build big beautiful buildings so that individuals can make it rich; au contraire. Ironically, gambling was now his wife's habit. He was complaining she gambled too much and wasted money, even though they both went to the gambling casinos. Here's my point. They too were partners in crime. My father was happy and willing to go along with his wife as long as they were winning. Wild horses couldn't keep him away from the casinos. Just as Adam shifted the blame to his wife and God, my father shifted the blame to his wife. Listen. There is nothing good about gambling. It is a diabolical system set up to destroy lives and families. The idea of winning big or getting rich quick is the drawing card. Unfortunately, once a person gets started, they often become hooked and their lives are wrecked. From a biblical standpoint, it breeds a form of covetousness. My final point: there is always a repercussion for sin. Adam and Eve's act of disobedience brought sin, and sin brought shame; thus, they hid themselves from God. But here is the beauty behind the story: God didn't leave them that way. He covered their nakedness and removed their shame. The Holy Scripture declares,

> *Unto Adam also and to his wife did the Lord God make coats of skins, and clothed them.* —Genesis 3:21

This was God's covenant love, a foreshadowing of the substitutive atonement for the sin of the first Adam. So then, if He showed the richness of His mercy to Adam and Eve who ran from Him and hid themselves, how much richer mercy will the Lord God show us who run to Him through His Son, Jesus Christ our Lord? Glory, hallelujah!

SATAN, A MASTER OF DISGUISES

Obviously, the woman didn't know that Satan used the voice of the serpent and trickery to beguile her. He is a master of disguises. The Bible declares,

> *And no marvel; for Satan himself is transformed into an angel of light.*
>
> —1Corinthians 11:14

Make no mistake about it—Satan is super-duper convincing. We are no match for him, at least not in our own power. He disguises himself as the real thing (truth) but in reality, he is a counterfeit. For centuries he has beguiled men by speaking to their minds, imitating their own voices. Having said that, there is no language on Planet Earth that the devil does not speak. Whether it is English, Spanish, or Chinese with all its dialects, he speaks them all. The day he spoke to Eve, Satan must have been speaking snake pit language. Yes, he is the mastermind behind much of the evil in our world today. The violence of murder, rape, thievery, genocide, and so on—all starts with the voice of a devil.

I watched the miniseries by Stephen King called *Storm of the Century*, and found it to be similar. The devil, disguised as a man, walked onto a small island located off the coast of Maine. At his arrival, this entity began wreaking havoc. Although the character was fictitious, his characteristics were very good examples of the traits of Satan. The townspeople were absolutely oblivious to who and what they were dealing with.

Night after night, what appeared to be a man would get into the minds of individuals, speaking lies and coaxing them to do horrific things completely out of character. Murder and suicide were his ultimate aim.

Just as the actors in the movie were unconscious of their perpetrator, so it is with persons in real life. Many are unaware of the enemy's wicked devices and fall prey to his trickery.

This, beloved, is his chief aim. I strongly warn you. Beware, he is real, and he lives and works in the darkness. Many lives are cut off without even the slightest knowledge of their assailant. I'm sure you have heard people say, "I don't believe there is a devil." Well, if they don't believe in the existence of the devil, they surely don't believe there's a hell. This is exactly what Satan wants you to believe. I tell you the truth—hell and the devil are real.

In retrospect, I can see that this invisible enemy had my whole family in a pit of some sort. The abusive behaviors were perpetual, and caused a lot of pain. I get the fact that families are going to have typical family issues, but my family was in no way typical. When it came to my siblings, it was hard to watch their abuse, even though I was hurting as well. One evening I walked in the house and I saw my father disciplining my brother Craig for reasons I don't know. My father was always harsh when it came to Craig. As I walked by, I saw my brother crying. He was standing in a pitiful, crouched position and had no shirt on. As I looked in, I saw that my father was very angry. He grabbed my brother by the skin of his chest, picked him up, and threw him against the bathroom wall. I stood in shock as Craig fell to the floor. He got up, whimpering and in pain. I could see the finger impressions in his chest where Father grabbed him. No doubt, he was fearful of what our father might do next. In spite of that, my brother walked up to him, wrapped his arms around his waist, and said, "Daddy, I love you, I love you . . . I just want you to love me." Father stood there rigid with his arms down straight to his side, with a look of hate in his eyes.

All I know is, whatever Craig did, he didn't deserve that kind of punishment. For my brother's sake, I walked through at the right time, although I'm not sure if my presence abated the incident. Who knows what else Father planned to do to my brother. Yes, Craig acted feminine, but he deserved love just the same. After all, he was a victim of circumstance. It was because of the sins of the forefathers that the door of the demonic realm was opened in the first place. Satan came in and wreaked havoc on all of my father's children.

Speaking of wreaking havoc, when I was a young teenager, I felt a little strange. I could only relate it to what we called a tomboy. I was naive to lesbianism. That lifestyle wasn't a visible part of the culture in my youth. I thought my odd feelings were because I was thick-framed and a bit muscular for a girl, on top of the fact I was always teased about my body while growing up. With hindsight, it was a demonic attack via manipulation, to try to confuse me of my gender. Confusion is a spirit, sent by the enemy to create turmoil in the mind, to make one think he or she is the opposite of who and what they are intended to be.

As it was with me, my brother Craig didn't know what hit him. We were only kids struggling with the sins of our fathers that were passed on (generational curses). As I grew older, the feeling went away. But Satan didn't stop. Remember, I said he is a relentless predator. I understood that I was a female, there was no argument there. So being confused about my gender was not a weak point for me. But because of the sexual abuse, the devil would continue speaking his lies. I never questioned the fact that I was a woman. Many who have experienced sexual abuse as a child do, however this nonsense of a woman (or man) feeling like she is meant to be another gender but has somehow been born in the wrong body is ridiculous. Listen. I'm not saying that what they are feeling isn't real. I'm saying it's false. To accept the lie from the enemy that they are trapped causes one to fall deeper into the spirit of confusion. That is the real trap.

Society helps feed this lie by saying people are born this way. Well, I've got news for you—not hardly. Listen, we are all trapped in our bodies, and nobody can do anything to change it. You and I are stuck! I don't care how many hormones you pump into your body or surgeries you get, you can't change who and what God created you to be. Our Creator is the one who decided to make us male or female, and He didn't make a mistake concerning you and me. So whatever the gender, celebrate it!

Now, you might ask "What about those who are intersexed?" I feel it is important to mention a condition called, hermaphroditism, clinically known as ovotesticular disorder. In other words, babies that are born with both male and female sexual organs. This is not to be confused with the spirit of homosexuality. Rather, it is a birth defect, a fluke if you will. Something was off during the developmental stages, causing this confusion of genitalia, similar to an infant born with extra fingers and toes, or twins that didn't completely separate in the womb.

This is a very unfortunate occurrence. Things do happen that can't be explained or understood. However, according to medical research, the double sex organs are said to be external only. An individual's true gender is internal and can be determined as the child grows, at which time surgical intervention can take place to correct and stabilize the abnormality.

Whether you agree with this argument or not, the best thing any person can do is to give their life to the Lord Jesus Christ and find out who they are in Him. Amen? My goodness, if I could add three inches to my stature, you best believe I would . . . not happening.

Listen again, my friend, your identity is not on the basis of some confused feeling. Take a good look in the mirror; there would be a grand place to start and should be enough to convince you. What kind of world would this be if we all believed and did things based solely on what we felt? And how often do feelings change from day to day? Now, let me say this. If it had not been for the mercy of God to resist the devil's lies, I could have fallen prey just like anyone else. Here's why I say this. The devil lost a soul (me), and he wasn't going to walk away peaceably. Getting saved doesn't get you a trouble-free demon card. The devil wants back what he lost! The day I was baptized in the Holy Ghost was another great day of victory. Through Him I learned how to fight back.

FIGHTING BACK IS A MUST!

You recall my opening scripture of Ecclesiastes 3: *"To everything there is a season, and a time . . . a time of war and a time of peace."* I had to learn to fight early in life. As a child, I had to defend myself from a monstrous pedophile. I had no choice but to stand and fight. So it is when it comes to our souls. You needn't think that surrendering will bring peace to such a crisis. No, never! You must fight! Fight! Fight for your soul with every intention to win. It's the most precious thing you've got. Fighting back is a must!

Here's my story . . .

I had been saved for about three years and living celibate. One day I was sitting at my sewing machine making a dress for a friend, when suddenly, I was visited by an evil spirit. A voice spoke to me and said, "If you don't have sex, you're going to be gay." It was the most preposterous lie I'd ever heard. Not having sex doesn't make a person gay. It's a demon spirit called perversion. As with Eve, he tried to divert me from the commandment of God's Word. His strategy is to plant doubt. The Bible refutes such a claim and declares, "Because it is written, Be ye holy; for I am holy" —1 Peter 1:16. Satan doesn't want God's people to live holy lives. He wants to plant in your mind ideas that are impossible.

This is what I want to plant into your spirit, beloved. Salvation is a privilege freely given to us. Once you've been delivered from the hand of the enemy, you will have to fight to keep it. Let me remind you; this is a spiritual battle which usually begins in the mind. Your only recourse is to fight with the Word of God. You must discern and resist all the works of darkness; taking every vain thought captive to the obedience of Christ!

According to Ephesians 6 we are instructed to wage a strategic warfare. So I say to you beloved, *Be strong in the Lord and in the power of His might, putting on the whole armor of God; in the mighty name of Jesus: Amen.*

Of course, I've heard stories like mine, of women and men who were raped and molested when they were young children. As they grew up, they didn't want to have anything to do with the opposite sex, so they turned to a same-sex intimate relationship. No matter the twisted scenario, Satan is behind it. Same-sex relations are the epitome of confusion.

The scripture calls same-sex relationships an abomination (Leviticus 18:22). The Old Testament reveals that it is a detestable act in the sight of God (see also Romans 1:26-18). And we needn't think that He is indifferent about it today. Read the Bible—you will discover God's plan relating to humanity and sexuality has not changed. Same-sex relations are a clear violation of the law. In other words, man's misuse of original intent goes against the very origin of God's divine order and the sanctity of the union between a man and a woman. Once upon a time, American society held a standard against such sinful practices, which forced the perverted to remain hidden. Today homosexuality is rampant; rebels shaking their fists in the face of the Almighty as if to say, "I can live like I please and will indulge in whatever I want." Let me say this: an individual may consider living outside of the will of God, but not without severe consequence. Yet, it is not His will to condemn the lost, but to save; today God is calling men everywhere to repent. I plead with anyone who is struggling with a spirit of perversion, not to give in to the lies of Satan. But rather give in to the Lord Jesus who loved you enough to give His life on a rugged cross. Therein lies the answer. Only He can deliver and set free from this bondage of sin. But you must turn from all unrighteousness with your whole heart, unto God. The Lord Jesus loves you and has a great plan for your life.

I want to encourage you to start journaling if you haven't already. It is said to be very good therapy, and I agree. Writing about the stresses helped me to come to terms with them. It reduced the impact of the trauma on my physical health as I went through my process of healing. One day I sat down and made a list of everything I hated about my father. For the record, I want to warn you; it's a bit lengthy, and here it is.

I hated that:

1. He was a bully
2. He saw me as a sex object rather than a daughter
3. He couldn't be trusted
4. He was a liar
5. He was a manipulator, always trying to get one over on his wife and children
6. He always made me feel I owed him something
7. He made me work for affection
8. He went to church every Sunday but hadn't changed his ways
9. He never genuinely apologized for his behavior.

My father would always pull the "You don't respect me" or "You don't love me" card. He would manipulate—cover up for the real issue behind my intolerance concerning him. Here's a chief example. He and I would be sitting down, holding a decent conversation, when he would start playing with his privates and looking at me with lust in his eyes. It was clear that I couldn't trust him any further than I could throw him. He needed help, and after all these years, he still isn't willing.

Lust must be dealt with or it will destroy you. It has a domino effect leading to sexual sins, which lead to guilt and shame. Not to mention unwanted pregnancies or STDs, which could lead to death. I'm not just talking about a person who feels sexual urges from time to time.

For it is God who put sexual desires in us; they are normal human urges. A spirit of lust goes deeper than that. It's like a harness on the mind that directly jerks the senses toward unhealthy thoughts at will. From personal experience, it is an aggressive ongoing battle. As a baby Christian, I didn't understand that the adversary plants impure thoughts and images in the mind. His aim is to get you to yield and fall into temptation. In 2 Corinthians 10:5, Paul calls these imaginations; strongholds—arguments that one must constantly override with the weapons of our warfare. Bringing every thought into captivity to the obedience of Christ. Let me interject right here and say, everyone who has given their life to the Lord Jesus has had a "lust issue" they've struggled with at one time or another— sexual or otherwise.

That said, I wasn't alone in this. A precious sister in Christ began to speak freely about her struggles with lust. She happened to be a client of mine, and knowing that I was a minister, she opened up and started talking. I observed how frustrated she was. She said, "I was raped by my uncles and my brothers when I was a little girl, and now I have a hard time living for Jesus. I know I'm saved, but I constantly see images of nudity in my head." She went on to say, "I can even be at my church, when unexpectedly, I'd see images of naked people flash before my eyes." I understood her struggle and felt compassion for her, knowing the inward battle she had to overcome.

No doubt her open confession meant that she truly wanted help. I ministered to her through the Word and prayer, also sharing my testimony. For anyone who will be set free from the bondages of lust, confession is the first step. After I prayed, the bondages were broken off her, and she left my salon renewed. Unfortunately, she didn't keep it. A few years later, I saw her walking along with her lesbian lover. This young sister gave in to the lies of the devil. I don't know about you, beloved, but I refuse to let a devil have any part of me—on ANY level. He's a foul demonic spirit from the underworld, and I hate him!

Speaking of confessing, it was my first step to deliverance from lust, and I must say, it was hard for me at first. It was shameful and I didn't want to feel like a sinner. When a person has a genuine love for

Jesus, they don't want to be a disappointment to Him. But because I wasn't willing to confess early on, it took longer to get set free. In addition, forfeiting a refreshing in the soul which comes from the presence of the Lord. I would rather have bit my tongue until it bled than to say I had a spirit of lust. It wasn't until my spiritual life became stagnant that I had no choice but to deal with it head on. It must be dealt with, and the sooner, the better. Spiritual bondages don't just go away.

Many in the body of Christ are bound by the spirit of lust. There are larger numbers affected today, simply because the church doesn't preach holiness like it once did. In addition, everywhere you look, there are sensual suggestions, bam! in your face. You see it in shopping malls and on billboard advertisements. It's nothing to see larger-than-life poster shots of half-naked women and men modeling lingerie displayed in front of the store windows. Our TV stations are loaded with images of sexual innuendos, and instead of turning away many of the saints are falling for this filth—hook, line, and sinker. As I mentioned before, they are totally oblivious, unable to discern devilish tactics. Because of this, they let the filth of Hollywood into their homes and then wonder why their families are breaking up.

I must mention that the media has changed for the worse. Unless Christians take charge over what they allow in their environments right now, they will become desensitized to ungodliness. It is said, "You are what you eat." It's also said, "You are what you watch." Watch it long enough and you are in danger of becoming affected in some way. Okay, last thing on this. If images and words are not effective, why is it when we watch a TV commercial for fast food, we get the craving to have it? Images and words create an impulse to act out. Are you feelin' me? I hear Christians making the statement, "There's nothing else to watch." Okay then, this is where we need to ask the Lord to give us godly wisdom to direct our time. Herein are a few suggestions: Use the time to spend with your children, get a hobby, or get your Bible and read it. Do something–find another outlet that doesn't open your spirit to demonic filth! Here's another one: "I don't see anything wrong with it." This is the worst yet—married couples believe marriage makes porn acceptable. Um, no, there is nothing remotely close to that in the scriptures. These statements show many are already affected. It's better for you and your family to turn away from it. If it doesn't glorify God, then it's unholy and defiled. Here's my question to you. Would you like to see your son or daughter play a role in a pornographic movie? Probably not. Well, you're watching someone's child play a degraded role for YOUR entertainment. Pause and think about that.

I choose not to watch TV unless it's wholesome. King David understood the necessity of turning his eyes away from wickedness and declared,

> *I will set nothing wicked before my eyes; I hate the works of those who fall away;*
>
> —Psalm 101:3-4

What can I say about this psalm? It is crystal clear. David's righteous convictions were so strong that he refused to delight in wickedness for even a moment. He had no tolerance for it. We are called by God to live sanctified, consecrated lives. These two words are not heard of much today. Only with a stern commitment to live separate from the world will we guard our eyes from anything that will defile our inner lives.

Now, I have another confession. I didn't come to this decision on my own; the Lord had to help me. I learned to recognize the demonic filth that was infiltrating through the TV, no matter how subtle. He taught me how to identify lust and what was feeding it. I wanted to be free, truly free, but there were steps I had to take. First, I had to take control, meaning I had to allow the fruit of temperance to operate. As we all should. Second, I had to obey the voice of the Lord (receive and follow biblical instruction); and third, I had to hate all sin. I hope this doesn't sound "holier than thou" to you. If so, I don't know what else to tell you. What I am describing here is simply this: there is always a responsibility on our part, as believers, to walk in our deliverance.

Here's my story . . .

One night I was watching a miniseries, which seemed harmless in the beginning. It was one of those Disney childhood stories made into adult entertainment. I kept watching until I got hooked on the show. I'd rush in from church on Sunday night to catch the episode. Before long, it began to display magic scenes and witches casting spells and so forth. My Holy Ghost prompted me to turn it off, but I didn't listen—I was fascinated with it. Listen very carefully, because this is important. I had been seeking God, intensifying my prayer life, and studying the Word. I had been in the presence of God, under the anointing and witnessing on the street corners, telling lost souls about the love of Jesus. When I came in from church that night, I decided to watch the show, against my Holy Ghost once again. When I went to bed I began to struggle with the spirit of lust, which I had not been battling for a long time until that night. I mentioned earlier that we are no match for Satan. Be warned, subtlety is how the enemy sneaks in.

The next morning when I woke, I asked the Lord why I was attacked. Lo and behold, the following night He spoke to me through a dream. In the dream I was sitting on my bed when this woman, out of nowhere, walked through the walls. She looked like the old-time sanctified sisters. Her hair was teased up really big and she wore drab-looking clothes and eyeglasses. As she walked in she kept saying, "You have too many doors open. You have too many doors open." I asked, "Who are you?" She didn't respond. The woman kept repeating, "You have too many doors open." Then I screamed at her and again I asked, "Who are you! Where did you come from?" It was as if she didn't see or hear me. She went through my bedroom without ever looking in my direction, continuing the same speech, until she walked to the other side and disappeared through the wall.

When I woke up, I knew it was a rebuke from the Lord. What I thought would not harm, was harmful. I quickly repented and obeyed the Lord and closed all doors. Like David, I refuse to watch anything vulgar. I don't know about you, beloved, but my goal is to walk in righteousness and holiness before a holy God. If we will continue to profess Jesus Christ as Lord and Savior, we must keep our spirit-man clean.

I have had experiences with casting out demons. Let me tell you, not only are they hideous, they have the foulest, most detestable odor I've ever come across. They are unclean and evil, and when you understand just how foul a demon is, you won't want any part of it either. Not only so, but you won't want to watch anything that has to do with the dark works of the underworld. Listen, beloved, everything we do comes with a price. In the past, I lost my anointing for a few moments of sinful pleasure. What took me years to build through prayer, fasting, and seeking God was gone in an instant. It wasn't worth it—trust me when I tell you. I didn't know what I had until I lost it. Thanks be unto God, He gives us the grace to get back up and get back in the race.

> *He brought me up also out of an horrible pit, out of the miry clay.* —Psalm 40:2

Ah, this is one of my favorite psalms from my childhood. It strengthens me every time I read it. There is a story behind it. I mentioned earlier how my parents insisted that we go to church every week, and we also had to participate in something. This was a good thing. The family attended Grace Temple Baptist Church, where I attended Sunday school and sang in the church choir along with my siblings. It was fun, especially being in the choir. My family and I enjoyed singing.

The first Sunday we arrived I was a youngster, in the first grade. When we walked into the vestibule of the church, I saw the double doors with small windows leading to the sanctuary. I watched as different people walked up to look through the windows as they entered. I wanted to take a look as well, but I was too small to reach them. The doors finally opened to a sanctuary filled with people singing and organ music playing. I grew up in this church hearing the fortieth division of Psalms read every Sunday morning. The late Reverend I. C. Green was the residing pastor at that time. He would rise from his seat and stand at the pulpit to read the scripture as the choir followed with a melodious song. This passage stuck with me throughout my life. It wasn't until I came into the fullness of God that I understood what it meant, and every time I quoted the verse, I was speaking by faith to my future.

Earlier I mentioned there was no way out of a pit unless someone was there to pull you out. Well, David sings praises unto the Lord as the one who rescues him from the pit of despair, saying, *"For He has put a new song in my mouth, even praise unto our God."* So it was with me. Truly, He has given me a new song to sing!

Here's my story . . .

I was about the age of thirty when a sister invited me to a camp meeting in Virginia. During those years the repercussions of sexual abuse still lingered. I decided to go, and with great excitement I began to pack for the trip. When I arrived, it was nothing like I expected. It seemed all the saints there lived in a state of poverty. They showed no kindness, not even the slightest pretense. I couldn't believe the racial prejudice displayed among Christians. I couldn't help but wonder what Bible were they reading. Did they skip over the part of the Bible where is says, "Beloved, If God so loved us, we also ought to love one another"?

The camp thrived on an array of donations from different organizations, such as clothing, shoes, and toiletries. I noticed that once the donations arrived, all the white saints would gather around, picking and distributing items to themselves and their friends. In the meantime, the black saints stood waiting on the side for the leftovers, if there were any.

When mealtime rolled around it was no different. The white saints were assigned to the kitchen to serve everyone. A line was formed and when it was my turn, it was clear they didn't want to serve you if you were black. The server gave me a "you disgust me" look, dipped her serving spoon into a big pot of whatever it was called, and "plop!" onto my plate it went. No need for me to think I would get a smile or a head nod. At any rate, I got blocked bowels the first week I was there because the food was so horrible.

Nightfall was approaching and sleeping arrangements set. The mattresses and sheets were old and beat up, and the moment I lay down, I realized I was sharing the bed with the mosquitos. It was almost unbearable. All I knew was, I was so ready to go home. I was most miserable. But God had a plan.

There was this new wave in the body of Christ called "joy." Something called "laughter in the Spirit" was going around. During camp meetings the saints would go up for prayer and fall under the power of the Spirit and began laughing uncontrollably. I didn't want to dismiss what I saw happening as total nonsense, so I told myself, "This is not for me, and plus, all these folks falling out laughing are just silly, anyway."

One night, a preacher was expounding on bondages, and I was sitting right up front. He began to say, "Laugh at physical abuse. Laugh at incest." I became totally offended. Everything in me screamed, "*That ain't funny*!" He repeated it over again and I felt my anger rising. There was a war going on inside me that night, I tell you. At that moment I didn't realize what the man of God was conveying. But God was in control.

The minister preached an intense message. He said, "Call back those fragmented parts of you, call back your self-worth, call back your self-esteem and self-respect, call back your courage, call it, in the mighty name of Jesus!" I began to call back everything that was stolen from me.

After a while, something began to break. The Spirit of the Lord was all over me. I found myself getting up from my seat and moving toward the altar. The brother laid hands on me, and the next thing I knew, I hit the floor, laughing uncontrollably along with everybody else. I'd laugh a while and I'd cry a while. This repeated through the evening. When I came to myself, the bondages were broken off and I had experienced a new level of deliverance. I was filled with the joy of Lord. Everything I encountered prior to that night paled in comparison. Let me interject right here. What I needed, money could not buy. Only a divine intervention from on high could perform it. My experience left me wanting more of God's goodness. Oh yes, in the words of David, "He has given me a new song to sing!" A song of victory, hallelujah! I left that camp with my new, freshly delivered self, thanking God for the great work He had done in me.

A TIME OF THANKSGIVING

After a great victory, thanksgiving always follows. I never thought the day would come when I would thank God for my parents, but it did. In spite of all I endured, I was so thankful. I began to see things in a different light. What was meant for evil, God worked together for my good.

This also brings me joy. I began to realize it helped shape me into the person that God wanted me to be. You've heard the saying, "What doesn't kill you only makes you strong"? It's true; I'm a living witness. Listen to Romans 8:28:

> *And we know that all things work together for good to those who love God, to those who are the called according to His purpose.*

This verse is exciting to me because God truly worked all things together for my good. There wasn't one thing left out. Here's the beauty of it. The heavenly Father took away the pain of the pits and made me fit for His kingdom. If I had not been broken, if I had not experienced the pits of life, I wouldn't know the incredible love and healing power of God. If I hadn't been rejected, I wouldn't be able to identify with those who suffered with heartbreaks. If I had not been raped as a child, (not that God willed it to happen) I wouldn't be able to tell you that in Christ you can become brand-new, for Jesus said, *"Behold I make all things new."* Beloved, that includes you.

> *Therefore if any man be in Christ, he is a new creation; old things have passed away; behold all things have become new.*
>
> —1 Corinthians 5:17

Let me explain it like this. Here in the Arizona desert, there are plenty of cacti. One early spring morning I noticed a peculiar cactus with all its prickly sharp needles decorated with big, beautiful white flowers blooming all over it. Wow, I thought to myself, that's unexpected beauty. It's God's way of saying, "I can take your most prickly situations and bring out a beauty, that I may be glorified. Listen to the words of the prophet:

> *To appoint unto them that mourn in Zion, to give unto them beauty for ashes, the oil of joy for mourning, the garment of praise for the spirit of heaviness; that they might be called trees of righteousness, the planting of the Lord, that He might be glorified.*
>
> —Isaiah 61:3

He set my feet upon a rock and established my goings.
—Psalm 40:2

In our opening scripture, David declared three things: He brought me up, He set my feet upon a rock, and He established my goings. Prior, the king of Jerusalem cried out to God from a deep miry pit of agony. This Psalm provides a powerful example of how we, too, are to seek God when faced with troubles. God's promise is that He will hear the cries of the righteous. Taking a closer look at David's prayer, he did not offer a patty-cake invocation. He sought the Lord with his whole heart; he cried out. Then the Lord heard him and delivered him also out of the pit. Simply put, we cry, then God hears. Note the "also" it

It's God's way of saying,
"I can take your
most prickly situations and bring
out a beauty that I may be
glorified!

indicates that blessings of deliverance don't stop until He establishes our goings. There is something wonderful about how God establishes our path. Let's examine the word "establish."

In Hebrew, "establish" is KUN; *Strong's Concordance* defines it as "to stand firm, be established, steadfast, be fixed." David was destined to be king of Israel because God established his goings. Years passed and troubles seemed to mount. It didn't look like it was to happen. But when God establishes our goings, or our steps, they're fixed—nothing can overturn them.

I'm reminded of a shrub I have growing in my front yard. I never watered it. The only water it receives is from the desert rain on few occasions. It encountered the long hot droughts of summer. Once it was cut back so low, it looked like it was dead. Surely it can't come back now, I thought. To my amazement, the shrub came back in full force and grew bigger every time. The shrub blossomed and bloomed in its season. How was this possible? It was established. Its roots had grown far below the earth's surface. I believe it tapped into a water table deep in the ground. That's what our life is like when God establishes us. The adversities on the surface don't impede our destiny. Because when we are tapped into Him, the sustainer of life we are as a tree planted by the rivers of water who's leaves shall not shrivel, but will prosper in its season.

After the Father establishes us, we are encouraged to forget, along the way, according to Psalm 45:10–15. No longer are we identified with the pits of the past. Heretofore, we are now a part of royalty, representative of our King Jesus. We now have His spiritual blood running through our veins. With that said, once you learn who you are in the Lord, there mustn't be any slipping backward. No, we hold our new position with honor, worshipping Him:

> *So shall the King greatly desire thy beauty: for He is Thy Lord!*—Psalm 45:11

BROKEN FOR YOU

All human suffering in the world put together cannot compare to the horrific suffering of our Lord Jesus Christ. The only difference was that He volunteered. He knew what lay ahead, yet He was willing. During the Passover, He spoke to His disciples and said, *"Take eat, this is my body which is broken for you."*—Matthew 26:26

When I considered the pain inflicted upon Him, the shame He endured while the world mocked Him, spit on Him, slapped and beat Him, I confessed to my Father and said, "I couldn't endure such a heavy cross."

But Jesus did for us what we could not do for ourselves. Just before the passions of Christ, as mentioned in Luke's gospel, Jesus wept. My attention was drawn to all the tears He must have cried, and while He cried, the world laughed.

If anyone had a reason to hold a grudge, it was Jesus, but He didn't. He received evil for good. He was rejected, though He loved. The Holy Scripture declares:

> *"He was in the world, and the world was made through Him, and the world did not know Him. He came to His own, and His own did not receive Him."*
>
> —John 1:10–11.

The Son of Man was laid in the deepest, darkest pit for the sake of you and me, but God didn't stop there. You see, Jesus wasn't sent solely to do good deeds, suffer, and die (as some might suppose). Throughout the ages many individuals have such a reputation. This would not suffice as a means of redemption, because humanity's greater need would have never been met. But after three days, Jesus rose from the dead with all power in heaven and earth. He defeated the stings of life (sin and death's cruelty) so that we too could rise. Yes, we can arise from the pits of life. Jesus took upon Himself all our pain, all our sickness, all our diseases and even death. Why did He do it? LOVE. In His great act of love, we can be healed, delivered, and set free.

Herein is the beauty of His suffering. No one can look on the sufferings of Jesus and remain in the same condition. We can ask the Centurion soldier:

> *So when the centurion, who stood opposite Him, saw that he cried out like this and breathed His last breath, he said "Truly this man was the Son of God!"* —Mark 15:39

No doubt the soldier hadn't planned to make such a passionate confession. But one look changed his life forever. I must mention the effects the death of Christ had on those who were already dead. The Bible reveals this occurrence was so powerful that the veil of the temple was ripped from top to bottom, the earth quaked and graves were opened. Many saints were resurrected from the pit of death, back to life. While reading the scriptures I came across these words of John the Revelator:

> *And I looked, and behold, in the midst of the throne and of the four living creatures, and in the midst of the elders, stood a Lamb as though it had been slain.*
>
> —Revelation 5:6

I wondered what a slain lamb looked like. I too wanted to see Him. OH, then one day I saw a vision while praying. It was a brief moment. I saw Jesus, high and lifted up on a cross. His face was marred, and His arms were stretched out wide. He wore the crown of thorns upon His head as the blood ran down His body.

The glory and splendor was upon Him while He hung there on that cross. That one glance changed my life. I could only fall down on my knees in fear and holy reverence. My life will never be the same. So, I say to you who are in the pit of despair, you only need to look on Jesus and arise.

DEALING WITH THE PAIN

DEALING WITH THE PAIN

My heart is severely pained within me,
And the terrors of death have fallen upon me.
Fearfulness and trembling have come upon me,
And horror has overwhelmed me.
So I said, "Oh, that I had wings like a dove!
I would fly away and be at rest.
Indeed, I would wander far off,
And remain in the wilderness. (Selah)
—Psalm 55:4–7

My heart is severely pained within me —Psalm 55:4

There is no pain like the pain inflicted by those close to you, people in whom you put your trust. In this psalm, David expressed anguish so severe it is described as "a woman feels in her time of travail." So extreme was the psalmist's inner pain that he wanted to run away from it.

> *So I said, "Oh, that I had wings like a dove! I would fly away and be at rest. Indeed, I would wander far off, and remain in the wilderness. Selah.* —Psalm 55:7

We've all been at this place of wanting to leave behind painful experiences to search for a place of comfort, only to realize that there is no such place. I like these words of Charles Spurgeon:

> *We are all too apt to utter this vain desire, for vain it is; no wings of doves or eagles could bear us away from the sorrows of a trembling heart. Inward grief knows nothing of a place.*

Until emotional pain is dealt with, we may run here or flee there, but pain will show up everywhere. Addressing the issues that caused the pain is part of the healing process, though it is easier said than done.

THE SECRET IS OUT

Here's my story . . .

It was a Sunday evening. While I lay resting on the sofa, the Spirit of the Lord began dealing with me about the abuse I suffered as a child. I heard Him say with a gentle voice, *"The secret is going to come out."* As the Spirit continued to impress upon my heart, I perceived that it was time to confront our deep, dark family issues. Undoubtedly the Lord had a plan to bring much needed healing to the family, if those responsible for the damage would come clean and repent. No longer could my parents walk around pretending everything was normal while their children suffered in silence.

The emotional pain I felt was enormous. I didn't want to see my perpetrators' faces, let alone discuss the matter. To confront the issue would be like reliving my nightmares all over again. In anger and tears, I repeatedly asked the Lord why my father would do such a thing. How could he! Seeing my anger toward my father, the Lord spoke again, *"It wasn't your father. It was the devil."*

At that moment, a spiritual light came on and revealed the real culprit. Satan could no longer hide behind the face of a human. With holy indignation, I began to confess out loud, "Satan, I hate YOU!" The more I confessed the more empowered I became. Then the unexpected happened.

I heard the voice of Satan, spoken unlike any time before. He said, "Don't hate me. Hate God because He made me." Talk about a spiritual battle that night! While it is true that God made Satan, that's only a half-truth. The whole truth is found in Ezekiel 28:13–19; He wasn't created to be evil in the beginning.

> *Thou wast perfect in thy ways from the day that thou wast created, till iniquity was found in thee.*
>
> —Ezekiel 28:15

I didn't know how the Lord would allow this secret to come out; neither did I know what to anticipate. All I felt at that moment was serious pain. A few weeks followed and then I received a long-distance phone call from my baby sister. She mentioned talking with my elder sister. "Rhonda told me Daddy had sex with you two. Is this true?" she asked in doubt. My eldest sister had a habit of lying; you couldn't believe her half the time. "Yep, she's telling the truth on this one," I said. I told everything that happened, even the fact that I felt Mother was secretly aware of it all the while. Baby sister gasped in complete astonishment and quickly hung up the phone.

Immediately following that conversation, Mother called. "'Nita, I heard what happened. I didn't know stuff like that was going on." I used the word stuff to keep it clean. She kept up a good facade, acting surprised and hurt. It was sickening to hear her phony imitations of concern for my sister and me.

After Mother's many attempts to explain away her knowledge of the abuse, I was compelled to ask, "What would you have done if you'd known about it?" She replied, "I don't know." Buzz! Wrong answer, I said to myself. It was obvious my mother had no intension of standing up for her children against her husband's behavior, ever. Her denial was a disappointment and another added pain I had to deal with. And if that wasn't bad enough, the secret came out that my father raped my aunt Fredricka. She was only fifteen. OH, my gracious! I knew my father was a perverted creep, yet I was caught off guard with this one. As I explained earlier, her story was heart wrenching. After her rape experience, the pain drove her to drug use and it only escalated to a stronger substance. Fredricka had moved away from the country to live with her big sister Jonnye for a better life. Instead, she was emotionally scarred. The damage was so severe that Fredricka believed that every bad thing that had happened to her was well deserved. In other words, she felt she needed to be punished. She became accustomed to being abused by others, which is a condition called the Stockholm syndrome. She married a verbally and physically abusive man who beat her unmercifully. Her only deliverance from physical abuse came by way of death. Her husband died of a drug overdose.

A TIME TO HEAL

It is said in the medical field that the body has a fascinating self-healing mechanism. There are three phases in physical wound healing: 1) the inflammatory phase, 2) the proliferative phase, and 3) the maturation phase. Inflammation is the beginning stage of how physical wounds are healed. The body attempts to stop the bleeding that occurs at the time of injury. Over the next few days, the body begins to clean up the wound and protect itself from bacterial invasion. The skin swells, which is why they call it the inflammatory phase. Therein lies the pain. The wound seems to be getting worse instead of better. You know what it's like; it's so painful that the slightest touch makes you scream, but touch you must. As more time passes, the body begins to replace lost tissue and rebuild itself.

The proliferative phase is the second wound-healing stage. The wound begins to be rebuilt with new, healthy granulation tissue. At this stage, the wound is a reddish pink color along with secretion. Even though it looks a sight, it is healthy, and the bandages have to be changed often.

The maturation phase, also known as remodeling, is the last stage of the wound-healing process. It occurs after the wound has closed up and can take as long as two years. While it may appear that the wound-healing process is finished when maturation begins, it's important not to neglect it due to the risk of it breaking down dramatically.[2]

Dealing with physical wounds is easier because you can see it and go right to the hurt. This is not so easy with emotional wounds, which makes it harder to stop the emotional bleeding. What's needed first and foremost is love and patience, which are hard to come by these days.

Second, the wounded must be willing to go deep into those sensitive areas, exposing all the hidden ugliness of spiritual proliferation that has one bound and broken. Note that spiritual healing comes in stages as well. There are times when I thought I was healed in a certain area until something came along and hit it just right, then OUCH! I thought I was over that, I'd say. The only course of action was to go back and revisit the sore spot within my soul. Unfortunately, many people take the unending scenic route, trying to numb their pain with substance abuse, which only makes matters worse. The use of alcohol, drugs, sex, or even cutting themselves may temporarily ease the pain, but they can never remove it. One must be willing to take a walk down "Hurt Street." Are you ready?

LET'S FACE THE PAIN OF THE PAST ONCE AND FOR ALL

In an earlier chapter I talked about the pits of life. No one comes out of a pit unscathed, but there is hope. Listen again to the sweet words of King Solomon: *"A time to heal"* (Ecclesiastes 3:3).

We can all give high praise to God for our time of healing. In the Bible we find the story of the woman with the issue of blood who suffered with a painful disease for twelve long years. She'd heard of a man named Jesus walking the streets of Jerusalem and recognized her opportunity (see Luke 8:43).

This woman's story reveals that she tried many physicians, only to be left uncured and penniless. How often do we seek help from an unworthy source, leaving us helpless and bankrupt? No doubt the woman had to deal with emotional pain as well. Desperate yet determined, she pressed her way through the crowd. This was not a simple task. More than likely she had to get on the dusty ground and be trampled on. If this woman were here today, I believe she'd say:

In vain I sought my healing from men,
Only to be left broke, in debt to depend.
Jesus came to do the impossible, so I heard,
With nothing left to lose—my faith emerged.
If only I could get just one touch, was my hearts' plea,
Determined to move forward desperately
Hard pressed was I, to join the thronging crowd,
To receive virtue from the Master, so endowed.
My healing came instantly to my humble surprise.
Then He turned and looked about with discerning eyes.
"Who touched me? said He.
No one understood that question but me.
In fear and trembling I arose
To hear my Lord speak words of comfort composed.
"Go in peace, thy faith hath made thee whole."

—Anita Joe

When it comes to healing emotional pain, the process may take longer for some than for others. For me it took a really long time to get over a lot of the stuff inflicted on me. First, I didn't realize the depth of the damage. Second, I had to get out in order to see that what I encountered was not the norm but abnormal; and third, because the kind of healing I needed, like the woman with the issue of blood, would take an intervention from God. I too was hard-pressed to receive my healing. God had to first undo all the mess that was done over the years.

I like the definition for "undo." According to *Webster*, it means "to make of no effect or as if not done: make null: reverse." Just as the body is designed to stop the bleeding and reverse the damages, so it is with God when it comes to our soul.

Apart from saving me, He stopped my heart from hemorrhaging. Aw, a time to heal—I love the sound of that. What better time than now?

The heavenly Father is ready, willing, and able to heal you. Although healing entails pain, one must go through it to be made whole. Overcoming the pain of rape is a battle that many women, and even some men, face today. The act brings on a multitude of internal issues. In 2 Samuel 13, we find the familiar story of Tamar, who was raped by her brother Amnon. (See what I mean by close hurts?) The scripture says,

> *After this Absalom the son of David had a lovely sister, whose name was Tamar; and Amnon the son of David loved her. Amnon was so distressed over his sister Tamar that he became sick; for she was a virgin. And it was improper for Amnon to do anything to her. Then Ammon lay down, and pretended to be ill: and when the king was come to see him, Amnon said unto the king, "Please let Tamar my sister come and make a couple of cakes for me in my sight, that I may eat from her hand. And David sent home to Tamar, saying, "Now go to your brother Amnon's house, and prepare food*

> *for him." Then Amnon said to Tamar, "Bring the food into the bedroom, that I may eat from your hand." Now when she had brought them to him to eat, he took hold of her and said to her, "Come, lie with me, my sister." But she answered him, "No, my brother, do not force me, for no such thing should be done in Israel. Do not do this disgraceful thing! And I, where could I take my shame? And as for you, you would be like one of the fools in Israel. Now therefore, please speak to the king for he will not withhold me from you." However, he would not heed her voice; and being stronger than she, he forced her and lay with her.*

Tamar experienced something that no woman should ever have to go through, especially being that she was a king's daughter. A young virgin girl, had been sexually violated by an unforeseen malicious villain. The culprit; her own flesh and blood. Listen again to the psalmist's words:

> *For it was not an enemy that reproached me: then I could have borne it: neither was it he that hated me that did magnify himself against me; then I would have hid myself from him: But it was thou, a man, mine equal, my guide and mine acquaintance.*
>
> —Psalm. 55:12

Tamar never would have suspected her own brother to behave in such a heinous way. He mistook lust for love. You don't plot to rape someone that you profess to love unless something is wrong mentally. I am sure she asked herself the question a thousand times over in her mind. "Why would my brother do this to me?" or "What did I do to bring this on myself?" I asked the same questions. It was mind-boggling to think of why my father would commit such a crime against his own daughters, especially with my sister and me being babies at the time. It's unfathomable. That is the epitome of perversion—acts that can't be explained or imagined; and what's worse is when the act is perceived as normal or right in a deranged mind.

In Greek, perversion is DIASTREPHO; *W. E. Vine's Expository Dictionary* defines it as "to distort, twist: to turn aside, corrupted." In order to understand it fully is to see the definition for *corrupted.* It is the Greek word DIAPHTHEIRO: *dia*, "thorough, intensive," meaning "to corrupt utterly, through and through"; when said of men, "corrupted in mind." In layman's terms, it is the mind-set of a person who has become morally bankrupt. Let's read on.

> *Then Amnon hated her exceedingly, so that the hatred with which he hated her was greater than the love with which he had loved her. And Amnon said to her, "Arise, be gone!" So she said to him, "No, indeed! This evil of sending me away is worse than the other that you did to me." But he would not listen to her. Then he called his servant who attended him, and said, "Here! Put this woman out, away from me, and bolt the door behind her." Now she had on a robe of many colors, for the king's virgin daughters wore such apparel. And his servant put her out and bolted the door behind her. Then Tamar put ashes on her head and tore her robe of many colors that was on her, and laid her hand on her head and went away crying bitterly.*

This sounds all too familiar. As it was with Tamar, my elder sister and I were treated disdainfully. My father was a mastermind manipulator, plotting and planning his moves on us. Afterward, he would tear us down with his words, making us feel small. One might think my sister and I would have been brought close in all of this. But no. My father managed to keep us at odds with each other.

At times I'd catch him watching me. This made me very nervous. I wish I knew then what I know now, to never make eye contact with a twisted-minded devil. Eye contact was a come-on for him. Back to Tamar, the rape left her broken and full of pain, the pain of shame;

and if that wasn't bad enough, Amnon rejected her. This is a double whammy from the enemy.

What is shame? *Webster* defines it as "a painful emotion caused by consciousness of guilt, short-coming or impropriety; to force by causing to feel guilty [shamed into confessing].

There are two reasons why a person feels shame. One reason is because of some personal wrongdoing. This is called "warranted" shame. We know, biblically speaking, that shame is the consequence of sin.

Another reason for shame is mislaid or "unwarranted" shame, shame we shouldn't have because there is no just reason for it. Whatever you are feeling ashamed of doesn't bring reproach on the name of God, such as in Tamar's case. She was overwhelmed with grief and shame because she was now considered soiled, but she was innocent, and her shame unwarranted. Amnon shifts the blame to his half-sister, disgracing himself and his father's house and, most of all, the God of Israel. Truly, something sinful happened, but this young daughter didn't have a sinful hand in it. She suffered at the hands of a maniac.

I can identify with Tamar. When the so-called secret came out, neither of my parents wanted to take full responsibility. Even though my father admitted what he did was wrong, he would try to justify his actions. Mother didn't accept any responsibility for her part of the abuse.

She did manage to twist my words, though. One day she walked into my salon and started talking. "It's not my fault. I didn't have nothin' to do with that. It's not my fault, and I won't be sorry for none of it. I'm not apologizing, nope! Cause I didn't have nothing to do with it!" This was her way of trying to exonerate herself. All the while Mother talked, her back was turned. She couldn't even face me. I used to ask myself, *if you didn't know about the sexual abuse, why did you mistreat your daughters?* My mother's whole life was one big denial. I felt nothing but pity for her. I never made such accusations, but it was obvious to me that she was privy to it. I guess my parents didn't think their actions would come back to haunt them, but they always do. Jonnye Ruth went to her grave in denial.

The ordeal left me having to juggle a great amount of shame; ashamed of having been molested, ashamed when I saw my elder sister molested, ashamed of how my body looked because I had been touched, ashamed of the times when I had to urinate and couldn't because the pain was so great, ashamed of having a father who was a pedophile, ashamed of bearing his last name. When I was out and about, I would meet someone in passing and start a conversation. They would ask my name. After telling them, they'd say, "Oh, I know your Dad!" The voice of shame would whisper inside my head. "They probably know the family secret." Then, I was ashamed of the dirty jokes my father used to tell, ashamed of what people thought about our family, ashamed when my mother would bring her women friends to the house to visit. My father would act inappropriately as always, flirting right up in their faces. Oh, my! All that was going on inside, and I dared not tell anyone. The pain of shame makes you want to isolate yourself, as the psalmist expressed. You tell yourself, *Keep silent because people will judge you.* Ah, but one day something happened.

God began to set me free from shame. It was during the time I was pastoring a small church in Atlanta. We were preparing for a women's conference and had invited speakers from different parts of the country. Our theme was "Walking in the Light." I was scheduled to minister on the last night of the conference. But to my amazement, God had not spoken a word to me for the people. No, not one thing! The last night had arrived, and still I had not heard a word from the Lord as to what I should speak. I became a little concerned.

That night, as I was sitting in the pulpit, I heard my Holy Ghost speak to me and say, "Tell your story." Everything in me wanted to say "NO!" But I knew deep down I had to obey God. As I rose to the podium with tears running down my face, I could barely get through the song I started with. As I began telling my story, all eyes were fastened on me. When I finished, yokes of bondages were broken and many women were set free, starting with me. Blessed be the name of Jesus!

As I walk down memory lane, fettered under a daunting spirit of shame
Two-thousand years ago Christ beheld me and said, I will go
With joy He bore upon Himself, that horrid display
Shame now destroyed, and the battle is over—how could I ever repay
Free to walk, free to talk, free to be me; oh the cost!
Due praise belongs to my Lord so dear,
overflowing from a thankful heart of cheer
A simple thanks doesn't seem quite enough,
but that's all I'm required to give
To my God and King forever, to praise I will live

—Poem by Anita Joe

I began to walk in a freedom I hadn't experienced. I could walk in the light of honor, with my head held high because the Lord had rolled away the reproach of incest. God knew what was needed during that conference. Just one simple act of obedience caused me to be set free by the power of God. Beloved, obedience is the key no matter how dark things may seem at the present; obey God.

 My prayer for you today is

that you will be loosed from the demonic power of shame,
in the mighty name of Jesus!

Shame was only a branch of the problem; rejection was at the root. I learned later that the spirit of rejection was a stronghold in my life, which also desperately needed to be broken. Let's revisit Tamar's words: *"And Amnon said to her, 'Arise, be gone!' So she said to him, 'No, indeed! This evil of sending me away is worse than the other that you did to me.'"*

Tamar's experience of rape brought on shame, but a worse pain would follow, the pain of rejection. Amnon raped his sister, then cast her out like a soiled rag.

Before I move on, let me interject that Tamar's brother Absalom was outraged and plotted the death of his brother. Absalom is my hero because he did what his father, David, should have done. Incest was punishable by death (see Leviticus 20:17). Tamar was so crushed and ashamed that she was willing to marry her rapist to cover her shame, a man who wasn't remorseful on any level. Pause and think about that! He flipped the script, making her feel as though she was the culprit. This is exactly how the devil works. He is an accuser of the brethren (see Revelation 12:10). All the more, when attacked to this magnitude, it's such a struggle to overcome. It's not the act itself; he sends all of his demon spirits that have been assigned against you to torment your mind.

In Tamar's case, there were levels of injury. The enemy stole away her purity and dignity and destroyed her reputation, a low blow to a woman in her day. When a person has been violated, there is an interruption in the soul, mind, and body; an intrusion, if you will. If you've ever had your home broken into, you can grasp my meaning. It's like walking into your home and seeing everything in disarray. Your mind starts racing while you are trying to figure out what just happened. You gather yourself together and slowly begin to clean up the mess, wondering, *Who entered my domain and put their hands on my belongings without my permission?* And wondering, *Will the intruder come back? Am I safe?* You proceed with your life, but you're still shaken inside as you relive the trauma. Are you feeling me now? Exactly as one's home has been broken into, so it is with one's soul. Once you have been traumatized, it is a battle getting back to normalcy.

I must reiterate: who was Tamar? A king's daughter! Satan doesn't care who you are or what your status in life is. He knows your address, and just as sure as you live, he's coming. No doubt Tamar was fragmented by this one act of wickedness, and then rejection deepened the wound. The Hebrew word for rejection is MAAS; it means "to despise, to abhor and to cast away." *Webster* defines it as "to throw away, set aside, or discard as marred or worthless."

Rejection is another spirit straight from the pit of hell, one of the chief arsenals of the enemy. In our society, rejection is displayed everywhere—rejection from family and friends, rejection from a spouse, rejection on the job, even rejection from within the churches, places where it should not be.

People experience rejection for many reasons, mostly superficial. We are fragile beings, and the effects of rejection go deep. This demonic attack destroys your self-esteem and courage. It makes you feel as though something is wrong with you. Once your self-esteem is attacked, there goes your self-worth. Yes, it makes you feel worthless. As a result, you have the tendency to become a doormat for people, which I feel Tamar would have been for Amnon had she married him, simply because her presence would be a constant reminder of his crime.

I experienced rejection from my parents on a regular basis growing up. Being the bomb hairstylist that I was, Mother would frequent my salon. She had a standing appointment and would often show up pissed off about something, or perhaps at me. I wondered why she'd come in the first place. I would try and overlook her and strike up a conversation, to share an exciting event or a plan of some sort.

Shortly into my conversation, Mother would make a gesture of disgust. She'd grunt, turn up her nose, wave her hand, and blow me off.

Mind you, she was at my salon, getting her hair dressed by the daughter she despised. Mother always gave me the impression that I owed her for being born. Guess with that mind-set, she felt everything I did for her was owed because she was my mother, no need in me expecting any gratitude from her. In my adulthood, it affected my self-confidence and esteem greatly. I couldn't comprehend her reasoning. Being older helped me to see more clearly. I saw that my mother had low self-image also. Well, living with a man like my father, it's no wonder. This would explain why she called me out of my name often. A statement she made confirmed this. "I used to not like my nose when I was younger, but now I'm okay with it," she said one day while waiting to get her hair done. When she saw me, it was like looking in the mirror, and she didn't like it. You see, she dumped all of her pain of self-hate on me.

My heavenly Father saw me and began to work on my behalf. One Sunday morning I went to visit a church where a couple whom I'd met previously attended. When I walked in, I noticed them sitting near the back. I went over and sat in the seat behind them. As I took my seat, I greeted them. To my surprise, they both ignored me, giving me the cold shoulder. Wait a minute, I thought; this couple and I are acquainted. They had been to my house for dinner. The wife frequented my salon. I mean, I was her stylist, for goodness sake! What in the world was going on? I began to feel offended. As usual, I wondered, what could I have done wrong or what was wrong with me. Abruptly, the Holy Ghost interrupted my thoughts and said, "And you better not get offended. I want to show you something." The Lord opened my eyes, and I saw for the first time what was happening in the spirit realm. He showed me there was a spirit of jealousy operating in the wife; in order to keep peace in the home, the husband went along with the wife and they both shunned me. It's funny now, but then, not so much. After I saw by the spirit the hearts of this couple, He spoke again, saying, "You see, there's nothing wrong with you. They're the ones with the problem." I hadn't felt more liberated in all my life. That day the feeling of rejection began to be stripped away simply because the Lord opened my eyes once again.

The time had come for my healing. Just as God spoke to me in Ecclesiastes 3:3, *"To everything there is a season, A time for every purpose."* Being that there is a time for healing, it speaks to the fact that it is God's will to heal us, whether it be physically, emotionally, or spiritually.

My question then is, what is the purpose? Ah, would you like to know? Go with me to the Gospel of John:

> *Now as Jesus passed by, He saw a man who was blind from his birth. And His disciples asked Him, saying, "Rabbi, who sinned, this man or his parents, that he was born blind?" Jesus answered, "Neither this man nor his parents sinned, but that the works of God should be revealed in him."*
>
> —John 9:1-3

Listen beloved, by now you should understand that the heavenly Father likes to show off. He works on our behalf for His glory. What works? His wonderful mercy and awesome grace. Everything I suffered was so that the works of God would be manifested in me.

This passage of scripture is paramount simply because it helps us understand the Father's ways concerning our well-being. Our infirmities do not limit God's abilities, neither is He turned off because of them. It is because of our infirmities that He is so eager to reveal Himself. Ya gotta love it. Thinking back on it all is like breathing in fresh air. Oh shoot, you ought to hear people's comments when I tell them my story. "Wow, you don't look like you've been through anything like that" is what they say. With that said, I encourage you to look into the biblical perspective of healing. In Hebrew, the word for healing is RAPHE'; it means "to cure, heal, repair, mend, restore health."

Only God knows how desperately we need all of the above. I cannot express enough the healing power of God. Heretofore, we must look to Him to cure all that ails us. Speaking of a cure, I'm reminded of when I was very young in the Lord. I developed a skin fungus. It was working its way over my whole body. The fungus was itchy, with a burning sensation, plus it discolored my complexion. I was most miserable. I went to the doctor about my condition. All he would do was to write a prescription for a particular cream, which only temporarily subdued the symptoms. It never really worked. I decided to believe God for my healing. I started talking to Him about it in prayer: "Lord I want to be healed. I don't want to be soothed with medicine." When it didn't happen right away, I went back and forth in my mind. One day I'd believe and the next I was going to the doctor.

Frustrated with my wishy-washy mind-set I determined to believe God once and for all. I stood on the principle of the Word and declared I was healed by faith.

One Sunday morning, I got dressed as usual for church. When I arrived, the secretary was standing at the podium making the announcements. I walked up the aisle to my normal spot, third row from the front, and took a seat in the pew. The order of service changed as all the saints began to testify and sing songs. Worship service was high-spirited, which I always enjoyed. During the offering I casually looked down at my arms and I gasped with surprise—the fungus was not there! I was so excited; I couldn't wait to get home. Church service ended and I flew out of the double doors. My ride was waiting out front. "Thank you for the ride home," I said as I walked up to the car. I got in and away we went. Sitting in the back seat, thoughts of my encounter raced through my mind. "What will I find when I get home—will the fungus be completely gone?" We finally pulled into the parking spot and I said my goodbyes. I rushed into my apartment, undressed, and began to examine the rest of my body and saw that it was totally gone. I had been healed by the power of God. He'd heard my prayer.

Wait. God did such an amazing work that it was as if I'd never had the fungus. There was absolutely no trace of it. Are you feeling me, beloved? If He has the power to heal our physical bodies, He can also heal our broken hearts.

ANGER FOR HEALING?

Then said the Lord, Doest thou well to be angry?
—Jonah 4:3

Anger is an important subject to discuss. There is a right anger and a wrong anger, and we need to understand both. The wrong kind of anger is driven by the flesh and is sinful. We know according to the scripture that those who operate in the flesh cannot please God. This spirit of anger can spin us completely out of control, causing harm in a way that impairs, if we do not practice self-restraint. On the other hand, we do well if we understand righteous anger and the good reason for it.

The Bible declares, *"God is angry with the wicked everyday"* —Psalm 7:11. We read about Lot, a righteous man who became vexed because of the wickedness of the immoral people surrounding him (see 2 Peter 2:7). We should absolutely be angry at sinful practices and injustice perpetrated in our society against fellow humans. So it is with personal abuses. We need to ask ourselves the same question the Lord asked Jonah: *"Doest thou well to be angry?"* Yes, you will need to get angry—downright mad! It too is an important step to the process. It wasn't until I became an adult, I mean good and grown, that I had a right to be angry about my abuse and my abusers. I had a right to stand up for myself. To put a stop to it even if it meant refusing their company. You see, if I allowed them, they would continue their abuses, as if I was the same fifteen-year-old child. One day I was driving along and I began to think about all that stuff I'd suffered at the hands of my parents.

With all the molestation, the degrading name-calling, the rejection, and the stress they put me under, something happened within me. The next thing I knew, all of the "how dare yous" began to flow out of my mouth. I cried with tears of mixed emotions, screaming at the top of my lungs, "How dare you mistreat me! How dare you call me ugly and make me feel bad about myself? How dare you make me feel I wasn't good enough? How dare you sexually molest me and turn your guilt trip on me and make me feel it was my fault? How dare you reject me, I was my father's seed, the man you chose to be intimate with—I came from your womb! I was a part of you. Didn't you know when you rejected me you were rejecting yourself?"

Oh, I had a good cry that day. I was determined not to take it anymore. There's the old saying, "Even dogs get tired." If my great-grandma were here, that's what she'd tell you. From then on, I was going to demand my respect. Let's revisit Tamar's words again. "This evil of sending me away is worse than the other that you did to me."

Rejection is the nuclear giant of the enemy, posing to gravely threaten or damage our confidence. We will all face giants in our lives at one time or another. A dream I had lends itself to this reality. I saw myself carrying around a decapitated head by the hair. I walked into a certain room and placed the head on top of a table, then began to finger-comb the hair as though I was prepping a mannequin in my beauty college days. I was talking and showing this head to certain persons in the room, but I couldn't see who the head belonged to. Neither could I hear what I was saying. But when I turned the head around, I saw it was my mother. I went from house to house showing it off, when suddenly I woke. In astonishment, I asked the Lord, "What was that about?" Immediately He responded to me and said "Goliath!" This is what rejection is like, I said to myself. A defiant giant that must be slain! In the story of David and Goliath, we see that toleration breeds justification. In other words, the longer persistent misuse is tolerated, the more justified the perpetrator feels. This was true with David. But something happened when he heard the defiant words of Goliath repeated over and over; he became angry. A holy indignation rose within and he slayed his enemy, never to rise again.

SEEING THINGS AS THEY ARE

Things began to fall into proper perspective. I started seeing things as they were and not as I wanted them. You can't make people love and accept you; you can only try. In the event they don't, it's their loss. I realized something—as a woman of God, I was a good daughter, and with all of my love and talents, I had a whole lot to give. My mother never did accept me, but I came to terms with it.

So that's what
rejection is like,
I said to myself.
A defiant Giant
that must be slain!

Nevertheless, I wasn't going to let anyone's negative opinion define me, not anymore. Okay, so what am I saying? Get angry, but don't stay angry. Get angry enough to rise above your haters, and start moving forward.

The Bible is clear about the right kind of anger:

> *Be angry, and do not sin… do not let the sun go down on your wrath, nor give place to the Devil.* –Ephesians 4:26

According to *W. E. Vine's Expository Dictionary*, anger is "any natural impulse, or desire or disposition." Webster defines anger as "a strong feeling of displeasure toward a person or thing that opposes, annoys, harms, or mistreats one." Well, I'd had enough abuse for my lifetime, and I began to rise. Of course, my family had a hard time with the new me. Regardless, I knew the time would come when I'd have to stand up for myself. My mother had a bad habit of calling her children names, and if you weren't her favorite, you got it worse. One day I went to the family home after church service. Everyone was gathered in the kitchen, preparing for the usual early Sunday dinner. I forget what led up to her need to demean me in front of my siblings, but she went there, calling me Blackie, as she did when I was a child. I wasn't taking it anymore. I looked at my mother and said, "Will somebody tell Mrs. Jonnye that she's black too!" After all, she and I were of the same complexion. Well, she never called me that name again. I recognized the abuse, rose, and challenged the enemy of rejection to his face and stopped his mouth. Listen. Anything that makes you feel bad, hurt, and demeaned is abuse. You can't make excuses or overlook them with sayings such as, "Well, that's just the way they are," or "perhaps they're having a bad day." No, you must recognize abuse and put an end to it, no matter who the abuser is. This behavior is driven by the enemy. Therefore, you must take authority over it in the power of Jesus' name. You're probably wondering if I let the sun go down on my wrath. I wish I could say that I didn't, but I'm certain I did, though it was not intentional.

Only by God's grace did I overcome the anger and resentment I felt all those years. I really did love my family; unfortunately, they had deep-seated issues and were in desperate need of salvation. Getting through to them was difficult because they were stubborn. "Like talking to a brick back," as my father used to say.

FLASHBACKS

No one goes through the healing process without having to deal with the pain of flashbacks. The clinical definition is "a sudden and distressing vivid memory of an event in the past, typically as the result of psychological trauma." For instance, when going through a casual day, suddenly something triggers a memory of repressed feelings. It could be a smell or a sound. It could be a color of some sort or something repeated from your past. Along with being painful, flashbacks are emotionally wearisome. They are designed to break you down by reliving the moments over and over again in your mind.

There were times when a flashback would come while my husband and I were intimate. I would find myself in the bathroom, crying in silence. Christmas holiday was drawing near when my then-husband asked, "What do you want for Christmas?" "An exercise bike." I replied, What a nice gesture, I thought. Especially with us being newlyweds and all. Waiting anxiously, that day couldn't come fast enough. Without any more delays Christmas arrived. I awoke early that morning, with enthusiasm. Stepping out of bed I slipped into a pair of house shoes and shuffled into the living room, expecting to see my new bike. At first glance, I was let down. The dude went to a secondhand store and bought me a used piece of equipment. I was madder than a hungry junkyard dog, on Christmas morning. Here's the thing that triggered it. Years earlier, my mother decided she'd buy me a Christmas gift. That was odd, as she never bought Christmas gifts for me. I certainly wasn't expecting anything from her; that's for sure. I happened to be in the kitchen washing her dishes when she walked in with a box in her hand. She didn't bother with gift-wrapping. It was an old brown box that had been used for something else. She handed it to me and said, "Merry Christmas, I got this for you. Maybe you can use it on one of your fashion designs." Turning around, I took the box and pulled out a used fox fur collar that was terribly unappealing.

The price tag said two dollars and ninety-nine cents. It was a mess. It's not that I'm above secondhand, depending upon what it is, but let's be real, *for Christmas*? At that moment, I wanted to be vindictive and wrap it up and give it back to her the following Christmas. I so wanted her to feel what I felt. My heavenly Father dealt with me and I let it go. Thank the Lord.

When I saw that used bike parked in the front room that morning, I relived a moment of my past and I was way pissed off! Now, that was a different emotion; usually I would be brought to tears, but not this time. I thought about how I put my all into shopping for my husband and made sure he got top-of-the-line. When you love someone, you give them the best gift you can; you know what I mean? What was that? A flashback. Another instance was the time Mother came into the salon to get her usual set and style. I didn't mind caring for my mother's hair, even though she couldn't appreciate it.

The relationship she displayed between us was affectation. Even the times she was nice weren't genuine. Close family members began to notice and made their subtle comments. Anyway, she came and sat in my shampoo chair, and I laid her head back in the bowl. I reached for the hose and turned on the water, testing it to make sure that it wasn't too hot. As I began to gently shampoo my mother's hair, I'm having a flashback moment of when Mother used to shampoo my hair. I was about six years old. She would shampoo all of her daughters' hair in the kitchen sink, as would most mothers back in the day. Mother lifted me onto the countertop and put my head under the running water facedown. For a young child, this position was terrifying.

I felt like I was going to drown. As I screamed to the top of my lungs out of fear and tried to pull my head away from the running water, Mother forced my head down and with an acrid tone, she said, "Get that head back under there!" Looking back, it seemed as though she was trying to punish me somehow. Mother's approach was different when she shampooed my younger sisters, she would gently lay them on their backs and lower their heads in the sink, which allowed the water to run down away from their faces. When I came to myself, I was feeling a low-grade surge of malice. I said to myself, "Lord, it's a good thing I'm saved right now."

Then there was our "family picture day." Everyone moved about the home sprucing themselves up for the Olan Mills photographer. The boy's dressed in their Sunday shirt and tie while the girl's followed suit, adorned in their own special attire. My mother combed my hair straight back to make me look bald. The baby girls, on the other hand, were given hairstyles with beautiful curls combed to one side, cascading over their shoulders. What was that? A flashback.

I was thirty-four years old at the time; that had happened twenty-seven years ago, but it felt like only yesterday. Another incident occurred when my father was in the Air Force and the family had to get vaccinated. This was one of the worse experiences of my little life. We arrived at the air force base hospital. The place looked colorless and desolate, and the smell of rubbing alcohol filled the air. I couldn't have been more afraid. There I was, with my parents in front of the doctor, and he was about to stick a needle in my arm—a three-year-old black child screaming bloody murder while her mother is smacking and pinching her on her behind to get her to sit still—which only made things worse. No doubt my cries were heard all over that hospital. You might think my mother would have shown some TLC, like, "Come on, baby, everything is going to be all right. Mama is here with you." There was absolutely no comfort nor understanding of my fears, not even an ounce. When I became an adult, the idea of having a needle stuck in my arm was still a distressing moment for me.

What was that? A flashback. Another flashback moment happened when I saw some large, beautiful seashells on display at one of the department stores. They were nicely polished, the color of the sand with a salmon-pink interior. My mind went to the time when our family lived in Guam, located in Oceania. My father had been stationed in the Philippines for about a year while we resided on the island in base housing until his return. On this little island, my siblings and I got acquainted with fresh coconuts and sandy beaches. With our many trips to the beach, Mother became fond of seashells and had a beautiful collection of different sizes and shapes.

One day our father had planned a family day trip to the beach. He loaded up the car with fishing gear while our mother prepared a lunch basket. Soon we were on our way. He drove up on the sand and parked the car, and we all got out. Mother and Father gathered all their gear and headed toward the ocean. I stayed on the beach, watching them in the distance. I had no desire to go out into the water. I was only four years old at the time and couldn't swim. But there was a big problem. An infantry of wild mosquitoes flew in and began to attack my flesh. I felt as though I was being eaten alive. I was no match for them. Adding to my distresses was a chilling wind blowing in off the ocean. The family car was the only escape, but the doors were locked, there was nowhere to run.

Time passed, and the pain of every bite was unbearable. I didn't know what to do to get away from this torture. I saw my parents in the shallow water a short way out, along with a few of my siblings. Mother and Father were bent over, collecting shells from the sea floor. I began to walk out into the ocean in sheer panic, crying frantically. With every step I took, I could see the little sea monsters as we called them, moving around in between the rocks under my feet. Besides being ambushed by the mosquitos, the sea creatures made me even more afraid. One thing I noticed though, the further out I went, the fewer mosquitos were attacking. I walked up to my parents, shaking with each little step. They stared at me in disgust, as if to say, "What are you crying about!" Looking back on it, you have to ask where their parental concern was.

When I became an adult, I brought up the incident and asked them why they didn't come to my rescue. "You saw I was hurting, yet left me crying," I said. "Why did you let that happen to me?" My mother looked with embarrassment, not really sure what to say. So my father stepped in quickly and said, "We didn't know." That was the head of the household's common lie. As I dealt with the pain of the past, to my surprise, it began to ease.

One Sunday I was teaching the children's class at my church. I enjoyed teaching them; they were always wide-eyed and eager to learn about Jesus. While teaching, I held baby Janice in my arms. She was a little over two years of age and had fallen asleep. After class was over I sat holding her, waiting until her parents arrived to pick her up. In the meantime I gazed upon her little body. Seeing how beautiful she was, my mind flashed back to the time when I was her age. I wondered how anyone could sexually abuse this precious gift. My only thoughts were to love, protect, and guard her, and she wasn't even my child.

Herein is the good news. This time, when I flashed back to my past abuse, there was no pain. It was now only memories. Oh! How I used to reflect on that unrighteous plague of emotional trauma; an ongoing mental battle throughout the day tearing me up inside. By late nightfall, I would be filled with sobbing. Lying prostrate on the floor, I'd cry out to my heavenly Father for help. He would always come to my aid. His presence would fill the room and His love would fill my heart. Divine encounters like this brought about my healing. Every level of healing and deliverance I received was like a new wave of refreshment. Yes, beloved, it gets better, until pain becomes a thing of the past. How did I know I was completely healed? God sent me right back to the place of my pain.

Here's my story . . .

I received word through one of my siblings that my mother was very ill. She had been diagnosed with lung cancer. Immediately, I made preparations to go and see about her. At the time, I was living in Phoenix, Arizona, which was only an hour-and-a-half drive. After a few visits, I moved back home to care of my parents. It's always that one sibling who willingly steps up to the plate.

I loved them despite their ways. Spiritually, I had matured a lot and felt honored to care for them, especially my mother, who was by now in her seventies. Despite her age and illness, she looked good. I observed she didn't have much fight in her to battle the cancer. Her mind was dwindling; she wasn't able to articulate even the simplest verbiage. When it came to eating right and exercising, I had to use a whole lot of encouragement. I was happy when she would finally decide to participate.

One particular morning she agreed to get out of bed. I helped her get dressed, and we walked up the street hand-in-hand. The neighbors waved with smiles as we passed by. It was a cool spring morning, with sunny blue skies. I noticed dandelion seeds blowing in the wind.

My mind went back to the time when, as a child, I'd run after the little white fuzzy seeds to catch them. My mind journeyed back to how I used to play up and down these same streets and walking to and from school many a day. I used to babysit for the neighbor's kids, though most of them have come and gone. Hmm, I made fifty cents an hour back then. So many memories passed through my mind as I focused on the seeds blowing to their destinies by the force of the gentle wind. I wondered where their final destinations would be, especially since they had no choice in the matter. Suddenly, a dream came to me. It was one of those vivid night visions that seemed like real life. I saw myself walking along the roadside when a gust of wind came up behind me and jolted my body up into the sky.

The impact was so strong that even though I was asleep, I felt pain as it jerked me away. Up, up, and up I went, flying very high, feet first, with my face upward and my arms lying flat against my side. I looked around and saw many other people being blown with the wind as well. They were of all different genders and nationalities. The wind took me over mountains and valleys, and I could see green and gold-colored fields below. After a while the wind let me down, and I had begun walking along a different highway when I woke up.

After seeing the dandelion seeds, I understood the dream. Symbolically, our lives take the same course as the seeds. As the seeds are blown toward their destiny to be planted, flourish, and grow, so the wind of the Spirit blows each of us in the direction of our destiny.

As the seeds are
blown toward
their destiny to be
planted, flourish,
and grow, so the
wind of the Spirit
blows each of us
in the direction
of our destiny.

In the midst of caring for my parents, I asked the Lord why He'd sent me back home, a place where there was so much pain. Not that I was resentful in any way, although it wasn't an easy task. My parents hadn't changed their ways at all, and we still had obvious friction. I knew within my heart that out of all their children, I wasn't the one that they would have desired to be their caretaker when the time came. Whenever my father became angry with me, he would threaten to put me out of his house. My decision to leave my job and lifestyle to care for them didn't amount to much as far as my father was concerned. He finally told me to leave his house, knowing I didn't have a job or money. I began to pack up my belonging once again, hoping that perhaps this time Mother would stand up for her child in her final hour. Perhaps I was hoping for too much. But I was right all along—she was weak. When I handed my father the house key, he snatched it away. As usual, Mother stood by his side. I walked past them as they lay together on their bed. My parents didn't hide their emotions. They were awfully upset with me. I left without uttering a word, shaking my head, wondering how he made my mother's crisis all about him. She was the one who needed special care. I found my way to another women's shelter and quickly found a position in a salon. But it would take time to build a clientele. Again, this was not easy.

A few weeks passed when I got word that Mother's health had declined. Late that evening I drove across town to visit her from the women's shelter where I had been residing. I walked in her bedroom where she lay in bed. Mother immediately perked up when she saw me, but couldn't express it with words. I saw she wasn't going to live much longer. I really didn't know how to feel. I prayed for her while I combed her hair and massaged her back. I kissed her on the cheek and said, "Mom, I don't hold anything against you." I left and returned to the women's shelter. She died later that night. I returned to the family home early the next morning. I walked into Mother's bedroom where she lay in the same position as when I left. I lay across her now lifeless body, which was cold and stiff. I began to weep. I thought about the words I wanted to say when she was alive, but didn't. They were better left unsaid. I thought about all the attempts I'd made to bridge a broken relationship, now over. My mother was gone . . .

But here's where it gets good. After all I encountered up to my mother's death, I saw the hand of God and the work He had done in me. One morning I lay on my bed, meditating upon the Lord's goodness, when I realized there was no more emotional pain. Years of praying and confessing the Word concerning forgiveness had worked. The anger and resentment I had toward my parents was completely gone, and I felt not even the slightest sting of the memories. Once again, joy flooded my heart.

I'm truly healed!" I said to myself. This was a great victory for me. I confess, months before I knew of my mother's condition, my Holy Ghost dealt with me about going back to Tucson. I was resistant because of my awful experiences.

Only in going back to the place of my pain did the Father reveal that I had conquered my enemies. I was able to love the ones who hated me, care for the ones who didn't care for me, walk hand in hand with the very one who rejected me, and yes, feed the one who molested me. Listen. Dealing with the pain and getting past it is vital. You will understand as I disclose my next revelation. In the midst of it all, the Lord opened my eyes and showed me that His divine plan for my life was about to unfold.

God was taking me somewhere, to the very place chosen by Him, where I would flourish indeed. You see, beloved, it's not about where you come from; it's about where you're going. What GOD had in store was too wonderful, too glorious for me to continue holding on to past hurts!

Apostle Paul speaks to us in Romans 8:18:

> *For I reckon that the sufferings of this present time are not worthy to be compared with the glory which shall be revealed in us.*

THE BEST IS YET TO COME!

I thought it was ironic, after God called me into the ministry, that He spoke, saying, "I have called you to do a work, to declare my name, and I will be your front. I want you to love my people and love them unconditionally and walk in my favor." While I hadn't experienced true love then, He commanded me to love. Beloved, God is love. It is impossible to be in Him and not show love. The day I said "yes" to the Lord and gave Him my life, I chose love. I don't know about you, but I wouldn't have it any other way. Let me say it on this wise: if I stay broken and you stay broken, what do we have? Continued chaos. Somebody has to rise and be the initiator, declaring boldly—*the cycle stops here!*

When we walk in love, the Word says we are mature, displaying our Father's character. In seeking the Lord, I learned through revelation what true love is. God is glorified when we love, not hate; in kindness, not anger; in forgiveness, not bitterness; in truth, not deception. Unconditional love is to undo the works of the enemy by the power of the gospel. I had to learn that it doesn't mean allowing people to walk all over me. Yes, it is kindness, and yes, it is patience. But it is also *loving a person enough to tell them the truth even if they don't like it.* It's *loving them enough to see them repent of their sin and change their detrimental habits.*

Listen, beloved. When you walk in love, you experience the richness of peace and the favor of God on your life. In the Body of Christ, we hear a lot taught on favor. For example: "a seven-step formula to divine favor" or "confess it over your life" and all those things. While it is true that we must confess the Word, herein is the principle: walk in love and you will experience the favor of God. It's just that simple. We walk in the higher places of life when we walk in love. I challenge you to rise to the occasion and watch God. God not only takes us back to our place of pain; as I stated before, He wants to take you to a place you never thought of in your wildest dreams. Listen to the story of Mephibosheth:

Now David said, "Is there still anyone who is left of the house of Saul, that I may show him kindness for Jonathan's sake?" And there was a servant of the house of Saul whose name was Ziba. So when they had called him to David, the king said to him, "Are you Ziba?" He said, "At your service!" Then the king said, "Is there not still someone of the house of Saul, to whom I may show the kindness of God? And Ziba said to the king, There is still a son of Jonathan who is lame in his feet." So the king said to him, "Where is he?" And Ziba said to the king, "Indeed he is in the house of Machir the son of Ammiel, in Lo Debar." Then King David sent and brought him out of the house of Machir the son of Ammiel, from Lo Debar. Now when Mephibosheth the son of Jonathan, the son of Saul, had come to David, He fell on his face and prostrated himself. Then David said, "Mephibosheth? And he answered, "Here is your servant!" So David said to him, "Do not fear, for I will surely show you kindness for Jonathan your father's sake, and will restore to you all the land of Saul your grandfather, and you shall eat bread at my table continually." Then he bowed himself, and said, "What is your servant, that you should look upon such a dead dog as I? And the king called to Ziba, Saul's servant, and said to him, "I have given to your master's son all that belonged to Saul and to all his house. So Mephibosheth dwelt in Jerusalem, for he ate continually at the king's table. And he was lame in both his feet.

—2 Samuel 9:1–7; 13

Mephibosheth's life is an example of how the wind of the Spirit—in one swoosh!—takes one from the pain of brokenness and shame to eating at a king's table. Beloved, whether your destiny is sitting with dignitaries or standing in a pulpit, God, in His divine wisdom, knows how to get you to the place that will ultimately reveal His glory in you in the end.

PERSONAL REFLECTIONS

Everyone has experienced brokenness on some level.

- Reflecting back, describe your brokenness in a few sentences.

    A. How long ago did it occur?

    B. If you were to explain your present season, where would you say you are emotionally and spiritually?

- What is the first step to becoming whole?

A. What are the two pertinent parts that you as the believer are responsible for?

1.

2.

- Why does the Father command us to forgive?

- What are the dangers of walking in unforgiveness?

  A.

  B.

  C.

- Life is not always fair. Sometimes it can be downright harsh. Jesus stated that offenses are inevitable. How does the Father aid us in overcoming pain?

- With the understanding that becoming whole is a process…

  A. Where do you feel you are in the process of recovery?

  B. What do you feel is your deepest need right now?

  C. How does your need relate to the woman with the issue of blood in Luke 8:43?

D. What would you like to see different in your life and for those involved?

- It is the will of the Father to establish his children. Explain how and why he establishes us.

NOTES

CHAPTER III

DARE TO RISE?

Rejoice not against me, O mine enemy: when I fall, I shall arise.
—Micah 7:8 KJV

HOPE

HOPE

But thou art He that took me out of the womb; thou didst make me hope when I was upon my mother's breast.
—Psalm 22:9

Ah, HOPE, how sweet the sound.

Hope is of highest significance to the life of the believer. For hope sets the tone of endurance, fearlessly pronounces survival, and boldly proclaims accomplishments.

The psalmist speaks of our Lord Jesus in this text. He is our example of hope. At a tender young age, while on His mother's breast, Jesus hoped in God, His Father.

Since hope is so significant, what does it mean? In Hebrew, the word is BATACH; it means "to attach oneself, to trust, confide in, and to feel safe." Many have placed their hope in persons or things temporal or superficial. Much like a raveling cord during a crucial moment of rescue, inevitably one will wind up disappointed.

So then, what is hope? Real hope is Christ; He is the hope of glory. If I were to express it in my own words, I would say it is the ability to believe beyond the present, without worry and anxiety.

I experienced a hope moment when I was just a kid. I couldn't have been much older than three years of age. My elder brother and I went walking to the corner store. Our parents had given us some small change to buy what every child craves—candy.

When we arrived, there was a beautiful red balloon that captured my eye. I bought it, along with a few candy treats. On the way home, we walked through the rocky side streets. With my balloon in one hand and coins in the other, I slipped and fell and the balloon burst spontaneously.

I cried out of embarrassment and pain, while my brother laughed me to scorn. Somehow I found the strength to collect my little self. I lifted my hand that held the coins and said, "I still got some more money!" Hope was already at work inside me, even then. I learned very early in life that no matter the circumstance, believing and trusting for a brighter day sparks indescribable strength that causes one to rise, shake off the dust and forge forward. This, beloved, only comes from the Lord. My question is, does God really cause little children to hope? I would say so. When I was about the age of nine, I desperately wanted the acceptance and approval of my parents. I wanted to hear the words "I love you. You're beautiful and special." Well, I never did.

One day I was in my bedroom, standing in front of the mirror, staring at my reflection. I began to hear my mother's voice, her words playing over and over in my head. "You're so ugly. Look at that big nose you got. It's bigger than mine. You're so black!" From deep within, I began to speak back words that were totally the opposite. As I stood there, I gave myself a smile and said, "One day I'm going to be pretty." I said it again and again. Here's the amazing thing about it—I believed it. Not having an understanding of the power of words then, I was contending with the negative words spoken over me. Words were used to break me, and it would take words to build me up again (see Proverbs 18:21).

But how did I know to say those words? How was this possible at a young age? Where did the words come from? I believe it was HOPE.

Because I didn't get nurturing from my parents as all children should—proper nurturing that causes one to grow up having healthy thoughts, good self-esteem, and courage—my heavenly Father deliberately stepped into my life very early and fostered me.

The psalmist goes on to say,

> *"I was cast upon thee from birth. From my mother's womb You have been my God."*
>
> —Psalm 22:10

It would be years later before I would come to understand that I was specially handpicked from my beginning for His glory. And because I was chosen, the omnipotent God would preserve me from the perils of the enemy.

Here is my story of hope . . .

Telling this story brings me much joy, which is what hope does. I thought about my bishop in Houston, Texas, Henry Melvin Bolden. He was an old-school holiness preacher, a man of faith. He didn't just talk faith; he lived it. He understood the fickleness in man, especially when it came to the truth of the gospel. Speaking the truth is not popular; it never was. A preacher could easily lose his or her supporters if they didn't like what was preached. Bishop Bolden would say, "As long as God's green earth grows cotton, I'll have a suit, and as long as God makes cows, I'll have a steak!" His faith was so powerfully evident that I hungered and thirsted for it.

I grabbed ahold of that same faith, and I too began to walk it out; believing God wasn't difficult for me. He was all I had. He was all I knew. If God said it, I believed it, and by faith it was going to happen. I was securely locked in. Nothing seemed impossible.

Faith and hope go hand in hand. Faith caused me to expect that which I hoped for. Despite the lack of nurturing, the abuse, and the victimization, I had hope—a hope that does not disappoint.

This virtue is inherent in every soul on the planet; it is a gift from God. He put it there for one simple reason, so that we would reach for someone and something beyond ourselves, that someone being Himself.

Now, here we pose a question. If God put this wonderful gift in every man, why are so many living in hopelessness?

HOPELESSNESS

> *But I don't have the strength to endure. I have nothing to live for.* —Job 6:11

I don't think you can talk about hope and not mention hopelessness. It is when one feels that to hope is nothing more than pure vanity, that things will never get any better than the present. The reality is, the pain of a tragedy can become so severe that it is possible to lose hope. This mindset destroys any possibility of hope and brings one to a place of giving up. Once that state of mind takes hold, it will lead to a road of utter self-destruction. In this situation individuals are consumed with depression. They often become so desperate to feel better that they attempt to solve their passing issues with the permanence of suicide, adding more trouble to the initial problem.

Despair knows no boundaries, race, or gender. Whether you are a confessing Christian or a ranking sinner, the issues are real. It happened to Job, a God-fearing man, blameless and upright. You see, when you are in the midst of it, it's hard to see your way out of it.

Hopelessness comes by way of discouragement. If you don't know how to fight using the Word of God, you will walk around under a dark cloud of sadness and doom. Sadness and depression can become chronic, causing one to succumb to the idea that failure is the sum of life.

Many live in hopelessness today. When I am on the streets witnessing for the Lord, I often see people who have given up on life. It's one thing to see it from a distance, but when it hits close to home, the effects are even more heart wrenching.

I think of my brother Craig who now is deceased. His life was cut off at the early of thirty-three. Craig died of the horrible HIV that he contracted while incarcerated. His childhood experience was no different than mine, really; he too was hated by his father from childhood. After reaching adulthood he lived a homosexual lifestyle, though I don't believe my brother wanted that orientation. In part, he was driven, and in another part, he was deceived.

This young man experienced the onslaught of Satan in his life from the time of his birth. Of course, no one had the spiritual insight to discern what was happening to him. This is why it is so important to have godly parents who pray for their children, covering them with the Word of God. Our family was a far cry from that.

We all picked on Craig, calling him a sissy, among other names. This was not unusual for the family. Everybody was picked on and called out of their name. It depended on who was the victim for that day.

We learned this negative behavior from our parents. My mother's reasoning for it was absolutely absurd. In her words, "You're going to be called names when you get out in the world!" So I guess, in her mind, she was taking us through boot camp to get us ready. Which begs the question, where is the logic? There is none.

We were all victims of circumstance. Yet I still felt bad about all the name-calling and abuse we put on each other. As I stated in an earlier chapter, my father was abused by his father, and my father passed on the abuse to his children. I'm sure the cycle runs way back.

My brother Craig and I both suffered abuse and longed for affection. Though we were raised under the same roof, we took different paths in life. I chose the way of the Lord, and he rebelled and went to the dark side.

Why is it that I made it out and he didn't? Perhaps it was partly because of the degree of his brokenness. He became hopeless, coupled with anger; there's really no simple answer or quick fix. He made bad choices, which led to his demise.

In retrospect, all my brother needed was love, especially from his father. Well, he never got it. My brother probably felt that no one cared anyway. He likely thought, "What difference does it make what I do or what happens to me?" At least that's the way he lived his life. One thing is sure—every negative word that was spoken over Craig became a reality. He lost hope, and his life spiraled out of control.

My brother was a petite young man, handsome with pretty brown skin. He liked agriculture. You know, digging around in the dirt and watching things grow. His father was an athlete, the rough and tough guy. Many fathers want their sons to be like them in order to be proud of them. Craig was the complete opposite, and his father despised him because of it.

I believe the lack of love from his father drove him to drugs, and from there to homosexuality, to prison, and to HIV. Our father provoked his children many a day. Although the Bible states, *"Honor your father and mother"* —Ephesians 6:2, he made it awfully difficult to respect and honor him as a father. The respect we did show him was mostly out of fear of punishment. I prayed for Craig often, hoping he would accept the Lord Jesus into his life. The few times he came to visit I'd invite him to church. After the service, we would talk about God, but his heart wasn't open. It saddens me to say, Craig was a skeptic. He had only negative things to say about what was preached.

I had been residing in Atlanta, Georgia, when the Lord revealed to me in a dream that Craig was sick unto death. I awoke with tears running down my face. I didn't want to receive it. For days I cried out to the Lord on his behalf.

A few weeks had passed when a phone call from my family delivered the bad news concerning my brother. In confirmation of my dream, they said Craig was dying. My sister explained that he had contracted the HIV. Everyone was shaken by the news, especially Mother. She took it the hardest and didn't want to believe it either.

I loved my brother and would do my best to encourage him when he would listen. Unfortunately, he succumbed to the dark world of drugs and sexual perversity around him. These became a stronghold in his life.

Listen, beloved; hopelessness is no joke. If you can imagine a tiny ship in the middle of the stormy sea without a sail, tossed by the waves and driven by the wind, so it was with my brother. He existed in an ocean of utter despair, only to be dashed against the rocks of calamity and broken into pieces. Total destruction, cut off without remedy—that's what life without hope is like.

During all of this, I began to feel the pull of God that I would be leaving the city of Atlanta. I received a profound word of knowledge affirming this: "You will be going to a place where your winters would be like spring." Soon I realized I would be going back home. I closed the church and my salon, packed up all of my belongings, and headed west.

Once I arrived, I visited my brother in the bedroom where he grew up. The disease had already taken a toll on his body; he was skin and bones. My prayers went up before God continually for Craig's healing, it became apparent that it was about the saving of his soul.

I had a dream about my brother and me at this time. I was holding on to his hand and began walking up his arm with my hands until I reached his shoulders, clinching very tightly. I would not let him go.

When I awakened from the dream, I wasn't quite sure what the Lord was showing me until I heard the doctor's report. The medical test showed Craig should have been dead by now. Then I realized the meaning of my dream. My prayers had sustained my brother; they were his life line, if you will. God was allowing my brother time to come to Him and come to Him right.

Craig died about two years after his diagnosis, but on his deathbed, he did indeed repent. One day he said to me, "I wished I had done like you." My brother had done some soul-searching. He'd finally come to the end of himself. Craig was sorry for the choices he'd made in the short time he lived on the earth. Nevertheless, the Lord's arms are always wide open to receive the penitent heart.

After the funeral I began to really miss my brother. Not only that, I wished I could have done and said some things differently. The amazing thing about God is that every time I cried from sorrow of heart, the Lord Jesus would show up and comfort me. As the famous quote says,

"Earth has no sorrow that heaven can't heal"
(Thomas Moore, 1779–1852).

It was as though with His presence He was saying to me, "Don't cry. I'll be a brother to you." The Lord did this repeatedly until one day, in the midst of my tears, I saw by the spirit a vision of my brother's healed body as he was being raised into the heavens. With all that the enemy had done to destroy him, God intervened, and Craig got the victory in the end. Like the words of Jesus to the penitent thief, *"This day thou shalt be with me in paradise"* —Luke 23:43, I will see my brother again. Halleluiah!

A few years later, following my brother's death, I met George, a man seventeen years my senior. During our courtship we found out our families knew each other through church fellowship. He attended Phillips Chapel CME. I was evangelizing at the time and attended a Pentecostal church in the city.

We married eight months later. I stepped into marriage unprepared and naive. As a Christian, he was "more out than he was in and more down than he was up." Six months into the marriage, I saw George wasn't the man I had married. He was very disrespectful, as were his children and his family. Like my father, he had no respect for women.

After a few years, George's attitude had changed for the worse. As a result, I found that working in ministry and dealing with all the foolishness at home had become extremely arduous. It kept me on my knees, though; that's for sure. I continued praying, while asking God to fix the marriage. In retrospect, George's treatment of me said, "I don't love you."

A certain kitchen incident would prove this. I had cooked a slammin' dinner and was about finished, so I started setting the table. I cooked one of our favorite comfort foods, mashed potatoes with cheese topping. Oh, it was so good! I didn't cut any corners. Using heavy cream, garlic, and real butter, this wasn't a dieter's delight. To top it off, I would always add shredded cheddar cheese, then place it in the oven to slowly melt.

I filled the glasses with ice and poured the tea. Everything was ready. I removed the steamy pot of potatoes from the oven and set it on the stovetop and began to fix our plates. I spaced out for a moment and reached for the pot handle with my bare hand. Yes, the one I had just removed from the oven. My hand was on fire! Oh, the pain! I immediately dropped the pot and potatoes went everywhere, including on my body. My chest, stomach, and hands were covered! I went into shock, unable to move or scream. It seemed as if things were moving in slow motion.

In the midst of all this, I noticed my husband in the background. There was no sense of urgency to help, or any concern at all. He kept doing what he was doing, preparing his dinner plate, acting unaware of my dilemma. There was no "Baby, are you alright? Here, let me help you." Not one word!

I was finally able to muster up enough strength to remove the scorching potatoes from my burning body. Now I understand how Al Green felt with the hot grits. I felt numb as I left the kitchen to take care of my wounds. Thoughts of this man's behavior raced through my head. Earlier in the relationship George had told me he was a mean man. I should have listened.

That was not the first time I was hit with this cold, callous treatment by him. It was Saturday morning, and he and I had finished breakfast. We were sitting in the den watching TV, when out of the blue I was overtaken by a feeling of nausea.

I jumped up and ran to the bathroom while holding my mouth. Next thing I knew, I found myself bent over the toilet stool, puking my guts out. We all know what that's like—your head feels like it's about to explode, and just when you think you can't throw up any more, you do. I slowly gathered myself, washed my hands and face, and reentered the den. Needless to say, I looked pitiful after such an incident.

My husband was still lying calmly on the sofa when I reentered the den. I sat down on the floor, feeling so weak. I laid my head backward and rested it on a cushion when I heard my husband say, "Ya got sick, huh?" I mean, call me sensitive if you like. But how could you hear someone violently vomiting and not utter a caring word?

It behooves me to mention the passive-aggressive behavior slowly coming into play. Oftentimes a spouse has a tendency to overlook this behavior because it is indirect bullying. For example, if we were in close proximity while he was getting dressed or combing his hair, I'd receive an elbow to my chest. Each time, it was made to appear like an accident.

One early morning we were in the bed, asleep. Straightway, I was awakened by a blow to my ribs. Bam! I looked around to see what in the world had happened. My then-husband supposedly turned over in his sleep. Nobody turns over that hard, I thought. I made sure that didn't happen again. I moved to the spare bedroom and stayed there until I moved out. No doubt the dude was working up the nerve to start a full-fledged beating, but I wasn't going to stick around for it.

I began to feel afraid for my life in the sense that I was in the presence of a ticking time bomb that could explode any moment. There were too many incidents like this one, along with his infidelity. When I realized the relationship was over, I began to move forward mentally. I needed a plan. No doubt the Lord endured much patience as I eventually came to reality.

Looking ahead, hope is what I needed
for the journey I was about to undertake…

HOPE WAS WHAT I NEEDED

As a child of God, one comes to realize the most important thing in this life is his or her relationship with the Lord, and His presence. In my moment of discouragement, I said I didn't want to preach anymore. I told myself that no one wants to hear me anyway. How well I recall Jeremiah's words:

> *Then I said, "I will not make mention of Him, nor speak anymore in His name." But His word was in me like a burning fire shut up in my bones...* —Jeremiah 20:9

To tell you the truth, I felt as though God had thrown me out to the wolves. I was tired of all the rejection and unthankful-hearted folk. I would reach out to help those who in the end would turn against me. Oh, it seemed as though God was asking too much!

I walked away from the ministry and decided to open a boutique designing clothes instead. At least I wouldn't have to deal with church folk.

Months passed before I started missing my time with the Lord, the experience of His wonderful presence, and the wonderful fellowship we had together. *Ah, what had I done?* I thought. I made up my mind right then that I would never allow anything to come between me and my relationship with my Lord Jesus. I was willing to go through whatever it took.

Looking ahead, hope is what I needed for the journey I was about to undertake, subsequently I titled this part of the chapter.

FIFTY WAS A WAKE-UP CALL

Life is filled with twists and turns. They often come at times when we least expect them. Here I am at the age of fifty, going through a divorce after fourteen years of marriage. During this time, God, in his graciousness, gave me the word "hope."

Daily I'd meditate on the word, and it couldn't have come at a better time. Amazingly, the message of hope started showing up everywhere I went. It happened that Pastor Jackie McCullough, a very anointed teacher and preacher in the Body of Christ, began teaching an intense series on the subject. I would listen to her online broadcast consistently. I hung on every word; it was my lifeline.

There were times I turned on the TV and other ministers would be expounding on hope as well. I was getting a double dose, though spiritually I felt so weak. There were times when fear crept in, too. I needed all the strength I could get to pull me through.

While working in a salon for a major department store, I signed up for training in advanced coloring. The stylists came from different salons across the Phoenix metropolitan area. Everyone gathered in the assigned room prepared by the instructor. She was a very pleasant lady who happened to be a Christian. She pulled out some virtue reflection cards and asked everyone to pick one. "Don't look at your cards until I give the okay," she said. After everyone had chosen their cards, we were permitted to take a look. To my amazement, there it was on my card, typed in big, bold letters—HOPE. *Here it is again*, I thought. You just know when there is a reoccurrence of the same thing that God is talking, and talking he was.

This was a season full of uncertainty. I set a prayerful plan in motion and struggled to accomplish it, to no avail—I was right in the middle of a tanking economy. I had two businesses, neither of them making enough money to cover expenses. No matter how much effort I put forth to make things work, everything started dwindling away.

The Lord had a divine plan that would propel me in a direction that was completely different from what I could imagine. I soon realized my steps had been ordered. There wasn't the slightest hint or question, it was time to leave the marriage. George had been waiting long for this moment as well, but he wasn't man enough to make the first step. I guess the Lord just helped him out.

Yes, fifty was a wake-up call for me. I had a startling realization that I had lived out half my life. In retrospect, I wondered if I had anything to show for all those years—whether I had failed myself or, most importantly, failed my God. In the grand scheme of things, fifty years on earth is not very long. Time is so fleeting; you wonder where it all goes. Is God going to keep His promises? Little did I know I was about to embark upon the journey of my life, and I needed hope to get me to the next level. The omniscient God knew it, and He was there to see me through it.

I drove off to Phoenix in a U-Haul truck with only ninety-three dollars on my credit card. I had only been gone a few months when I began to receive phone calls from George. He apologized, explaining that he wanted me back. They always do. But it was too late.

STARTING OVER AGAIN

STARTING OVER AGAIN

Do not remember the former things, nor consider the things of old. Behold, I will do a new thing, now it shall spring forth; Shall you not know it? I will even make a road in the wilderness and rivers in the desert.

—Isaiah 43:18-19

There are benefits to starting over again. Learning from our past mistakes is prime, because you certainly don't want to repeat them. But what can I say about the great advantage of starting with a clean slate? Isaiah encourages us to forget the former things. In other words, don't dwell on yesterday! Beloved, it is impossible to move forward looking behind. To be more precise, the "former things" haven't a placement in our future. For this reason, our only choice is to forget so that we my walk into our divine destiny, with the understanding that God is doing something far greater for us, in us and through us. Yes, it takes guts. Many have done it, with success, including me. Although I was fearful of the unknown, I didn't let that stop me.

Here's my story . . .

With hindsight, I realized that I had put all my apples in one basket—the wrong basket. My marriage left me empty on many levels. I had nothing to show for the time spent. Nevertheless, understanding that divorce was inevitable, I had to figure out a plan to move forward.

One morning I decided to write my then-husband a written request for a small portion of our finances. After all, it was due me for all the years I had put in. I gladly took off my gold band and placed it on top of the letter and left for the long drive to work, which was now in Phoenix. As I drove off I thought surely he'd agree; besides, it was much needed. My portion would help me easily transition to my new single life. *What a relief,* I thought.

I arrived home after work and opened the garage to pull my car in, but, there was no way in. There was furniture stacked to the ceiling. While I was away, my then-husband conceived of a plan of his own. Separating my belongings from his, he'd moved everything out to the garage. Consequently, I had to park on the driveway.

When I entered the house, he stood waiting for me. "I packed up all your stuff, everything you came in the marriage with. Take it and leave, that's all you're gettin'," he said.

No sense in arguing about it, I thought. Plus, after ripping and running up the highway to Phoenix and back, I didn't have the energy to fight. It was just as well. The Lord had already given me the green light to move on.

In spite of the marriage laws, my then-husband didn't feel I deserved any portion of the settlement, so I walked away empty-handed. And let me tell you, I was BA-ROKE!

I knew that if my soon-to-be ex was going to give up my portion of the finances, I'd have to fight for it. Meanwhile, I racked my brain about how to pursue it until the Lord, with His wonderful self, visited me again in a dream. He showed me the ugliness of what I would encounter if I were to push for a divorce settlement without the promise of getting anything in return.

No doubt God was speaking. He conveyed to me, "You can stay and fight and go through all the hell, or you can receive my peace and a greater future." Trusting the Lord, I made the choice to follow after peace.

You know the song, "Can't Nobody Do Me Like Jesus"? It's true. What I wanted and needed at that moment, all the houses, cars, or money couldn't give me.

When it comes to possessions, you can replace them. If not, oh well. I know that many people wouldn't even dream of walking away from the years they'd invested in a relationship. I had different people encouraging me, saying, "Girl, you better get your half!"

They may have meant well. But what they didn't understand was that I was a God-seeker. And when you seek God, He will reveal what eyes have not seen or ears heard. Then He will turn around and back it up with His Word to confirm it. Honey, you can't help but be strengthened to rise and move forward. Yes, even if it means walking away from everything you have ever known.

Here's what I mean. One day something supernatural happened while I was on my walk through the neighborhood. I was feeling terribly despondent about my present life and the choices I'd made. With a penitent heart and tears, I was talking to the Lord in my prayer language when I noticed sparks flying from a very tall palm tree. It appeared as though it was on fire.

I shook my head and questioned whether it was burning with fire or if I was seeing lights. There were sparks flying everywhere. "For sure, this is fire," I said to myself. I began to pick up speed. *OH my, someone's house will burn down!* I thought. I had to go and warn the homeowner. As I moved closer to the palm tree, I saw that it wasn't fire at all. It was the presence of the glory of God on that tree. He showed up for me in the middle of my despondency as if to say, "You may have messed up, but I still want to use you."

You're familiar with the story of Moses when he slayed the Egyptian? He buried him in the sand, hoping no one would find out. As a result, Moses had to flee for his life. What do you think brother

Moses took with him? Nothing, I tell you, except the clothes on his back. He too had to start over, leaving behind all the riches of the palace. He took up residence in the desert until the Angel of the Lord showed up in a burning bush. It was there that God began to reveal to Moses what was in store for his future and his people. Beloved, we serve a God of second chances. Hallelujah!

While starting over can be very beneficial, this transition wasn't at all what I thought it would be. Not realizing I'd embarked upon a completely different season and time of my life, the old methods of getting out and pounding the pavement to accomplish my goals were no longer working. In the past, my plans would always prosper easily. With God at the wheel, I was destined to undergo a rocky uphill journey. And yet, there were more lessons on the horizon that the Lord was sure to teach.

Feeling terribly anxious, I began filing the divorce papers, which were filled with probing questions that caused me to relive unpleasant moments. The strain of it all was like standing before a judge and jury who demanded an account of my entire life. To make matters worse, loneliness had invaded my world. OH, how I yearned for a friend, a shoulder to lean on, a voice of encouragement.

I had no one to turn to except my heavenly Father. With the strength of God, I put my emotions aside. I gathered myself and kept looking forward, never to return back. I won't say I wasn't tempted, especially when I ran out of my beauty cream and didn't have the money to buy any. Ole slew-foot would speak up and whisper, "Go ahead, call him up. Ask him to buy it. Tell him you'll pay him back." Even though it appeared to be a small thing, I knew it would swing open doors to an ungodly relationship from the past, and I was not eager to forfeit my future blessings. I was determined to remain focused.

I made a few grueling trips back and forth to the downtown Courthouse. Finally, the papers were filed. It didn't take long for the divorce to become final. Six months later I received a phone call that shook me to the core. George was dead. After this happened, I say death is cruel. I wouldn't wish it on my worst enemy. For two long days, he lay on the floor with no one by his side. When he was found, he'd left a trail of how he had succumbed to his fatal end. How sad that there was no time for final goodbyes, hugs, or kisses. Yes…it was too late.

Let's look into the scripture and see how starting over was essential for the entire human race.

> *And God saw that the wickedness of man was great in the earth, and that every imagination of the thoughts of his heart was only evil continually. And it repented the Lord that he had made man on the earth, and it grieved him at his heart. And the Lord said, I will destroy man whom I have created from the face of the earth; both man, and beast, and the creeping thing, and fowls of the air; for it repenteth me that I have made them. But Noah found grace in the eyes of the Lord. The earth also was corrupt before God, and the earth was filled with violence. And God looked upon the earth, and, behold, it was corrupt; for all flesh had corrupted his way upon the earth. And God said to Noah, The end of all flesh is come before me; for the earth is filled with violence through them; and, behold, I will destroy them with the earth. For yet seven days, and I will cause it to rain upon the earth forty days and forty nights; and every living substance that I have made will I destroy from off the face of the earth.* —Genesis 6:5–8, 11–13; 7:4

After all the wonderful works God had created, He was proud, as well He should have been. For He beheld them and said, "It is good." But as time went on, something drastic happened, through no fault of the Creator. The Holy Scripture declares, "And God looked upon the earth and, behold, it was corrupt." —Genesis 6:12

God, who is holy, could no longer have a relationship with His own creation. The people of Noah's day were unsalvageable. He didn't do anything wrong; everything was right and good. Perhaps in your case it was the same. You obeyed God, your plans were perfect, but things still turned out disastrously.

Let's look at our Creator. He lost a whole creation because it had become wicked. This grieved His heart and He had to take drastic measures and destroy all living things.

Yet, it did not alter God's plan for humanity. Herein is what I want to convey to you. God had to start over. The head of the universe, the Creator, started all over again! So then, if He started over, how much more might we, as mere humans, have to start over again? And yet again. Get this—afterward, He didn't look back, not even once.

Prior to this event, He searched the whole earth until He found the one man who was righteous, a man that would be willing to carry out His will. His name was Noah. He was faithful, walking in harmony with God.

One man? God was satisfied with one man on the entire planet? Pause and think about that! Some of you brothers and sisters who are trying to hold on to toxic relationships ought to grab hold of this revelation right here and now. Many relationships have become so bad that it's like trying to utilize hazardous waste. It's dangerous to you, your health, and the environment. The only thing one can do is dispose of it. Let me give you a "for instance."

Years ago, while pastoring a congregation, the Lord gave me a dream concerning a particular sister. She was married to a man who was not trustworthy, but she was in love with him and wanted the marriage to work. One night in a dream the Lord spoke a word of warning to me on her behalf indicating that the husband was "unclean." I ministered to the young sister the same word and prayed for her protection. Regrettably, she didn't listen. As a result, she contracted a venereal disease. Understand what I mean by toxic? This is not God's will for His children.

God in His wisdom had to cast out the hazardous waste, if you will, because our eternal future depended upon a righteous bloodline through which Jesus the Christ would come. Now here's the question.

Who else on earth has lost an entire creation? Who on earth has lost more than God? I don't know of anyone. Yet here we are, crying over spilled milk. You hear it all the time with divorcées: "I lost my house to my ex" or "I lost my money to my ex" and so on. So what. Rise and start over. I'm sure you know as well as I do that sometimes you have to lose in order to gain. Besides, you won't be the first and certainly won't be the last. Stuff can always be replaced. Perhaps you might be saying, "But Lord, I'm old!" Noah was six hundred years old when the floods came. You might be thinking, *men don't live that long anymore.* Well, Moses was eighty when he met the Angel at the burning bush. Beloved, don't count God as slack. He is able to restore in one moment what it took you twenty years to build. But you have to trust Him (see Joel 2:25).

FROM YOUR WORST TO YOUR BEST

> *According to my earnest expectation and my hope, that in nothing I shall be ashamed, but that with all boldness, as always, so now also Christ shall be magnified in my body, whether it be by life, or by death.*
>
> —Philippians 1:20

The time came when I could barely make ends meet. But I was believing God for better days ahead when one day I saw a homeless woman. She was pushing a grocery cart stacked full of all her belongings. I walked over to her, and as I drew close I could see this lady had been homeless for a long time.

Her skin had been weather-beaten by the overbearing heat of the Phoenix sun, and her clothes were drab and ragged. As I looked into her empty, lifeless eyes, I wanted to minister to her. I asked if I could pray for her, and she was more than welcoming. After I prayed I went away, hoping I would see her again so that I could give her some money from the little I had. But as I turned to walk away, I heard a voice say, "This is going to be you." *What? Not so!* I said to myself. Immediately I started rebuking the Devil. To tell you the truth, I was puzzled by those words, and I tried to shake them off, but couldn't.

During my morning walk I saw this lady again. I walked up to her and gave her some money and asked, "What is your name?" She looked at me and said, "Anita." I was flabbergasted. "Can't be!" I said to myself. First, I hear a voice telling me I'm going to be homeless. Then this woman says her name is Anita, too. Oh no, this is not possible. Perhaps she heard me say my name or something, I told myself. How likely was it that she had the same name as me? I didn't know what to make of it.

Shortly thereafter, darker days came upon me. All my efforts and prayers to the Lord asking Him to turn things around were of no avail. Every door was closed shut. Just when I thought it couldn't get any worse, the unexpected happened. The very words that I heard in my spirit came to pass and I became homeless. I was forced out on the street.

Homelessness is something I thought I'd never encounter. Like the tale of Alice in Wonderland, it was as if I had walked along one day and fallen into a dark hole, except this was not a dream.

The Lord already had me in a very hard place, yet it was a good place because I could see His hand at work everywhere I turned. *God has a way of taking you through the worst to get to your best.*

This was my wilderness experience. Everyone has to go through it for discipline purposes, so I wanted to make sure that I kept my attitude in check. I didn't want to wander in the wilderness any longer than was scheduled.

To my amazement, it was in this season that the Lord revealed audibly the purpose for which I was called. It left me astonished for weeks. This was the second time in my life I'd heard His voice in this manner. The thought of the experience causes me to tremble all over. People who say they hear the voice of God and act very nonchalant about it make me wonder.

Moving on with my story, I found myself out on the street, sleeping in the backseat of my car. I was parked on the side of the road, eating out of a can. I was thankful to the Lord that it was wintertime. I don't think I could have survived the sweltering summer heat of Phoenix. My eyes were opened to a whole new walk of life I hadn't really seen before. I mean sure, you see a few transient persons in passing and wonder how they got there, and then the thought passes. This was different because it was me.

One morning after I awoke from my sleep, I got myself together and sat looking out of the window. It was pretty cold that morning, and only a few people scurried around. I noticed an Indian woman who had been thrown into homelessness walking into the park.

She positioned herself on a park bench for sleep with a blanket to keep warm. My heart went out to her, wishing I could comfort her somehow. All I had was a car and a food box. I decided to make a peanut butter sandwich to give to her, along with an apple. I walked over to her and asked if she wanted something to eat. She said yes, and I sat down next to her and began to tell her about Jesus. She opened up and told me her story and that she had a relationship with the Lord. I could see in her eyes that she was hurting. "May I pray for you?" I asked. "Yes," she replied. As I began to pray, she cried silently; tears streamed like a river down her face. I don't think I've seen so many tears before. I felt her pain. This woman was a victim of brokenness. I walked back to my car and was so thankful to God for it.

Though I was homeless, at least I had a piece of shelter to lay my head down in. Plus, I knew it was temporary. I wondered when the Lord would raise me out of this pit of total uncertainty. I was convinced in my heart He would. I knew my future was bright despite the present picture. I had hope.

Let's revisit one of the definitions of hope. It means "to attach oneself." The word "attach" reminds me of the old metaphor of the little boy and his kite. As the story goes, on a bright sunny day, with the wind just right, he flies his kite so high that it's no longer in sight. Then a man walks up to him and says, "Son, what'cha got there?" The little boy replies, "A kite." The man says, "Ya can't see it. How do you know it's out there?" The little boy replies, "Because every now and then I can feel it tugging at my string." So it is in real life. Hope tugs at the strings of our heart, even in our darkest hour. God says, "I'm still here" and *"I will never leave thee nor forsake thee."*—Hebrews 13:5

Days passed as I made my way out of my car to the park's water fountain. This was my means to take a wash off. I could not help but notice people staring at me; it was embarrassing. I looked up to the heavens and said, "Father, you know I am doing the best I can."

After being on the street for two months, I finally made my way to a Catholic-run shelter. Upon my admission, I was greeted by the sister of the house. As she began to explain the rules of the shelter, I shifted my attention to observe the statues in the waiting area. There was one huge in size depicting Mary with the baby Jesus sitting at her feet. My first thought: someone went to a lot of trouble in a vain attempt to thoroughly address deep human need. I zoomed back in to hear my assigned bed, and permission to take an early shower. I hadn't had a shower in weeks, not to mention a decent hot meal. My body had become so thin I could barely stand to look at myself. The thought I might starve to death came to mind. But the Lord had mercy and allowed me to live through it.

The moment I stepped into the shower, it felt like the next thing to paradise. The discomforts of living on the streets were so depleting. I'd been mainly living on adrenalin. After sleeping cramped up in my car for two months, I welcomed the privilege of reclining on a mattress which afforded me to stretch out my legs. Even though my stay was temporary, it would aide in some sense of order. You can rest assured I was thankful for everything! The next morning I went out to my car for four o'clock prayer time. This was my routine regardless of being homeless. The Lord's presence was incredibly weighty, and as I basked in His glory, the Spirit graced me with strength to carry out my daily ventures. After prayer, I'd slowly drift off to a tranquil sleep. Before long, I was awakened by the voices of the women as they made their exit. The rules of the shelter mandated, all residents to be out by nine o'clock a.m. and in by three o'clock p.m. When three o'clock rolled around the women were allowed to reenter the shelter. We all gathered in our sleeping quarters, waiting for daily prayer followed by evening supper. Knowing how the Catholics prayed, I thought, *this should be interesting*. We all gathered around the table. I saw other professing Christians besides myself. The sisters' sole purpose was to convert everyone who came through the shelter to Catholicism. Uh-huh.

After we gathered around the table, the sister asked me if I wanted to read the prayer that evening and to do the rosary. "No," I said firmly. She asked the other Christians if they would read the prayer (which was directed to Mary), and they agreed. They were willing to do it with the hopes that they would be granted a longer stay in the shelter, but that never happened. The shelter only allowed a thirty-day stay and then you were out. There was not time to lollygag. Whatever you needed to do to get back on your feet, you had to do it quick. Much to their surprise, they were asked to leave at the thirty-day mark right along with everybody else. You see, submitting to the devil never pays off. *"For it is written, you shall worship the Lord your God and Him only you shall serve.* —Luke 4:8

After a few days in the shelter, I got acquainted with some of the women. Like myself, a few were experiencing homelessness for the first time. As I looked at them I wondered where their families were and why they could not go home. For me, my being homeless was divinely ordered. Call it discipline or the chastening of the Lord, I knew that the hand of God was on me, so much so that He gave me a heart of compassion for the women there. I truly saw them through the eyes of Jesus. As Mark 6:34 declares, *"And Jesus, when He came out, saw much people, and was moved with compassion toward them, because they were as sheep not having a shepherd."*

If Jesus were here today, these are the people with whom He would hang out. And just like Jesus, I felt their hurt and saw their brokenness. They desperately needed a savior and a hope. No futile attempts of man's idea of religion would bring either. Being homeless was a completely different world—a forgotten world, is what I called it, a place where people look on you with disdain, where you are fed the leftovers of the leftovers, and sometimes even spoiled food. It's a place where mercy is scarce, except from the few who really have the heart of Jesus.

I met one of the volunteers, an older Sicilian woman in her seventies. She was endearing, and she spoke with a New York accent. She loved working at the shelter and candidly expressed her dedication to Catholicism. She was born and bred Catholic. She walked into the dining room with a smile and sat down next to me. "What brings you to the shelter?" she asked. We began to talk about the Lord, and I explained how I arrived.

While we talked she looked into my eyes and said, "You are glowing. I can see it, and I know God is with you." And with me He was. One couldn't help but commend the sisters for their work of charity. But for me, it wasn't about what I could receive. I purposed in my heart that I would earn my keep. I was a servant of the Most High God, so I presented myself to the nuns. "I am a servant. How can I serve?" I asked. "If you need any cleaning or mending done, I can do it for you. I sew for a living. Should you need my assistance, I am here." They were hesitant at first, and I'm sure my resistance to the Catholic rituals played a part, but they soon saw my stern commitment to the Lord Jesus and decided to give me a try.

I continued with my four o'clock a.m. prayer time. I'd leave the shelter to go to my car and spend time reading my Bible, praying, and singing to the Lord. One morning I heard a tapping on my car window. I looked up and saw that it was the head sister. "I have been looking for you. What are you doing out here?" she said. "Praying. I have early-morning devotions," I replied. "Oh, you're welcome to come and pray with us," she said. This was the beginning of invitations to their events. I had never attended a Catholic anything before. Their annual Catholic retreat was coming up, and the volunteer invited me to go with them. I agreed. It was good to get out of the shelter and eat good, fresh food for a change. Upon arrival, we all walked into a meeting room that was casually decorated with soft creamy white walls and several rows of cushioned chairs. It was filled with people exchanging hellos and formal introductions. And ah, yes…there it was, on the other side of the room, a buffet arrayed on tables. I hadn't thought about much else during the ride over. The presiding priest made his entrance dressed in a long black robe accented with a red cummerbund and tassels. He began working through the crowd, greeting everyone with a smile and a handshake. A very pleasant fellow he was – tall and robust. Yet, his mannerism displayed purposeful flagrant femininity. With a wrist flip gesture and switching with each step. It appeared no one was bothered by it. On the way back to the shelter I asked the sisters if they had the ability to discern the spirit of an individual.

They were very uncomfortable with the question, so in a round-about way, they alluded to the idea that even if they knew, they weren't sayin'.

THE PURPOSE OF GOD

After years of ministry and waiting on God for instruction, the purpose of God was unfolding before my eyes—I knew that I was called to minister to the brokenhearted. The Lord had allowed me to experience the devastation of homelessness for this purpose. At least that's one reason. I had to become more like Jesus. The Holy Scripture declares, *"For we have not an high priest which cannot be touched with the feelings of our infirmities."*—Hebrews 4:15

I too had to be touched so that I could understand their struggles. As I experienced these devastations one after another, I came to realize that what the enemy meant for evil, the Lord was working all things out so His glory could be seen in me.

My talent earned me an extra month's stay in the shelter, which worked right into the plan of God. The sisters not only wanted their sheets mended, but also asked if I would make curtains for the entire shelter. I gladly said yes. As the Holy Scripture declares, *"A man's gift maketh room for him."*—Proverbs 18:16

I was close to finishing the curtains when one day, while sitting on my bed, I felt a strong pull to go back to Tucson. I knew it was the Lord speaking to me. Still resisting, I replied, "Lord, if I go home, they will say, 'She came back because she didn't have anywhere to go.'" But God was in control of my steps, and little did I know He was working in a roundabout way to get me back to my hometown. During the short while I was in the shelter, the Lord gave me favor with the sisters. The volunteer asked me to teach Bible class and to pray while she prepared food for us ladies. I was put in charge while the sisters were away and I had the privilege of staying in the shelter during the day. What a blessing. If you know anything about the climate in Phoenix, it gets extremely hot. It can easily climb up to 116 degrees.

After being in the shelter for almost two months, I'd had my fill and I told the Lord I was ready to go, and boy, did He move swiftly. I found the yellow pages and started searching through them for a job, designing clothing. The sisters didn't believe in any modern technology; the only thing available was the phone book. I was thankful for it.

After thumbing through the pages, I found a high-end boutique in North Scottsdale. I decided to call to ask if they needed a clothing designer. To my surprise, they did. The owner set up an interview to meet me, but again, God worked it out so that I started working right away. It so happened that a bride came through who needed express alterations on her wedding gown. The owner skipped all the prerequisites and hired me over the phone. I wondered what the boutique owner would have thought had he known I was a homeless fashion designer.

Shortly after, the sisters had a 110-degree heart change and gave me the boot. I had to scramble quickly to find myself some kind of residence. So I packed up my belongings and found myself working out of a hotel room. It was amazing to see how God was now moving me forward.

After a few weeks, I finally got settled into an apartment again, and for a moment, I was living my dream. I was designing dresses for the elite of Scottsdale, Arizona. The ladies loved my dresses, and I was over-the-top excited when I sold my first three-thousand-dollar dress. Other sales followed. The Lord had truly turned things around, I thought. In all of my excitement, I had completely forgotten about the Lord's plan to get me back to Tucson. He brought me through my darkness, protected me while I slept on the street, and fed me when I was hungry. Little did I know at the time that it was all a setup. Herein is the beauty of it all:

> As blood flow to the heart, so is life. *The hope of the righteous shall be gladness.*
>
> —Proverbs 10:28

Ah, HOPE, how sweet the sound.

- It is the sound of a snowmelt trickling down a mountainside, slowly forming a small channel until it becomes a mighty river.
- It is the sound of a young warrior's slingshot swooshing through the air as he prevails over a giant Philistine with one stone. It is the sound of a borrowed sword, drawn out of the sheath of the slain (1 Samuel 17:49–51).
- It is the sound of a sojourner with a strong heartbeat of faith springing into action, who hoped against hope.
- It is the sound of praise sung its loudest when there appears no reason at all to hope (Romans 4:18).

Dear beloved, I pray to the Lord Jesus on your behalf:

> *Now the God of hope fill you with all joy and peace in believing, that ye may abound in hope, through the power of the Holy Ghost* —Romans 15:13

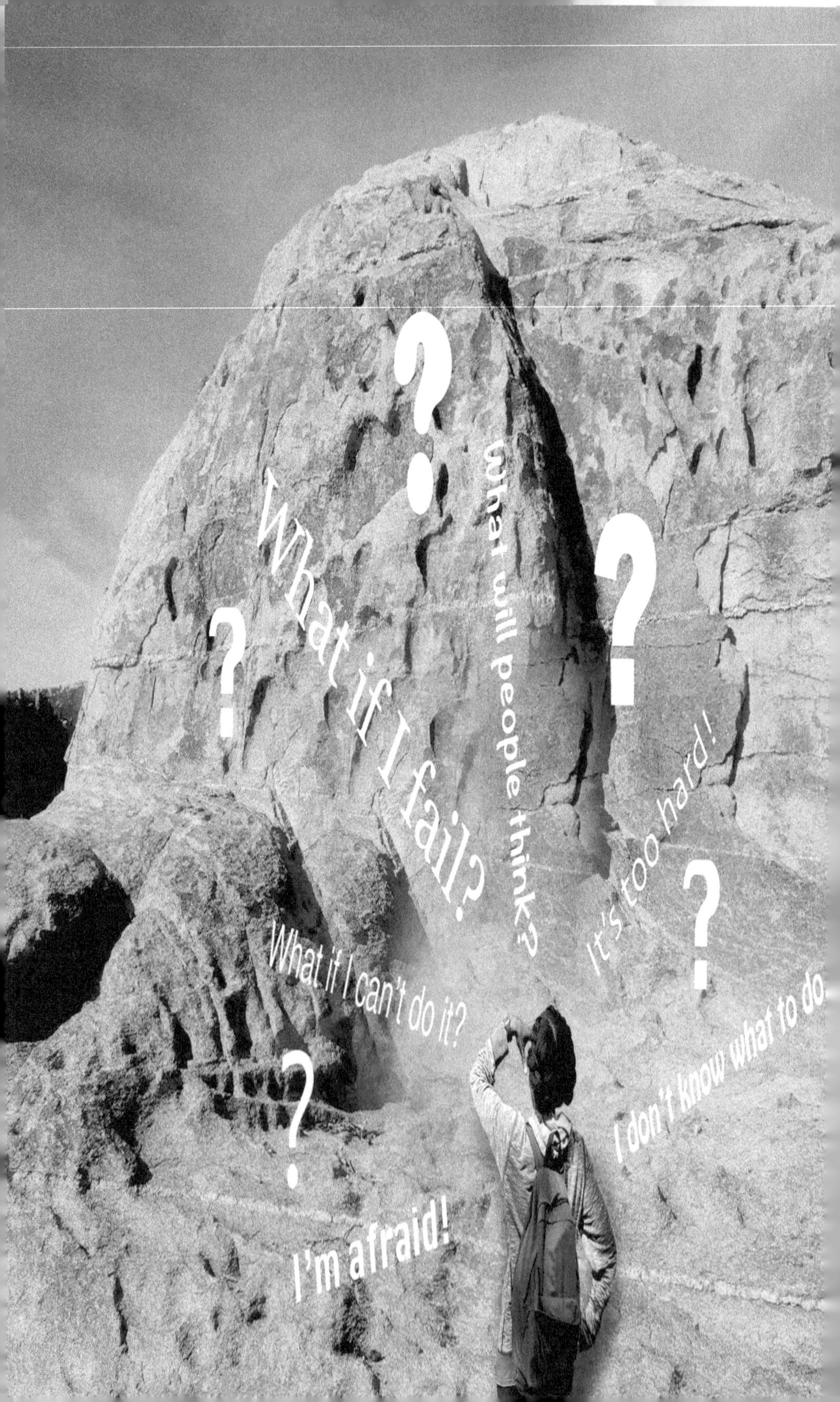
What if I fail?
What will people think?
It's too hard!
What if I can't do it?
I don't know what to do.
I'm afraid!

DARE TO RISE?

Now there were four leprous men at the entrance of the gate; and they said to one another, "Why are we sitting here till we die? "If we say, "we will enter the city, the famine is in the city, and we shall die there. And if we sit here, we die also. Now therefore, come, let us surrender to the army of the Syrians. If they keep us alive, we shall live; and if they kill us we shall only die." And they rose at twilight to go to the camp of the Syrians; and when they had come to the outskirts of the Syrian camp, to their surprise no one was there.

—2 Kings 7:3–5

And they rose at twilight to go to the camp of the Syrians; and when they had come to the outskirts of the Syrian camp, to their surprise no one was there. —2 Kings 7:3–5

This familiar story of four leprous men in 2 Kings is a display of great courage. They were desperate; their lives were between a rock and a hard place, to say the least. As they assessed their situation, they had three choices: 1) go into the city gates where there was famine; 2) sit still and die of hunger; or 3) run into the Syrians' camp and expect to be captured, perhaps even slain by the sword. Neither choice appeared advantageous.

As with the lepers, our lives are full of challenges, whether we are willing to take them on or not. Of course, some are more difficult than others. In grade school, we all played the game of dare. We played it to prove our courage and that we were not scaredy-cats. If we hesitated, the others would double-dog-dare us, which meant we'd do it or be a wuss to the rest of our classmates.

This game is much like an incident that happened when I was in beauty college. We had completed a haircutting workshop when one of my classmates challenged me to jump off the stage onto a folding chair positioned in the middle of the classroom floor. Another student volunteered to hold it if I jumped.

Well, I was the type who liked challenges, and if you told me I couldn't do a thing, I'd make it my aim to prove you wrong. With all my might, I took a leap and wound up on the floor, flat on my behind. I could have been seriously hurt. Most of the time, taking a dare left you looking silly, but you did it anyway because of peer pressure.

Of course, we all know that was a kids' game; real life is much more serious. It takes more than a childish dare in order to rise and face challenges.

Webster defines DARE as "to be sufficiently courageous; to challenge [someone] to do something, especially as a proof of courage or ability; To be bold enough to try; To meet boldly and defiantly."

What can we say concerning these men scourged with leprosy, a disease dreaded and considered highly contagious in those days. The Bible doesn't mention their names or their ages. The little we know is that they had a disease. Everyone who was suspect was excommunicated from the camp, which meant they were dependent upon the generosity of others. These men hung around outside the gate, hoping someone, *any*one, would throw food over the wall.

But it was a time of famine, and not likely that food would be coming their way anytime soon, even from their own family members. After all, they were but lepers. Their situation was dire; nevertheless, something had to be done.

They asked themselves a very pertinent question: "Why sit here till we die?" It seems to me that the worst thing a person can do about their predicament is to do nothing. In the minds of the lepers, doing nothing was claiming defeat. They knew that to sit meant sure death. In conclusion, they decided it was better to die trying. And try they did.

I am amazed at their courage. If anyone had reason to give up and die, they did. This horrible disease would be comparable to the HIV of today. You see, once the disease of leprosy was discovered, your name became Leper, and you were considered cursed. Leprosy was debilitating and contagious, so a person was shunned by family and peers. As the disease progressed it became unsightly, and people kept their distance out of fear.

As far as these four lepers knew, everything was working against them. Yet they would dare to rise. The scripture reveals they chose to surrender to their enemy, the Syrian army. Risky, right? No doubt they had some level of fear, but they rose and moved forward anyway. When they made it to the outskirts of the camp, they were surprised—NO ONE was there. What happened? Well, let's read:

> *For the Lord had caused the army of the Syrians to hear the noise of chariots and the noise of horses—the noise of a great army; so they said to one another, "Look, the king*

> *of Israel has hired against us the kings of the Hittites and kings of the Egyptians to attack us!" Therefore they arose and fled at twilight, and left the camp intact—their tents, their horses, and their donkeys—and they fled for their lives. And when these lepers came to the outskirts of the camp, they went into one tent and ate and drank, and carried from it silver and gold and clothing, and went and hid them; then they came back and entered another tent, and carried some from there also, and went and hid it.*
> —2 Kings 7:6–8

To their favorable surprise, the God of heaven had gone before them. Wait a minute! Do you see how God intervened for these leprous men, the outcasts of society? He had a plan for them all along. And not only so, but God would work through them for all of Israel's sake.

This is a compelling illustration of God's attitude toward courage. Think for a moment. If the lepers had decided to remain in their current position, they would have decided to just sit and die, they would have missed God's divine opportunity of provision for them.

Choices are a part of life. This was a tough one for those afflicted with leprosy. This shows us that our character is proven by the choices we make. Hard choices require sacrifice, and the harder the choice, the greater the sacrifice to be made.

I used to wonder how my mother could stand by and do nothing, knowing her children were being sexually abused. Until it came to me one day—actually, she had done something. She made a choice and decided to look the other way. Still trying to wrap my mind around it, I ask the Lord, "What kind of attitude is that?" "Selfishness," He replied. The Bible says that in the last days men will be lovers of themselves, lovers of money (2 Timothy 3:2). My mother wanted the appearance of a prestigious lifestyle. It was all about the superficial. Being the wife of an airman; having a house and cars. Her children came second, perhaps third. Because her priorities were mixed up, Jonnye Ruth failed her children, especially her girls. I don't judge her, but this is how it was. She used to tell me half a man was better than none.

What I'd like to know is, what is half a man? For the record, there is such thing. But for the sake of understanding, this comes from an old saying: "Half a loaf is better than none." In other words, a person may have wanted something more, but they didn't get it, so they decided to settle for less.

Less could mean a whole lot of trouble, especially in a marriage. Because once the relationship pattern is set and accepted, there is no need for the "less than" partner to change. From my own experience, when you settle for less, you always get less than what you settle for.

Needless to say, my parents' relationship wasn't the prototype for marriage. Although both had their issues of extreme selfishness, my father's actions ruined the entire family. He didn't give much thought to how detrimental they would be to the generations to come. My father made selfish choices to have his cake and to eat it, too. He had extramarital affairs outside their marriage union, came home and raped his daughters, and continued to have sex with his wife whenever he felt like it. Not a pretty picture, is it? But it was reality.

In a brief discussion, my elder brother opened up and shared his personal experience with my father's nasty ways. "When I was a little boy, he used to take me around his women and had sex right there in front of me," he said. I could hear the anger in his voice as he spoke. You call that half a man? No . . . that's a D-O-G.

We all have the power to choose to rise above our circumstances. A documentary on the Uruguayan Flight 571, told by a journalist, left me in amazement. It was a story of extreme courage in the midst of extreme devastation. The article reported that forty passengers and five crewmembers were on board when the flight fell to the ground. Included was a rugby union team along with their friends. The plane crashed in the Andes in 1972; over half the crew died, and a few others succumbed to severe cold and injury.

With high hopes, the survivors listened via radio for a search team to come to their rescue. Days continued to pass by. Little did they know, it would be over two months before they would be rescued. With very little food, they had to go into survival mode. Staying alive meant huddling together in the cold of night and eating on dead corpses—their friends who had died around them.

After weeks of listening to radio reports, they heard news that would crush their hopeful anticipations. The reporter announced that the search for them was called off, assuming by now that everyone was dead.

One survivor's father would not give up. His father's intuition kept him pushing on, telling the authorities, "Please keep looking! I know my son is still alive. I know he is!" The remaining survivors came to the conclusion that they had to do something. They chose three young men who would journey across the rugged mountains in the snow to get help. Mind you, these men were malnourished on top of the fact that they did not have proper gear to make such a trip. But they rose anyway and off they went.

They trekked ten whole days across the icy cold Andes until they spotted a Chilean shepherd. He aided them, giving them food and water and alerting the authorities. The shepherd described them as walking skeletons. "There was not an ounce of muscle on their bodies, just bones and flesh," he said. News reporters were in awe of them, saying, "It is not possible that they could make such a trip, especially in their condition." The Lord was with the lepers, so He was with the men in the Andes. When these Chilean men recovered, they were thankful to God and testified that He was the reason for their survival.

Beloved, God honors courage. The scriptures are full of His commandments to be strong and to fear not.

In the first chapter of Joshua we read that God gave Joshua specific instructions to lead Israel into the Promised Land. *"Now therefore arise . . . Be strong and of a good courage."* God promised that He would be with Joshua.

Joshua arose, obeyed the voice of God, and began to move forward. He and his army conquered nation after nation, even those that were mightier, with God fighting for them.

It behooves me to mention the story of Melba Pattillo Beals, who wrote *Warriors Don't Cry*. She also was born in Little Rock, Arkansas.

Her story chronicles a continuous epic battle to integrate Little Rock's Central High in the fifties. Melba and eight others were selected for such a task, and what a task indeed. Now, these children weren't randomly selected. Those young teenagers voluntarily signed up, not knowing the full repercussions. Their lives would be changed forever. They would have to endure the undue hatred and cruelty of fellow humans because of the color of their skin. Before the school year began, they received terrible phone threats on their lives. Even with the landmark 1954 Supreme Court ruling, Brown v. Board of Education, integration in the school would be hard-won for them. In 1957 the young teenagers rose to the challenge and headed toward Central High.

The first year would prove to be the worst. Melba and her friends had to live with the idea that they could be hung by a rope or shot to death simply because they wanted a good education. With no help from law enforcement, these young black children were left to fend for themselves. It was frightening, to say the least.

Opposition was so intense that soldiers from the elite 101st Airborne Division were called in to restore order. As Melba gave a riveting account of her junior year at Central High, each morning the children made gallant steps and stood against a mob of white mothers and fathers shouting the "N" word. Joining the crowd were police officers who looked the other way, even with fireballs, acid-throwing attacks, and economic blackmail.

For Melba and her eight friends, those steps marked their transformation into reluctant warriors—on a battlefield that helped shape the Civil Rights movement.

Quoted from Melba Beals' book *Warriors Don't Cry*:

> *With the help of her English-teacher mother, her eight fellow warriors, and her gun-toting, Bible- and Shakespeare-loving grandmother, Melba survived. "Dignity," said Grandmother India, "is a state of mind, just like freedom."*

And incredibly, from a year that would hold no sweet-sixteen parties or school plays, Melba Beals emerged with indestructible faith, courage, strength, and hope.

The courage that these young men and women displayed was paramount. They rose with the audacity to face their oppressors. Beloved, are you ready to rise and to sign up for the task ahead?

What are these examples of courage saying to you and me? To arise is a conscious choice; one has to DARE to arise.

As I grew up I could see my mother was weak, and I resented her for it. Listen, my friend, your children need to see strength in you in the time of difficulties. This helps them to see they can depend on you, trust in you, and model after you.

As I aforementioned, rising is not easy, but rise we must. Having said that, each person's situation may differ; nonetheless, it calls for the courage to try.

A REASON TO RISE

- For some, rising may mean separating from family members because of their insistent ungodliness (see Genesis 12:5; 19:12–16). While every attempt is made to intervene, they are unwilling to repent and change their ways.

Just because a family frequents the church house doesn't make them godly people. You have to rise, turn them over to God, and shake the dust off your feet.

It is unfortunate, but there will be families in hell. Jesus tells the story of the rich man in hell as he makes a plea for his brothers.

And he cried and said, Father Abraham, have mercy on me, and send Lazarus, that he may dip the tip of his finger in water, and cool my tongue; for I am tormented in this flame. Then he said, I pray thee therefore, father, that

> *thou wouldest send him to my father's house: For I have five brethren; that he my testify unto them, lest they also come into this place of torment." Abraham saith unto him, "They have Moses and the prophets; let them hear them." And he said, "Nay, father Abraham: but if one went unto them from the dead, they will repent. And he said unto him, if they hear not Moses and the prophets, neither will they be persuaded, though one rose from the dead.*
>
> — Luke 16: 24-31

- Perhaps for you, rising may mean leaving an abusive marriage.

Years ago, the church used to teach married Christian women to submit to their abusers. It was a sign of suffering for the sake of Christ. The battered women would sing their songs and testify how they were beaten for wanting to go to the house of God. Ministers would preach from the pulpit and instruct them, saying, "That's your husband. Go, submit to him and pray for him." The Bible says a sanctified wife will sanctify her husband. Because this one scripture has been misinterpreted, it has led to erroneous teaching and unwise counsel, and women have died as a result. Today, there is a better understanding. Not only is it unbiblical, it is against the law to batter your spouse. If you are in an abusive situation today, I'm telling you, this is not acceptable. You must rise and run for your life!

- Rising may mean you need to change your friends; the people who aren't going anywhere in life and have no plans or goals. They do not want you to succeed. These kinds of folks are not your friends.

Perhaps you've had a friendship over the years, but it's one-sided. What do I mean? One person seems to have more invested emotionally in the relationship while the other thinks they're doing you a favor by being your friend. This was the story of my life. I didn't know how to pick friends. This scenario happened everywhere I went. Different places, different faces, but the same results. I finally came to the conclusion that I had to change; I was letting in the wrong kind of folks.

The Lord began instructing me in the scriptures concerning the wicked behavior of people. I was in my sewing room when I heard the TBN Praise the Lord program coming on. Benny Hinn was about to teach, and I thought I would listen while working. But the Lord wanted my full attention.

All of a sudden I felt the Spirit of the Lord take hold of my arms. He drove me into the next room and sat me down right in front of the TV. It was an intense moment; it felt as though I was glued to the chair.

To my surprise, the title of the message was "What Kind of People to Avoid." Listen. As this brother began to expound on the Word of God, my mouth hung open in amazement. *Avoid people?* I said to myself.

It was not a coincidence that I had recently gotten over a terrible so-called friendship. Brother Hinn taught from the book of Proverbs on how to avoid the angry man (Proverbs 22:24–25); the gossiper (Proverbs 20:19); and the flatterer and the liar (Proverbs 26:28; 27:14). The one scripture that stood out the most was Proverbs 27:4, the danger of jealousy, a spirit that can never be appeased.

I had never heard the subject taught in depth, but that day it was crystal clear. It was time to rise and to take heed of what the Lord was saying. My Father made a believer out of me.

Apostle Paul speaks to us from the New Testament, giving us a list of persons with evil behaviors with whom true Christians should not fellowship, not even to sit and share a meal.

> *But now I've written unto you not to keep company, if any man that is called a brother be a fornicator, covetous, or an idolater, or a railer, or a drunkard, or an extortioner: with such an one no not to eat.* —1 Corinthians 5:11

There were times when the Lord would even show me their character and I would ignore His warning, partly because I wanted a friend so badly. Well, being naive didn't help either. I always wound up getting my feelings hurt in the end. I believe my heavenly Father looked down on me and said, "I really gotta get in her face and help this one!"

It was about time I got over the foolishness of being needy. Herein is the wisdom: "You can't bring close everyone you meet," simply because close relationships are not easily valued. The majority of folk can't handle who you are and what you're meant to be. They don't understand. Besides, there are only a select few who deserve your company anyway.

Let me share a rather unpleasant involvement I had. Some years back, I befriended a pastor and his wife. It appeared that they were struggling financially. I wanted to help, so I welcomed them into my home, treating them with love and kindness. Before I became acquainted with them, the Lord visited me in a dream, showing me the wife had a jealous spirit. Still, I moved forward with the relationship. I learned the hard way that when the Holy Ghost gives a warning, you'd better heed it.

As time went on, her character began to show. This sister was not nice—at all. She made some of the most absurd comments. For instance, "I wish some rich person would give me their money and let me spend it on whatever I want." I thought, *That's a very strange statement. Who in their right mind would invite someone to do such a thing?* I hadn't realized she was hinting to me. My goodness, I wasn't even close to being rich.

One day after a church service we were in my home, enjoying a relaxed Sunday evening. Both she and I were lying on the floor of my living room, just chilling. I had my back to her when something compelled me to turn over and look her way. In that moment I saw her reach for my purse and attempt to look through it. Seeing that she was busted, she pulled away and lay back down.

I returned to my position without saying a word, but in my mind I couldn't believe what I had witnessed, especially since I had my total week's earnings in my wallet.

Most folk would have dismissed her immediately, but I didn't. I knew the Spirit of the Lord that day was trying to tell me what He had already revealed as He had many other times. I know that I've mentioned jealousy already. But, perhaps like me, you need to hear it again.

Make note beloved, when people are jealous of you, they want what you have, and they will do whatever it takes to get it. In some cases, jealous individuals will go as far as to tear you down with their tongue in an effort to tarnish your reputation. Even though I was a blessing to her and her family, it wasn't enough. They turned out to be vicious, covetous leeches. Listen to what Proverbs 30:15 declares: *The horseleach hath two daughters, crying, Give, give.*

You must beware of folk with whom you have to consistently prove yourself—your love and affection, your loyalty, etc. These are users. As long as you're doing the giving, they are happy. Mind you, they are not grateful, but happy . . . momentarily, that is. If by chance they decide to show a little generosity, there is always an ulterior motive. I learned the hard way not to ignore what the Lord would show me. My goodness, He was gracious enough to give me warning, for my own good.

Getting back to the program . . . when it was over, I was one shoutin' sister. I felt like I had grown ten feet tall that day. I had learned something new about my Father God that was monumental. He is a God of love, not of foolishness.

With the new knowledge I received, I instantly rose, trusting in the Lord to bring the right people into my life. Took me long enough to finally get it. No one needs a so-called friend that bad.

- Perhaps rising up for you may mean that you need to BELIEVE God.

It's just that simple—start believing! Focus only on Him and His word and believe! Believe every promise He has spoken over your life. No matter how long ago it was, just believe. This brings me to the story of Sarah:

> *Through faith also Sarah herself received strength to conceive seed, and was delivered of a child when she was past age, because she judged Him faithful.* —Hebrews 11:11

I'm not saying it will be easy; your faith will be tested. But God is faithful. He will fulfill His promises. He did it for Sarah, and He will do it for you. The scripture says Sarah laughed when she overheard the conversation between the Lord and Abraham about them having a baby. Perhaps she was thinking too many years had passed. Or perhaps she wondered when the Lord had last seen Abraham's body. The Bible says they were well stricken with age. Nevertheless, after years of waiting and years of expecting, surely Sarah reminisced on the Lord's mighty hand throughout their lives and she judged Him faithful. The question is, how do you judge Him?

- For some of you, rising may mean learning to say NO! Proverbs 1:10 declares, "*My son, if sinners entice thee, consent thou not.*"

The Bible gives wise counsel for individuals who find it difficult to say "no." You've heard of the advertising campaign "Just say NO." Well, some wrestle with the idea. Timidity is the cause for some, while other are considered plain old "yes" people. Even when it's apparent that they can't, shouldn't, and/or don't want to do what is requested of them.

Herein is the wisdom: everybody fits into a category, whether good or bad, from family members to associates. You have to discern their spirits and decide what kind of people you want in your life.

OPEN NOW MINE EYES

God is so wonderful in how He deals with us. With all of His discipline and chastening, God began to open my eyes and to reveal the great things He had in store for me. The Psalmist declares,

> *Open thou mine eyes, that I may behold wondrous things out of the law.*

—Psalm 119:18

Although David was a king, he understood the need for God to open his eyes. It reminds me of the old Helen Keller movie I saw the other day. For those who are not familiar with it, Helen Keller was deaf and blind. This was the result of an illness that struck when she was an infant. Her parents' love for her crippled her even further over the years. Helen was completely undisciplined, throwing tantrums if she didn't get her way. Her parents sought out help and finally found a teacher who would move in with them and work with the child.

The teacher had a battle on her hands from day one, given the child's handicap alone. Her fight was not only with the child, but with Helen's parents as well. None of them were willing to accept the teacher's method of instruction, clueless to what it would take to teach the child to communicate and to understand that there was a whole big world outside of her.

Helen's blindness was, of course, physical; for her parents, it was mental. What I liked most about the teacher was that she stood her ground; she was not easily intimidated. She was convinced Helen could be reached. With much patience and long-suffering, the teacher tapped into her, and a whole new Helen emerged.

This is the same way God has to deal with us, because oftentimes we are blind to what God's will is. We have a tendency to fight against Him. In His gentleness, He consistently deals with us until we finally get it.

I was like Helen at one time. I thought I knew what was best, and if God didn't do it my way, I would throw a tantrum. There were people around me who thought they knew what was best for me, too. For example, I always delighted in designing and sewing clothes. In my earlier years when I attempted to pursue fashion, the saints told me it was a sin to do so, even though the sisters pranced around in designer clothing during special church events, taking great pleasure in admiring and being admired.

What they failed to realize is that somebody with the same talent I have designed those dresses. You see what I mean? Blindness. God has to open our eyes to His word and His will; if not, we will miss out on the great things He has in store.

Let's examine the word "wondrous." It is the word PALA in Hebrew. Its basic meaning is "to be wonderful" and "to cause a wonderful thing to happen." Its first occurrence is found in Genesis 18:4: *"Is anything too hard for the Lord?"* Or too wonderful? This word, "pala," is used primarily with God as the subject. He does things that are beyond the bounds of human power or expectations.

Get ready, beloved. God is about to do exceedingly abundantly above all that you can ask or think (Ephesians 3:20). If you can think it, it ain't wonderful enough! If we ask, as David did, God will open our eyes so we may not only read about His wonders, but begin also to experience them.

Some years ago I met a beautiful sister in Christ by way of my evangelist travels. As we became acquainted, I got to know her story. She was in an abusive marriage for over twenty years, and I do mean abusive. She was a lovely, sweet woman inside and out. It was difficult for me to understand why her husband would treat her with such disdain. He'd physically and verbally abuse her in public. It was never ending. To make matters worse, he taught their children to disrespect her as well. He was not in any way ashamed of his actions. He was a devil without the blue dress, a spawn of Satan, the ultimate bully from hell.

They had four beautiful children together. I felt pity for her because she and her children were hurting from years of trauma. I would pray with her and share a word from the Lord to encourage her time after time, even though my own marriage was rocky.

Like many women, in my sister's case, she was bent on staying in that unhealthy relationship, which caused her health to suffer unnecessarily. Her nerves were so badly shattered that her hair was falling out, along with weight gain and so on. When she visited her doctor she explained painful symptoms, but they could never find anything wrong.

Her problems were no doubt stress related. This poor woman became so confused, always second-guessing herself. She couldn't discern friends from foes. Finally, she would make attempts to rise and have him dismissed from the home by court order, but she wouldn't follow through. She caved in and took him back.

Even with all of the encouragement and prayer, she was reluctant to move forward, fear being a root problem. Needless to say, this was not a good move on her part. Shortly thereafter, she mentioned in conversation that he said to her, "You are a stupid fool." I gasped! This man had absolutely no intention of changing his ways. To tell you the truth, he didn't have a reason to. As long as his wife put up with the abuse, her husband, or whatever you might call him, was going to dish it out. Isn't that just like the devil?

One day while I prayed for her, the Lord gave me a powerful word on her behalf. He said, "Turn to Me and trust Me and I will strengthen you; I will cause you to rise like the sun." You see, beloved, God wants to help us out of our distress, but we must rise up. He will not do it for us. My sister in Christ's constant refusal to rise turned into rebellion. She leaned on her own understanding of what she wanted instead of what God wanted for her.

Remember what I said earlier. Because we think we know what's best, we want what we want and feel God should put His stamp of approval on it. He will never go against His will—never.

Beloved, my prayer for you today:

The Father will cause you to rise in faith and yield to His will in every area of your life; in the name of Jesus. Amen.

THE CLIMAX

THE CLIMAX

As I come to the close of this book, it is only the beginning for you and many others who have chosen to arise from their brokenness and live a purposeful life. I want to pause right here and give scripture to back up the previous "rhema" word from the Lord.

Let's visit the scripture theme, Isaiah 60:1:

> *Arise, shine; for thy light has come . . .*

"Arise" in Hebrew is QUM; it means "to arise, stand up, come about." "Shine" in Hebrew is OWR; it means "to be [cause, make] luminous." I use the sun as a metaphor to describe these two words. Though it is something we see regularly, much of the time we don't consider the fullness of its strength nor its faithfulness.

In the book of Genesis, chapter one, we understand that in the beginning there was no sun. The earth was in total darkness until God created it by the word of His power. The Bible declares, *"And God made two great lights; the greater light to rule the day."* On the fourth day, God made the sun and set it in the firmament to give light upon the earth. This God-given power force was commanded to rule by day. That being said, it is the governing power of one of the most important essentials for the survival of all living things.

Think about it for a moment. At God's command, it rises and shines on the earth, or not (see Job 9:7). But we understand that it was created for a specific purpose; therefore, when it rises, it rises with purpose, declaring the glory of its Creator.

The sun is dangerously bright, so much so that anyone who would dare to stare into its brightness can become blinded by it. Now imagine what our world would be like if the sun had a mind like a man and refused to shine from here on out. What if the sun was afraid to come out of its chamber because it was shy and wanted to be left alone? Or if it decided to keep all of that wonderful light to itself?

Beloved, just as the sun was created to declare the glory of God, so it is with us. We too were in darkness until the power of the gospel came and shone in our hearts and we became illuminated with the glory of God. Just as the sun was created to rise and shine on the earth, so we were created to rise and shine in the earth.

Two things I want to mention. First, "Arise, shine" is a commandment that God never gives us to do in our own strength. Second, to arise is to take action. The question is, what are we commanded to shine with? The answer is "righteousness." That is the glory of our great King, whose righteousness is brighter than the sun. No man dare gaze upon Him without expecting to be left as a dead man.

Out of darkness, the Lord made the sun to be. Heretofore, let us no longer underestimate the word of His power. Dare to rise and shine dangerously bright, with the same righteousness of our Lord Jesus, the Christ.

Rising is easier said than done. Walking it out and talking it out is a horse of a different color. As I mentioned earlier, one has to take action. To help you understand that it is absolutely possible, we will examine the word "cause." Webster defines it as "a person or thing that makes something happen, that produces an effect." In Hebrew, the word "cause" is AT; as an adjective, it means "gently, meekly, slowly." The same meaning is used in Genesis 7:4, when He caused the rain to fall on the earth during the time of the flood. Just a side note: He was giving the people in Noah's day time to repent of their wickedness. In the same sense, God, in His sovereignty, gently graces us with strength to rise to the place of courage.

Another use of the word "cause" is found in the New Testament; Apostle Paul declares,

> *Thanks be unto God the Father who always causes us to triumph in Christ.*
>
> —2 Corinthians 2:14

In this instance, "cause" is that with which we are led by Father God into triumph in Christ. Through a sacrificial death and resurrection, Jesus disarmed principalities and powers. Everything that was against us (sin, Satan, and the world) was nailed to the cross and as a result Jesus has made us alive with Him. Only under His authority do we reap these benefits and privileges. Because Christ was and is triumphant; through Him we are also triumphant. Because He rose in victory, so we rise in the authority of Jesus' name and in the power of the Spirit.

RISE TO YOUR HERITAGE

> *And I will cause thee to ride upon the high places of the earth, and feed thee with the heritage of Jacob thy father: for the mouth of the Lord hath spoken it.* —Isaiah 58:14

Even though God is speaking to Israel, this can apply to us today. The promises of God revealed in verses 8–14 simply teach us that God is the power source behind all blessings from one generation to the next. He wants to bless His people with a wealthy heritage that is far beyond what we can imagine. We can anticipate the blessings of His presence, protection, healing, and prosperity. In order to receive them, we must rise and honor our Lord through single-hearted obedience. He will surely cause thee to ride upon the high places of the earth.

This is key, because God promises to honor those who honor Him. Why am I sharing this? The commandments of the Lord always include the promises of His blessings. You must recognize and realize that your light has come, and arise! Your heavenly Father wants to use you; don't let Him down!

You see, beloved, you needn't fret. Little by little, just as the sun rises to the dawning of a new day, God will cause you to rise. You know how it is? Early in the morning, just before the sun comes up over the horizon, you look up and see the darkness giving over to the blue sky.

Even though it is a bit obscure, you know something is happening. Then you wait a little while, and the next thing you see is a beam of light peeking over the mountaintops. Then a little more time passes and you look again. What do you see? The sun's rays begin to shine brighter and brighter. All of a sudden, you see the sun rising higher with each passing moment until it reaches its height of glory. It's not just shining for the sake of shining, but with purpose, its rays beam across the sky with confidence and strength, blessing and bringing life to everything it touches. So it is with you, beloved. As you determine to be what God has ordained, you too will rise with purpose, and everywhere you go, you will bring life and blessings. You will shine with the light of His glory for the world to see.

It's a new day and a new season to be all that God is calling for. No more procrastinating, no more doubting, no more excuses, no more fear of men. It's time to rise; this time, when you rise, you rise with the understanding that:

I am accepted.

> *To the praise of the glory of His grace, by which He made us accepted in the Beloved.*
>
> —Ephesians 1:6

Christ dwells in me.

> *Greater is He who is in me, than he that is in the world.*
> —1 John 4:4

I will rise knowing I don't have to fear.

> *There is more for me than against me.*
> —2 Kings 6:16

I must rise with the understanding that God is faithful.

> *He will be with me always, He will never leave me nor forsake me, and He will be with me to the end of the earth.*
> —Hebrews 13:5

I will arise with the understanding that I am a mighty conqueror.

> *Yet, in all these things I am more than a conqueror through Him that loved me.*
> —Romans 8:37

And finally, I rise knowing I am guarded by the armed forces of heaven.

> *No weapon formed against me shall prosper.*
> —Isaiah 54:17

So, my question to you, beloved, is . . .

Dare to Rise?

Dare to rise? Should it mean leaving behind
all you've ever known? Dare to rise? Even if
it brings you to a place called Alone.
Then suddenly I take a look, a good look.
What is that I see, a light? OH there is a light within.
It was shining with the light of my
Great King even way back when,
Like the dawning of a brand new
day, so my eyes are opened.
And what do I see—reality, yes, reality
What do I do with this I see
Continue as it were,
or dare to arise and declare victory?
Dare to rise? To the mountaintop so high.
Not many willing to pay such a
price, for it takes a sacrifice.
"How would one get started?" you might ask.
I would reply, look back and see
You have already started the task
The higher and higher you go,
only leads to the top, you know.
Dare to rise? How do I get there, you say.
If only I had someone to show me the way.
Ah! Finally, I'll say,
let me introduce you.
Meet Wisdom and Knowledge, for they are kin.
Together with them, you will win.
They are kindred, their paths are life and peace.
Make Wisdom your sister, she won't forsake you
She is faithful and true, her words

are simple and uplifting, too.
Wisdom? Yes—she's calling, saying,
"Come, come up here! You've been down long enough
I will teach you and give you strength to rise and shine
Only don't forsake me for there is not much time
With me are riches and honor and wealth,
and my purpose is always to give you the very best."
Wisdom? She's calling, saying move with haste
You must get to your God-given special place.
Rise like the sun, with its rays so bright
Rise with the glory you were given, it's your birthright.
ARISE! OH what awaits, whom, despite the fear, choose to rise.
Tis your season . . . Dare to rise?

—Poem by Anita Joe

Yet, in all these things I
am more than a conqueror
through Him that loved me.
—Romans 8:37

PERSONAL REFLECTIONS

- Name three things that this chapter reveals in order that you may rise. Define each of them.

- Give three examples of God's attitude toward courage.

- When faced with difficult circumstances, what should you do or not do? How can you avoid making the same past mistakes?

- Throughout the scriptures, God made promises to individuals. As they walked with God, He was able to make good on His promises because the individuals displayed: faith, obedience and ________________?

- What are the high things in life?

- Why is it important to understand the will of God for your life?

- Being that rising is a conscious choice, name areas in your life where you can make application.

NOTES

NOTES

SOURCES

- The Complete Word Study Old Testament (Word Study Series)
- Bible Translations: King James, New King James, New Living Translation, The Amplified Version
- W. E. Vine, Vine's Expository Dictionary for Old and New Testament Words
- Strong's Exhaustive Concordance of the Bible
- Charles H. Spurgeon, The Treasury of King David
- Webster's Ninth New Collegiate Dictionary
- Macmillian Dictionary

♦EXPRESSIONS OF WORSHIP 

—BY ANITA JOE

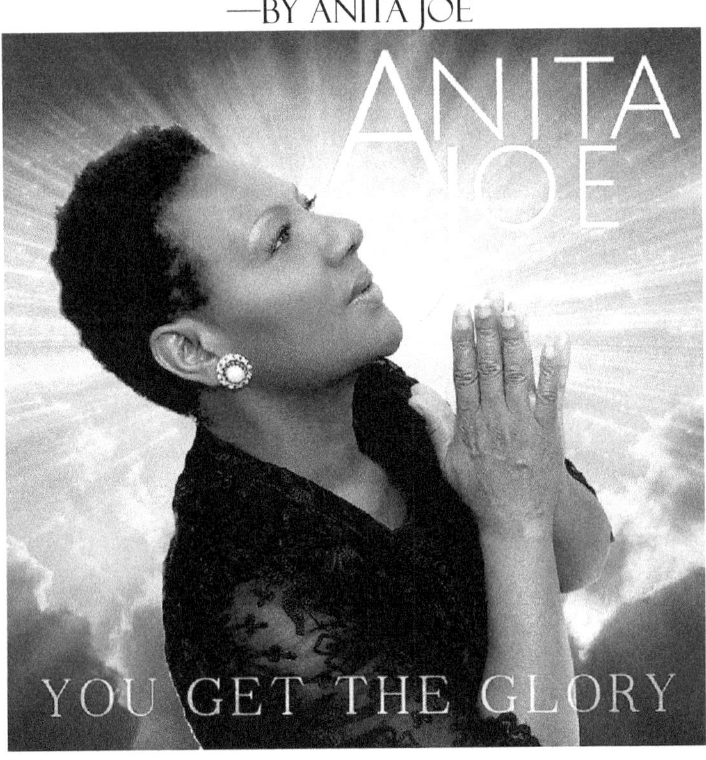

You Get the Glory is the sound of powerful ministry and expressions of worship straight from the throne of heaven. Mixing the old with the new, Anita introduces her album as a two-edged sword. The album features Anita Joe singing under the inspiration of the Holy Ghost. You are sure to rejoice with great songs like "You Alone," "Worship God," and the anointed "Hymnal Medley." It is a celebration of glorious praise that will lift your spirits. May this album bring a new depth of worship into your life.

Anita Joe, pastor/psalmist and singer, started singing gospel music in the church choir at a very early age. Over the years, as her relationship with her Lord Jesus grew, she realized her ability to write and sing under the unction of the Spirit. With strong conviction to spread the good news of the gospel through song, she adheres to her God-spoken mandate to "Bring My people into My presence."

In her personal pursuit of God's presence, Anita understands the importance of ushering in His glory. Therefore, spending much time alone with God, she receives from heaven, then releases worship that allows the river of God to flow in the midst of His people.

For orders contact: anitajoeministries@gmail.com or visit our website: anitajoeministries.com

ABOUT THE AUTHOR

Born in Little Rock, Arkansas and raised in Tucson, Arizona, Anita Joe received Jesus Christ as Lord and Savior and was baptized of the Holy Ghost at the age of nineteen. She was called into the ministry in her early twenties, God working mightily through her with ministry gifts of healing, deliverance, and prophecy. Experiencing abuse in her childhood, she was broken and desperately needed the healing power of the heavenly Father. Anita's life was supernaturally changed through His unconditional love and she now demonstrates this same love by the power of the Holy Ghost, through her preaching and teaching of the gospel to broken and hurting individuals.

> "In my travels, I see a world full of broken souls in need of the restoring power of Jesus Christ. No matter how severely shattered a person may be, He is able to heal, deliver, and set free by the power of His word." —Anita Joe

ANITA
JOE
MINISTRIES

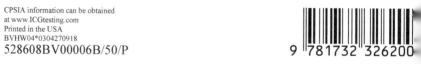

CPSIA information can be obtained
at www.ICGtesting.com
Printed in the USA
BVHW04*0304270918
528608BV00006B/50/P